THE FOUNDATIONS OF
THE AMERICAN EMPIRE

*William Henry Seward
and U.S. Foreign Policy*

THE FOUNDATIONS OF
THE AMERICAN EMPIRE

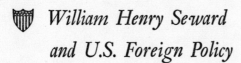 *William Henry Seward*
and U.S. Foreign Policy

Ernest N. Paolino

Cornell University Press | ITHACA AND LONDON

Cornell University Press gratefully acknowledges
a grant from the Andrew J. Mellon Foundation that
aided in bringing this book to publication.

First published 1973 by Cornell University Press.
Published in the United Kingdom by Cornell University Press Ltd.,
2–4 Brook Street, London W1Y 1AA.

International Standard Book Number 0-8014-0796-6
Library of Congress Catalog Card Number 73-8402

Printed in the United States of America by Vail-Ballou Press, Inc.

To Sophie

Contents

Preface

In the historiography of American foreign relations, the year 1898 has special significance. It was then, according to many historians, that foreign policy took a sudden and seemingly inexplicable turn. In Samuel Flagg Bemis' celebrated phrase, a Great Aberration seized the American people, and the United States government launched upon a novel and radical course in its relations with the outside world. Whereas previously, according to this view, Americans had been concerned mainly with filling out the continental boundaries (expansionism), beginning in 1898 with the Spanish-American War their interest turned outward, toward the acquisition of extra-hemispheric territory (imperialism). This new interest was formalized in 1900 by the Open Door notes, which officially marked America's emergence as a world power with interests and commitments far beyond the western hemisphere, especially in Asia.

Much historical investigation has been aimed at explaining this sudden reversal of attitudes. Economic, political, social, even psychological causes have been adduced. Fine distinctions have been drawn between the earlier "expansionists" and the later "imperialists" in order to establish the fundamental nature of the change. While all of these approaches are of great interest and possess historical value, they have in a real sense obfuscated the issue.

This book argues that the shift was neither as inexplicable nor as pathological as has been assumed, and that distinctions between expansionists and imperialists are more apparent than real. It seeks to do this by an intensive examination of the ideas, objectives, and policies of William Henry Seward, Secretary of State from 1861 to 1869. Although Seward has been most often regarded as an expansionist whose major objective was unrestricted territorial acquisitions in the western hemisphere, his private papers and government archives suggest quite different purposes. For by the time Seward had joined Abraham Lincoln's cabinet, he had already devoted a great deal of thought to the idea of an American empire that did not require the acquisition of vast tracts of terrain on the American continents. Since the empire he envisaged was largely commercial, it required the acquisition of only a small amount of new territory, essentially such strategically located areas as would aid in American domination of sea lanes.

This vision of American global commercial hegemony animated much of Seward's effort while Secretary. The scope of this vision was extraordinary, as can be seen in its mere outline: a network of commercial depots that would provide the way stations for trade, an intercontinental communications system under American auspices and control, the establishment of the American dollar as the primary unit of international trade, and an open door in China that would secure control of Asia's markets for the United States. To achieve this grand design Seward was prepared to commit the United States to international agreements on a scale greater than ever before and, if necessary, to commit American military power as well.

Although Seward's program, which was far in advance of

its day, would fail, Seward's brilliance and prescience cannot be denied. He clearly anticipated the objectives, if not the means, of the expansionists of 1898. Alfred Thayer Mahan, Henry Cabot Lodge, Theodore Roosevelt, and the other exponents of the Large Policy added little that Seward had not already envisioned. Seward's career as Secretary of State reveals the fundamental continuity of American foreign policy between 1861 and 1900, and demonstrates the inappropriateness of the efforts to distinguish expansionism from imperialism.

The scholarly obligations I have incurred along the way are so many that it would be impossible to list them all here. Some, however, are so personal and so significant that they deserve at least a brief mention. My greatest debt is to Lloyd C. Gardner, under whose direction I began this study at Rutgers University, and whose encouragement, patience, and thoughtful criticism have made it a far better work than it could otherwise have been. Richard P. McCormick and Warren Susman, also of Rutgers, provided indispensable assistance at various stages. L. Ethan Ellis aided me from the beginning with sage counsel, moral support, and helpful editorial advice. Needless to say, none of them bears any responsibility for whatever shortcomings remain.

I should like to thank, however inadequately, the staff of the Rush Rhees Memorial Library, Special Collections Division, of the University of Rochester, for their invaluable help with the Seward Papers, so splendidly housed there. I am also indebted to the staffs of the National Archives, Washington, D.C., the New York Public Library, the New-York Historical Society, and the Manuscript Division of the Library of Congress for their indispensable cooperation. My thanks go also to Mr. François-Xavier Grondin, Chief of the Public

Documents Division of the Rutgers University Library, New Brunswick, N.J., for unfailingly answering even my most obscure questions.

Special thanks are due to Anne McCartney, who saw the manuscript through an early stage and saved me from many errors; David L. Cowen, Rutgers University College, who generously lightened my teaching load so that I might devote more time to this study; to June Johnson, of the Department of History, Rutgers University College, for being the most efficient and understanding secretary imaginable; to Ronald J. Moss and Kevin E. Jordan for providing the leaven of humor which preserved my sense of proportion when the going got rough.

Beyond all these, however, one person deserves whatever credit there is for making this book possible. She has shared the arduous journey that everyone who writes a scholarly book must undertake. Her wise and good-humored criticism of the form and substance of this book makes her truly its co-author. For her sustaining faith, her imperturbable tolerance, and much, much besides, I owe her more than I can say.

ERNEST N. PAOLINO

New Brunswick, New Jersey

THE FOUNDATIONS OF
THE AMERICAN EMPIRE

William Henry Seward
and U.S. Foreign Policy

CHAPTER I

William Henry Seward—
Territorial Expansionist?

When, on March 4, 1861, William Henry Seward took up the duties of Secretary of State, an office he was to hold through eight of the most critical years in the history of the Republic, he brought with him a fund of invaluable experience and knowledge. For twenty years, beginning in 1831, he had represented the people of New York as state legislator, as governor, and as United States senator.[1] Throughout that period Seward had spoken and written extensively on the role of the United States in world affairs. He had long had a keen interest in what he once referred to as the "destiny of America," by which he meant its inevitable rise to the front rank of world powers.[2] Seward's knowledge of the world beyond the borders of the United States came not only through books, but also through travel abroad: in 1833 to the British Isles and the Continent; in 1857 to Canada and Labrador; in 1859 to

[1] Glyndon Van Deusen, *William H. Seward* (New York, 1967), pp. 14–22, 48–85, 110–96.

[2] George E. Baker, ed., *The Works of William H. Seward* (4 vols.; New York, 1853–1861), IV, 122. Hereafter cited as Seward, *Works*. A fifth volume, published under a separate title, *The Diplomatic History of the War for the Union* (Boston, 1884), will be cited as Seward, *Works*, V.

Europe and the Near East.[3] On occasion these trips led him to revise or reaffirm his views on America's role in world affairs. During his 1857 visit to Labrador, he wrote that the trip had compelled him to abandon the notion that Canada was "easily detachable" from Great Britain, and to discount as "mass national conceit" the American notion that she could be. He became convinced that Canada would be independent and that it was a "region grand enough for the seat of a great empire," an empire that might, he thought, one day even rival Russia.[4] In 1859, Seward was impressed by England's industrial and maritime capacity, evidence of which confirmed his belief that England would continue to be America's chief rival and that a great effort would be required to secure economic leadership for the United States.[5]

By the time Seward became Secretary of State, he had produced a large body of opinions and ideas on his version of an American "empire." During the next eight years, but most particularly in the post–Civil War period, Seward endeavored to implement these ideas and make them a reality. Before examining his efforts to this end, we need to explore Seward's definition of the American "empire" with some care.

As others have observed, Seward was not an original thinker, nor always a clear one.[6] Many of the ideas he expressed on the subject of empire had been put forth at one

[3] Van Deusen, *Seward*, pp. 22–23, 183–84, 211–13.

[4] Log of Seward's cruise to Labrador, entry for 10:00 A.M., Aug. 22, 1857, in Seward Papers, University of Rochester. Unless otherwise indicated, all references to the Seward Papers will be from this collection.

[5] Frederick William Seward, *William H. Seward: An Autobiography, with a Memoir of His Life, and Selections from His Letters* (3 vols.; New York, 1877), II, 380. Hereafter cited as Seward, *Memoirs*.

[6] There are two contrasting views of Seward's intellectual abilities. Frederick Bancroft (*The Life of William H. Seward* [2 vols.; New York, 1900], II, 79) thinks he was a man of "extraordinary intellect."

time or another by previous spokesmen for American expansion. Seward borrowed Thomas Jefferson's phrase "empire for liberty" when he called for "liberty and empire"; when he urged Americans to enlarge the "area of freedom," he acknowledged a debt to Andrew Jackson by enclosing the phrase in quotation marks.[7]

No single speech or piece of writing of Seward's sums up his major ideas; they must be pieced together from scattered comments extracted from literally scores of public and private utterances over a period of some thirty years. Although these utterances sometimes lack consistency and clarity, it is still possible to find in them the main outlines of Seward's thinking on American expansion and empire, and to trace the influence of his ideas on his conduct of American foreign policy in the administrations of Abraham Lincoln and Andrew Johnson. Certainly Seward saw the implications of his ideas, for he was prepared to follow their logic insofar as the exigencies of domestic and foreign conditions permitted him to do so.

Qualifying Americans for Empire

Although this book is concerned primarily with Seward's foreign policy, some note should be taken of his views on

---

Charles Francis Adams (*An Address on the Life, Character and Services of William Henry Seward* [Albany, 1873], p. 15) thinks he was "never a learned man" and of "imperfect education." Both may be exaggerations. Seward's contribution is to be found neither in his creative thought nor in his learning but in his ability to synthesize existing ideas. That he may have thought of himself in this light is shown in this comment, recorded by his son: "Most of the world would be surprised to know how few of our thoughts are really original with ourselves. What we write and say is, for the most part, a kind of mosaic interweaving of ideas and recollections gathered out of other people's talk or books. The combination and rearrangement of them is about all we can call our own" (Seward, *Memoirs*, III, 496).

[7] Seward, *Works*, IV, 601; III, 441–42.

domestic affairs, since for Seward, more perhaps than for most Secretaries of State, domestic and foreign affairs formed a continuum. He felt that no empire was possible or even desirable unless the people who aspired to it proved worthy. We must, he said, "qualify ourselves for our mission." [8] To be worthy, the American people would have to be politically united, economically strong, morally upright, and dedicated to democratic principles.

Occasionally, these goals clashed and Seward found himself in a dilemma that he could not easily escape. He was convinced that the American system was "equally cohesive in its parts and capable of all desirable expansion" if only "the American people shall remain an undivided nation." During the 1850's, he thus feared the loss of indispensable sections of the nation through secession or lack of sufficient interest in their retention by the government. Somewhat surprisingly, Southern secession concerned him less than did the possible loss of California, a development which to him would have meant the "dismemberment of the empire." In March, 1850, he urged the quick admission of California to the Union, for he could discern "only one danger of severance—and that is involved in the possibility of criminal neglect of the new communities of the Pacific coast." [9]

On the other hand, he was concerned that Americans qualify morally for empire. In an address delivered in 1854, he asserted that "no ignoble race can enlarge or even retain empire." He warned against the "seductions" of expansion, and cautioned the American people that their "own virtue and moderation must be renewed under circumstances so new

[8] Seward, *Works*, III, 409.
[9] *Congressional Globe*, 31st Cong., 1st sess., March 11, 1850, App., pp. 262–63; 32d Cong., 2d sess., July 29, 1852, p. 1976.

and peculiar." Consequently, one of the reasons he opposed the extension of slavery was his fear that it would render Americans morally unfit for empire. The destiny of America, he said, could be achieved only by "maintaining the democratic system of government." Slavery would pollute the land, and, as a result, there would be "no virtue in commercial and manufacturing communities." [10]

But like so many others of his time who were forced to choose between their desire to round out the national boundaries and their moral objections to slavery, Seward subordinated the moral question to material necessity. He could not abandon his commitment to the notion of an empire firmly grounded on the Pacific coast and conceded that, failing all else, he would vote for the admission of California "even if she had come as a slave state." [11]

So that the nation might be economically sound, Seward favored the rapid construction of a transcontinental railroad, a coast-to-coast telegraph line, government subsidies to shipping companies, a policy of cheap public lands, and liberal immigration and naturalization laws.[12] With the nation inter-

[10] Seward, *Works*, IV, 170; III, 24; IV, 326.

[11] *Cong. Globe*, 31st Cong., 1st sess., March 11, 1850, App., pp. 262–63.

[12] For Seward's views on railroads and the telegraph, see Seward to the Pacific Rail Road Convention, Oct. [8], 1849, in Seward Papers; Seward to S. B. Ruggles, Nov. 6, 1852, Seward Papers, Library of Congress. For Seward's views on the land question, see *Cong. Globe*, 31st Cong., 2d sess., Feb. 27, 1851, pp. 739–42, and the excellent analysis by Walter G. Sharrow, "William H. Seward and the Basis for American Empire, 1850–60," *Pacific Historical Review*, XXXVI (Aug., 1967), 325–42. On immigration, see *William H. Seward's Travels Around the World*, ed. Olive R. Seward (New York, 1873), p. 28. Hereafter cited as Seward, *Travels*. For a thorough discussion of Seward's domestic approach to empire, see Walter G. Sharrow, "Wil-

nally strong and healthy, Americans could then, confident of
success, turn their attention to wider horizons. The question is
whether these wider horizons meant unlimited territorial expansion, as is sometimes believed, or rather the achievement of
global commercial hegemony.

Standard Interpretations of Seward's Expansionism

The aspect of Seward's foreign policy that is most familiar
and most frequently commented upon is his presumed territorial expansionism. The essence of his imperial vision is
often reduced to his "undiscriminating voracity" for territorial acquisition, as Thomas A. Bailey puts it in his widely
used *A Diplomatic History of the American People*.[13] Samuel
Flagg Bemis calls Seward "a Republican apostle of Manifest
Destiny" who envisioned the "peaceful expansion of the
United States over the whole continent of North America." [14]
Julius W. Pratt, in *A History of United States Foreign Policy*, characterizes Seward as one of the "devotees" of the
"doctrine" of Manifest Destiny and confines his discussion to
Seward's proposals for territorial expansion.[15] In a more spe-
cialized study, *Manifest Destiny and Mission in American
History*, Frederick Merk also sees Seward primarily as a territorial expansionist and as one of those who sought to "resur-
rect" what Merk calls "continentalism," more familiarly
known as Manifest Destiny.[16] In an unpublished dissertation,

---

liam H. Seward, A Study in 19th Century Politics and Nationalism"
(Ph.D dissertation, University of Rochester, 1965).

[13] 3d ed.; New York, 1946, p. 399. In the 7th edition (1964), Bailey
softens his characterization of Seward to "an expansionist of hemis-
pheric appetite" (p. 360).

[14] *A Short History of American Foreign Policy* (New York, 1955),
p. 320.

[15] New York, 1955, p. 320.   [16] New York, 1963, p. 228.

Joseph G. Whelan has exhaustively catalogued Seward's efforts to secure territory, but his conceptualization never goes beyond seeing Seward exclusively as a territorial expansionist.[17]

That most historians have identified Seward as primarily, if not exclusively, a territorial expansionist is not surprising. References to territorial aggrandizement recur throughout Seward's speeches, which often enough are couched in the extravagant phraseology of his era.[18] Speaking at Columbus, Ohio, in 1853, he averred that the "borders of the federal republic . . . shall be extended so that it shall greet the sun when he touches the tropics, and when he sends his gleaming rays towards the polar circle, and shall include even distant islands in either ocean." Warming to his vision, Seward proclaimed that "mankind shall come to recognize in us the successor of the few great states, which have alternately borne commanding sway in the world." The American people, he claimed on another occasion, were "entering on a career of wealth, power and expansion." [19] He was not reluctant to do his part because, as he told the Senate in 1852, he had "the common pride of every American in the aggrandizement of my country. No effort of mine to promote it, by just and lawful means, ever was or ever will be withheld." Two years later he predicted that the "control of this continent is to be in a very few years the controlling influence in the world." Nor did he leave any doubt about who was to exercise that control, for Americans were no more moderate in respect

[17] "William H. Seward, Expansionist," University of Rochester, 1959.
[18] For a superb discussion of the mystique of expansionism in the pre-Civil War era, together with representative samples of the rhetoric, see Henry Nash Smith, *Virgin Land, the American West as Symbol and Myth* (New York, 1957), pp. 3–51.
[19] Seward, *Works*, IV, 122, 139.

to expansion than the British: "We are of the same stock, and have the common passion for domination." [20]

Seward claimed he could see prospects for expansion in almost every direction. Speaking at St. Paul, Minnesota, in 1860, he addressed a friendly word of encouragement to the Canadians, and advised them that it was "very well you are building states to be hereafter admitted into the American union." He called attention to the Russians in the Pacific Northwest and assured his listeners that those settlements "will yet become the outposts" of the United States. Looking southward, Seward hazarded the opinion that the capital of the United States would, in the not too distant future, be situated somewhere in Mexico. [21]

These few references could be multiplied several times over and would certainly seem to support the commonly held view that Seward was a thoroughgoing expansionist, that his version of empire was simply limitless territorial acquisition. And yet the ambiguities in Seward's expansionism raise serious doubts that it was, itself, a sufficient basis for the American empire. To see why this is so, we must ask three questions regarding Seward's putative expansionism. First, what territory did Seward intend to include in his expansionist schemes? Second, how did he mean to acquire this territory? Third, how did Seward's conduct in office square with his purported territorial objectives?

The Limits of Expansion

Despite Seward's numerous references to American expansion, it is not easy to discern how far he intended it to go. At

---

[20] *Cong. Globe*, 32d Cong., 1st sess., March 9, 1852, p. 247; 33d Cong., 1st sess., May 25, 1854, App., p. 770; 32d Cong., 2d sess., Jan. 26, 1853, App., p. 126.

[21] Seward, *Works*, IV, 333; III, 188.

times, indeed, he gave the impression that expansion would be limitless. A bit of verse in one of his letters suggests this:

> Our nation with united interests blest,
> Not now content to poise, shall sway the rest;
> Abroad our empire shall no limits know,
> But like the sea in boundless circles flow.[22]

On occasion, Seward gave the impression that expansion would have limits but would most certainly include areas outside the western hemisphere, as can be seen in his comment that "expansion will be made in adjacent regions if practicable; if not practicable, it will then be made in those regions, however distant, which offer the least resistance." [23] Those distant regions seemed to include even China and India, since Seward told Thurlow Weed in 1845 that the United States "shall begin to need more room there," but the evidence that he seriously wanted territory in those regions is not conclusive.[24]

At other times, Seward seemingly would have narrowed the scope of American expansion to the western hemisphere. He told an audience at Auburn, New York, in 1868, that "you are not to suppose, as many assume, that I am purchasing on government account, all the outlying territories in the universe, or indeed proposing to acquire dominion anywhere beyond the magic circle of the Monroe Doctrine." But whether this dominion was to include the entire hemisphere or only some portion of it he still did not make clear. Once he included "Canada and all British America to Behring's Straits, and Spanish America to the Isthmus of Panama, and perhaps to Cape Horn." Another time it was the "whole

[22] Seward to Philip Tomppert et al., May 10, 1867, Seward Papers.
[23] Seward, Travels, p. 357.
[24] Seward to Thurlow Weed, Dec. 20, 1845, Weed Papers, University of Rochester.

continent of North America from Hudson's Bay to the Gulf of Mexico, from the Pacific to the Atlantic coast." This included Canada, but did it also include Mexico? The question is debatable; in any event, Canada too seems to have been excluded in a speech in 1860, in which Seward said that the empire "shall reach from the shore of the lakes to the Gulf of Mexico, and from the Atlantic to the Pacific oceans." In this formulation the empire seems to be little more than the area now comprising the continental limits of the United States. These restrictions were confirmed in an 1860 speech at St. Paul, Minnesota. On that occasion Seward said he had changed his mind about the future capital of the United States being in Mexico, and that instead the "last seat of power on this great continent will be found somewhere within the radius not very far from the very spot where I stand." [25]

These contradictory and mutually exclusive ideas of American expansion indicate that Seward was never very sure just what the extent of that expansion should be. Quite possibly he tailored his views to suit the particular audience. A reading of his speeches to general audiences and those to the Senate appears to support the notion that the former were more extravagant than the latter, and intended to flatter local pride.[26] Whatever the reason for Seward's shifting views, it

[25] Seward, *Works*, V, 541; IV, 406; 395–96; 320. Seward's change of mind is not related by either of his biographers; they quote the original statement but not the later one (Bancroft, *Life*, II, 471–72; Van Deusen, *Seward*, p. 209). Seward had difficulty making up his mind. In 1872, the year of his death, he returned to his original idea, expecting to see the capital "in a more central locality, perhaps beyond the Mississippi, perhaps in Mexico," within the next hundred years (Seward, *Memoirs*, III, 484).

[26] For example, on his visit to Salem, Oregon, in August, 1869, he professed to see Puget Sound as "a base of future empire," forgetting

seems doubtful that such vague and conflicting formulations could serve as the basis for a viable foreign policy.

Methods of Acquisition

Besides being less than precise about what territory the American empire should include, Seward left unanswered the question of how this empire was to be acquired. He seemed to rule out conquest and aggression. "The sword," he said, "is not the most winning messenger that can be sent abroad." [27] His rejection of war as a proper vehicle for expansion was never more eloquently or forcefully put than in this comment, made in 1846, as war with Mexico impended: "I want no war. I want no enlargement of territory, sooner than it would come if we were contented with a 'masterly inactivity.' I abhor war, as I detest slavery. I would not give one human life for all the continent that remains to be *annexed*." [28] Twenty years later, with the horrors of the Civil War fresh in his mind, he was still convinced of the uselessness of war as a means of expansion:

I counsel no plans or schemes of military conquest. Not even the ancient plea of a necessity for the exhibition of our capacity for war remains. Wisdom, justice and moderation in the conduct

the prior claims of Mexico City and St. Paul, Minn. (Seward, *Works*, V, 574).

[27] Quoted in George E. Baker, *The Life of William H. Seward, with Selections from His Works* (New York, 1855), p. 288.

[28] Seward, *Works*, III, 409, emphasis in original. Seward was not always opposed to war. In 1856, he proposed issuing an ultimatum to Great Britain that if she did not "discontinue the exercise of dominion in Central America," the United States would declare war within a year (*Cong. Globe*, 34th Cong., 1st sess., Jan. 31, 1856, App., p. 80). His earlier comment that the United States would expand into those areas offering the least resistance seems to imply, at the least, a possible resort to force.

of our foreign relations make it easy to acquire by peaceful nego-
tiation, all the more than could be attainable by an unlawful aggression.[29]

Never, he said, would he advocate war except for "necessary defense." [30] Indeed, he seemed to have concluded at last
that territorial expansion might not even be desirable, for it
could lead to militarism at home. Although he remained convinced that American society was not inclined to militarism
still, democracies were "prone to war, and war consumes
them." [31] Seward believed that "centralization, consolidation,
and imperialism" were incompatible with American notions
of individual liberty and would require "standing armies in
time of peace." [32]

If war was not the proper instrument for achieving national
expansion, then by what means could it be brought about?
Seward was of the opinion that expansion would be pacific,
voluntary, and inevitable, in accordance with the laws of
nature. Contrasting favorably the budding American empire
with that of the British, Seward boasted that the United
States expanded without resorting to force.[33] War might add
territory, but the United States was "sure to be aggrandized
by peace." He therefore sought to discourage "this lust of
conquest, this seizing the unripened fruit, which, if left alone,
would fall of itself." [34] This view found expression in Andrew
Johnson's third annual message, in which, in a passage drafted

[29] Undated preliminary draft of speech, Seward Papers. Internal
evidence indicates that it was undoubtedly written sometime around
February, 1866, shortly after his return from a trip to the West Indies.
[30] Cong. Globe, 32d Cong., 2d sess., March 9, 1852, App., p. 244.
[31] Seward, Works, II, 83; III, 88.
[32] Seward to Count A. DeGasparin, April 7, 1866, Seward Papers.
[33] Seward, Works, IV, 169.
[34] Cong. Globe, 31st Cong., 1st sess., Jan. 30, 1850, p. 267.

by Seward, the President told Congress that it would be wise to leave the question of the absorption of the West Indies to the "process of natural political gravitation." [35]

But if Seward's imprecise notions of how extensive territorial expansion should be raise serious questions about how a foreign policy could be built on so uncertain a foundation, his concept of acquisition by gravitation also presents difficulties. The passivity inherent in such a doctrine contrasts markedly with the dynamism implied in the rhetoric of expansionism. If indeed gravity was to be the main mechanism of expansion, then there was no need of a policy at all—one had merely to bide one's time and wait for the inevitable. But Seward was no more consistent on this aspect of expansion than he was on the others. No matter how ineluctable one may consider the tendency of history, there is always a strong temptation to nudge it along by means of some appropriate action. Seward was no practitioner of "masterly inactivity." In the very message in which President Johnson asserted the wisdom of leaving the absorption of the West Indies to the forces of gravity, he also conceded, still speaking Seward's words, that the islands of St. Thomas and St. John were "immediately desirable," and therefore a treaty had been negotiated for their purchase.[36]

Although Seward rejected war and expressed confidence

[35] James D. Richardson, *A Compilation of the Messages and Papers of the Presidents, 1789–1897* (Washington, D.C., 1897), VI, 580, and Seward's draft of the State Department portion of the message in Seward Papers. Like so many of Seward's ideas, this was not original. See Albert K. Weinberg, *Manifest Destiny: A Study of Nationalist Expansionism in American History* (Chicago, 1963), pp. 224–51, for an excellent analysis of the idea of gravitation and its uses in American expansionist thought.

[36] Richardson, *Messages*, VI, 580.

in the inevitable operation of the laws of gravity, he was not altogether disinclined to use force if the objects of his diplomacy could not be achieved without it. In Asia especially, he employed a bit of gunboat diplomacy even if it did not fit in precisely with his previously expressed views.

Seward, then, wanted territory. But what territory? To discover this we must investigate how Seward's efforts to add to the national domain comported with his rhetoric on expansion, and how they related to a different vision—one of world economic hegemony.

Seward's Restrained Expansionism: Canada and Mexico as Examples

For a man who was described by a contemporary as "almost crazy on the subject of territorial acquisition," Seward's efforts in that direction seem curiously restrained.[37] Although early in his career he advocated expansion over the whole of the western hemisphere, when Secretary of State he appears not to have seriously entertained plans for the acquisition of extensive areas on the mainland. Toward Canada, for example, he maintained a circumspect attitude hardly in keeping with the grandiose claims he had made previously. True, as has been seen above, he at times asserted that Canada might well be absorbed into the United States, but by the time of his Labrador trip he seems to have abandoned this idea; at least he never proposed any overt action during his tenure as Secretary of State. Most certainly he abjured the use of force.[38] In fact, during the *Trent* affair he had specifically dis-

[37] Howard K. Beale, ed., *The Diary of Gideon Welles* (3 vols.; New York, 1960), III. 106.

[38] On this point, see Joe Patterson Smith, *Republican Expansionists of the Reconstruction Era* (Chicago, 1933), pp. 20–32. Patterson's study is concerned almost exclusively with the Canadian aspect of expansion.

avowed any aggressive designs on Canada.[39] One historian who has chronicled annexation movements from the Canadian side expresses some surprise that the "archannexationist" had "lost his appetite for Canada," and "almost completely ignored British America." [40] Not even the later opportunity afforded by the Fenian controversy tempted Seward from his abstinence.[41]

But if Seward had no intention of annexing Canada forcibly, he had not abandoned the hope that American influence would preponderate in Canada, and perhaps eventually she would voluntarily join the United States—on the principle of attraction, of course.[42] The means to this end were, significantly, commercial. Seward had, while in the Senate, supported trade reciprocity with Canada and had hoped for great things from it.[43] The reciprocity treaty of 1854, which had initiated mutually favorable trade between the United States and Canada, was abrogated by the United States in

[39] Seward to C. F. Adams, March 10, 1865, National Archives, Microcopy 77, Roll 79 (Instructions, Great Britain). Hereafter, references to microfilmed documents in the National Archives will be cited as follows: NA M—, R—, indicating microcopy and roll numbers.

[40] Donald F. Warner, *The Idea of Continental Union. Agitation for the Annexation of Canada to the United States, 1849–1893* (Lexington, 1960), p. 96.

[41] The only use Seward seems to have made of the Fenian controversy was as leverage for the settlement of war claims against the British. See Brian Jenkins, *Fenians and Anglo-American Relations during Reconstruction* (Ithaca, 1969), pp. 227–29.

[42] Preliminary draft of speech, undated, but probably Feb., 1866, Seward Papers.

[43] Bancroft, *Life*, II, 49. What Seward was hoping for might be gathered from a comment in a speech drafted on the subject of Canadian reciprocity: "The Commerce of the Continent is ours, and the Commerce of the world is becoming ours" (Seward Papers). The draft bears no date, but was probably written sometime in 1850. The speech was apparently never delivered.

1865, but Seward assured the British *chargé* in Washington that he would move quickly to open negotiations for its renewal.[44] He began to waver on the issue, however, primarily because he felt the United States was not yet in a position to gain all it could from a renewal of reciprocity. In a note to President Johnson, Seward outlined his ideas, suggesting that trade between the two countries might better be facilitated by the "adoption of a Zollverein or Customs' Union, similar to that which has secured great reciprocal benefits to the States of Germany." He expressed the hope that the Canadian provinces might become "coordinate members of the United States of America," eventually. But he did not press the issue, and left office without initiating any action to open the reciprocity talks.[45] Perhaps he was thinking along the lines suggested by a correspondent who advised him to *"Delay reciprocity, if you desire the annexation of these Provinces."* [46] Whatever the reason, Seward exhibited no great desire to hasten the annexation of Canada. If this was ever to be achieved, he thought it would come through some sort of economic arrangement and by the voluntary action of the Canadians. He was apparently content to let it go at that.

[44] Seward to C. F. Adams, March 10, 1865, NA M77, R79, recounting a conversation with J. Hume Burnley, "invited by myself"; also, Warner, *Idea of Continental Union*, pp. 40–41.

[45] Seward to Andrew Johnson, Feb., 1867, Andrew Johnson Papers, Library of Congress. Seward may have got the idea of a Zollverein from Isaac Buchanan, President of the Hamilton, Ontario, Board of Trade. In a letter to Seward, he proposed an American Zollverein to encompass "British America on the North and Mexico on the South" (Buchanan to Seward, Feb. 20, 1865, Seward Papers). That Seward did not, in his note to Johnson, include Mexico is interesting in light of his previous action there.

[46] J. Slocum to Seward, Nov. 5, 1868, NA M179, R290 (Miscellaneous Letters to State Department). Italics in original.

Mexico was another area that was sometimes within the scope of Seward's more expansive claims. As in the case of Canada, the claims were by no means unambiguous, even though he did at first try, in a revealing episode, to acquire Mexican territory.

At the outbreak of the Civil War, the Lincoln administration was confronted with the problem of sealing the borders of the United States against Confederate efforts to acquire supplies across them. The one weak spot was the southern boundary with Mexico, especially Southern California. The danger was heightened by the fact that Mexico was undergoing serious internal difficulties complicated by debt problems with England and France. Confederate incursions across the border could not be entirely discounted either.[47] Little wonder, then, that Seward was sympathetic to the proposal of his Minister to Mexico, Thomas Corwin, that the United States either seize Lower California from Mexico or purchase those Mexican states bordering on the southern part of the United States.[48] Given Seward's aversion to outright aggression, he naturally inclined to the latter method and instructed Corwin to buy Lower California to ensure that it could not "fall into the hands of the insurrectionary party of this country." [49] Corwin, fearing Mexican opposition to the alienation of her territory, countered with a suggestion that the United States assume the interest on the Mexican debt to England and

[47] Matias Romero to Seward, April 1, 1861, NA M54, R5 (Notes from Legation, Mexico), in which the Mexican Minister complains of "grave outrages" in Lower California.

[48] Thomas Sprague to Corwin, May 31, 1861, in Corwin to Seward, May 29, 1861, NA M97, R29 (Dispatches, Mexico). Sprague was the former Commercial Agent at La Baz, Lower California, who claimed that he had learned of a Confederate plot to seize the region.

[49] June 3, 1861, NA M77, R113 (Instructions, Mexico).

France, estimated at $62 million, at a rate of 3 percent annually.[50] Seward found this proposal acceptable and authorized Corwin to submit it to Mexico, adding that a six-year limit on the loan be imposed, and that failure by Mexico to repay it would mean the loss of "all her public lands and mineral rights in Lower California, Chihuahua, Sonora and Sinaloa." [51]

Corwin duly negotiated a treaty on November 29, 1861, which called for a loan of five million dollars payable in monthly installments of half a million dollars in return for the pledge of the lands and mineral rights previously mentioned, plus the forfeiture of church property, a feature Corwin had added. The treaty ran into trouble in the Senate, however, and despite the urgent appeals of Corwin, it was eventually voted down by the substantial margin of 28–8. Seward blamed the defeat on preoccupation with the war and economic stringency.[52]

This unsuccessful attempt at territorial acquisition points up several aspects of Seward's expansionism. First, Seward never really pushed very hard for the Corwin scheme. Possibly the Northern military reverses early in the Civil War distracted him from prosecuting the venture with as much vigor as he might have shown under more fortuitous circumstances. He certainly seemed less eager for it than Corwin was. In fact, he tried to restrain his sanguine Minister, who was apparently quite taken with the plan. Second, the episode was Seward's only venture in the use of "dollar diplomacy" to gain diplomatic leverage.[53] Third, American diplomats abroad

[50] June 29, 1861, NA M97, R29.   [51] Sept. 2, 1861, NA M77, R113.
[52] Seward to Corwin, June 24, 1862, ibid.
[53] This episode belies Van Deusen's assertion that Seward never practiced "nineteenth-century economic imperialism" (Van Deusen, Seward, p. 516). Seward's Mexican policy may be followed most con-

in the Seward years were, in many instances, exponents and practitioners of a different kind of imperial thinking from that which Seward himself espoused.[54] Finally, Seward never again made any effort to acquire territory in Mexico, despite his previous expansionist rhetoric; his version of the American empire did not require it.

Seward's later views on expansion into Mexico and his refusal to engage in such ventures were clearly stated in an 1865 communication to John Bigelow, who was Minister to France during the time when the French were attempting to establish a puppet regime in Mexico. Bigelow, like Corwin and others in the diplomatic corps, was more expansionist than the presumed head of the Expansionist Church himself. He proposed that Seward should not antagonize the French by insisting on their departure from Mexico. Friendship, he believed, could be maintained and France's failure in Mexico assured "by simple forebearance," until such time as Mexico would be "overrun and occupied by emigrants from the United States who will desire to share the protection and

---

veniently in James Morton Callahan, *American Foreign Policy in Mexican Relations* (New York, 1932), pp. 278–340.

[54] The recurrence of certain phrases in the history of American commercial expansion is revealing. For instance, George Robert Latham, Consul at Melbourne, Australia, advocated "an aggressive policy [toward Mexico] in the friendly sense of the term" (Latham to Seward, Sept. 26, 1867, Seward Papers). Seward himself had used a similar phrase when he referred to the time "when we gently coerced Japan into friendship with us" (Seward to Robert Pruyn, Nov. 15, 1861, *Papers Relating to the Foreign Relations of the United States, 1861–1872* [Microfiche ed., 1966], [1861], Pt. 2, p. 817). Hereafter cited as *For. Rel.* Tom Millard's "felicitous aggressiveness" in regard to American competition for dominance in China in the early twentieth century shows that the idea had lost none of its attractiveness. Quoted in Jerry Israel, *Progressivism and the Open Door, America and China, 1905–1921* (Pittsburgh, 1971), p. 39.

privileges of our govt." [55] Undoubtedly, Bigelow was envisioning another Texas.

Seward would have none of it. The United States, he replied, preferred to see a republican form of government in Mexico, but its efforts must be restricted to those of "moral influences." The American people, he continued, perhaps disingenuously, are not inclined to "political propagandism" and are even "more strongly disincline[d] from seeking aggrandizement by means of military conquest." Still, they might find it necessary to expand their boundaries, but if so, such expansion could occur only by the "annexation of adjacent peoples . . . through their own consent." They would have nothing to do with interference in the internal affairs of other peoples.[56]

Seward's mild rebuke to Bigelow had been foreshadowed in 1861 in the instructions he wrote to Allan Burton, newly appointed Minister to New Granada. Seward called Burton's attention to his predecessors' practice of giving advice on the internal affairs of the countries to which they had been accredited. "It belongs to the People of New Granada to regulate their own political affairs," wrote Seward. "A nation that cannot stand without foreign aid cannot maintain legitimate independence long after having become a client of another nation." [57]

By 1865, Seward had adopted a position that rejected efforts to acquire Mexican territory by any means except voluntary action on the part of the Mexican people themselves. But surely Seward was realist enough to know that

[55] Bigelow to Seward, Aug. 21, 1865, NA M34, R61 (Dispatches, France).

[56] Sept. 6, 1865, *For. Rel.,* 1865, Pt. 2, p. 413.

[57] May 29, 1861, NA M77, R45 (Instructions, New Granada).

such action was extremely unlikely. Engaged in a bitter struggle to redeem their nationality from the French, the Mexicans
were not likely to voluntarily surrender it to the Americans,
a people for whom they would feel little attachment. Despite
the expansionist prophecies and the abortive attempt to acquire Mexican territory early in the Civil War, Seward did
not think Mexican lands important enough to his plan of
empire to make any attempt to acquire any part of them in
later years.[58]

Toward Central and South America, Seward showed similar restraint. The only territory in Central America that really
interested him was the Isthmus of Panama. There the major
attraction was the possibility of an interoceanic canal, a project that had nothing to do with territorial expansion as such,
but was of vital importance for Seward's vision of commercial
empire. The mainland of South America interested him not at
all as a field for territorial expansion, and while Secretary of
State he made no effort in that direction.

One other aspect of Seward's expansionism requires discussion. Some historians have suggested that Seward sought to
acquire territory on the mainland of Asia, specifically in
China. The first to call attention to this claim, apparently, was
Frederick Bancroft. In his *Life of William Seward* he writes
that "persons not in sympathy with his prophecies had main-

---

[58] This did not prevent some from seeing Machiavellian motives
behind every Seward move. The editor of the *Army and Navy Journal* wrote to William T. Sherman that he "had an idea" that Sherman's
visit to Mexico in 1867 "meant more than was generally supposed.
Some of Mr. Seward's hints about the extension of our frontiers have
seemed very significant to me" (W. C. Church to W. T. Sherman,
July 26, 1867, William Conant Church Papers, Library of Congress).
Despite Church's fears, Sherman's activities were largely ceremonial
and quite innocuous (see Callahan, *American Foreign Policy*, p. 328).

tained that he was in favor of adding at least a part of China to the national domain." [59] No evidence is adduced for this claim, nor are the "persons" identified. Albert K. Weinberg and Thomas A. Bailey, following Bancroft, echo the claim.[60] The evidence for this view, however, is very tenuous and unconvincing. The only reference to acquiring land on the mainland of Asia in Seward's writings occurs in a letter to Thurlow Weed in 1845, which says that the United States "shall begin to need more room" in India and China.[61] But this claim was made very early in Seward's career and was not reiterated during the remaining twenty-seven years of his life. Other references that might be used to justify the claim are vague or open to different interpretations, such as the assertion that "our population is destined to roll its resistless waves to the icy barriers of the north, and to encounter oriental civilization on the shores of the Pacific." [62] The context in which this assertion was made suggests that Seward was thinking in terms of continental expansion to the Pacific coast and not to the shores of Asia.

One final statement bears on this point. This is the often-quoted prophecy Seward made to the American Minister to Russia, Cassius M. Clay, that Russia and the United States would remain on friendly terms "until, each having made a circuit of half the globe in opposite directions, they shall meet and greet each other in the region where civilization began." [63] The statement is ambiguous and does not make clear whether

[59] Bancroft, *Life*, II, 472.

[60] Weinberg, *Manifest Destiny*, p. 242; Bailey, *Diplomatic History*, 7th ed., p. 363. Bailey says that Seward desired "if one may believe his enemies, a part of China." The "enemies" are not identified.

[61] Dec. 20, 1845, Weed Papers, University of Rochester.

[62] Seward, *Works*, III, 409.

[63] May 6, 1861, *For. Rel.* (1861), Pt. 1, p. 293.

the confrontation would be physical—a doubtful prospect given Seward's attitude toward aggressive expansion—or commercial, which seems far more likely in the light of his customary policies.

This survey of Seward's ideas on expansion has sought to demonstrate that the generally held notion that he was an insatiable and inveterate territorial expansionist requires great modification. His proposals for acquiring territory were too inconsistent to afford a sure basis of policy. The methods he suggested for such acquisition—gravitation and voluntary adherence—were uncertain and time-consuming, if they would work at all. His practices as Secretary of State reveal that he was hardly voracious in his quest for territory.

But while the evidence demonstrates that Seward was not an unrestrained expansionist, to suggest that he was not an expansionist at all or that territorial acquisition had no place in his conception of empire would be inaccurate. He did indeed want additional territory, and would in time acquire some. But he never wanted to acquire just any territory; expansion was to be selective, not indiscriminate, and was to serve a larger purpose than mere land-grabbing. The kinds of territory and their geographical distribution were of great significance for Seward's idea of empire.

On the mainland of the western hemisphere Seward tried to acquire only Alaska and the Isthmus of Panama. All the other territory he sought was insular. The one exception was the land in Mexico in 1861, but that was wanted to avert an anticipated Confederate takeover rather than as part of an expansionist scheme. In any event, the effort was not actively prosecuted and was never repeated. Alaska, the Isthmus of Panama, the West Indies, and the Pacific were not ends in themselves. They were, rather, the means to an end. That end was not territorial hegemony in the western hemisphere, but global commercial supremacy. What Seward tried to do as Secretary of State is of far greater significance than what he said about territorial expansion in his earlier stump speeches. If one looks behind the rodomontade to Seward's actual policies and objectives, it becomes clear that to characterize him as "an expansionist for the sake of expansion" is to indulge in circular reasoning.[64]

Seward was not a one-dimensional man. His genius does not lie in his having played the changes on "Manifest Destiny" or in his single-minded pursuit of territory. It lies in the combination of familiar, if unclear, ideas of territorial expansion, deliberate, well-calculated acquisitions of terrain, and a profound insight into the true basis of empire: the commercial domination by the United States of the world's markets. Seward's conception of an open-door commercial empire and his efforts to achieve it are what make him the "central figure of nineteenth-century American imperialism" and the "greatest Secretary of State since John Quincy Adams."[65]

[64] Bancroft, *Life*, II, 490.
[65] Richard W. Van Alstyne, *The Rising American Empire* (Chicago, 1965), p. 176; Walter LaFeber, *The New Empire: An Interpretation of American Expansion, 1860–1898* (Ithaca, 1967), p. 25.

CHAPTER II

The Real Empire:
Commercial Hegemony

Unlike his ideas on territorial expansion, William Seward's views on commercial expansion were clear, logical, and supported by well-conceived programs which, if they did not entirely succeed in achieving their objectives, nonetheless laid a solid foundation for his successors to build upon. Throughout his twelve years in the Senate, Seward had urged his colleagues—and through them his countrymen—to improve America's commercial position in the world, and he actively supported measures to that end. He never ceased to proselytize for what he firmly believed was the only empire worth having: the commercial hegemony of the world. When he assumed the direction of America's foreign policy, he tried to implement his ideas under exceedingly trying domestic handicaps. He was to leave office fretting that he had not had enough time and regretting that he had not done more. But he had fairly launched the ship of empire and charted its course. It remained for others to pilot it to its destination.

The Empire as Commercial Expansion

Ideas of worldwide commercial hegemony must have come easily to one who conceived of the Constitution as having been framed largely for reasons of trade, a view Seward presented in his Phi Beta Kappa address at Yale in July, 1854. According to Seward, the states under the Articles of Confederation were free, sovereign, and independent. They guaranteed to their citizens the rights and freedoms enunciated in the Declaration of Independence. But something more was required. They

needed free and mutual commerce among themselves, and some regulations for securing to each equal facilities of commerce among foreign countries. A union was necessary to the attainment of these ends. . . . So a federal central government was established, which is sovereign only in commerce at home and abroad, and in the necessary communications with other nations.[1]

Given this view, it is little wonder that Seward would think that commerce was "one of the great occupations of this nation," and "the chief agent of its advancement in civilization and enlargement of empire."[2] Following closely on these assumptions, Seward could assert that one of the federal government's major functions was to advance commerce. In his words, it was for "the protection of commerce that they pass laws, make treaties, build fortifications, and maintain navies upon all the seas."[3]

Seward's meaning of gravity and the forces of attraction now becomes clear. For if, indeed, the "strongest bonds of cohesion in society are commerce and gratitude for protected

[1] Seward, *Works*, IV, 168. See also the draft of a speech ten years earlier in which he said that "Commerce, inland and foreign" was to be the "enduring motive power" of the new federal government (Speech at Union College, July 22, 1844, Seward Papers). This proto-"economic interpretation" of the Constitution has not been remarked upon by his biographers.

[2] *Cong. Globe*, 31st Cong., 2d sess., Jan. 21, 1851, App., p. 92.

[3] *Ibid.*

freedom," then why should they not be as effective abroad as at home? Thus, in what might be called Seward's Law of Imperial Gravity, he discovered the motive power of expansion in commerce, asserting that "attraction increases as commerce widens the circle of national influence." This law implies that commercial expansion would remove some of the stigma from territorial aggrandizement in "adjacent states," since it would "spare their corporate existence and individuality" while permitting domination of their markets.[4] His assertion that "political supremacy follows commercial ascendancy" may be taken as a corollary of Seward's Law.[5]

The empire as commercial supremacy was a theme to which Seward returned again and again. He put the matter succinctly in the Senate in 1853, when he asserted that "the nation that draws the most materials and provisions from the earth, fabricates the most, and sells the most of productions and fabrics to foreign nations, must be, and will be, the great power of the earth."[6] Adverting to the geographically advantageous position of the United States, midway between Europe and Asia, he concluded that it "must command the empire of the seas, which alone is real empire."[7] The real ob-

[4] Seward, *Works*, IV, 170.

[5] *Cong. Globe*, 31st Cong., 2d sess., Feb. 27, 1851, p. 740.

[6] *Ibid.*, 32d Cong., 2d sess., Jan. 26, 1853, App., p. 127. For a revealing insight into Seward's views on the significance of industrialization, see his introduction in William P. Blake, ed., *Reports of the United States Commissioners to the Paris Universal Exposition, 1867* (6 vols.; Washington, D.C., 1870), I, 3–6.

[7] *Ibid.*, 31st Cong., 1st sess., March 11, 1850, p. 262. The idea that the United States occupied a fortunate geographical position was a common one in this era. Commenting on a French map of global steamship and telegraph lines, the editor of a leading journal said that it put "America in the middle and the Eastern Continent divided into two, half lying on the right hand and the other half on the left

jective of the United States, he said, was "the commerce of the world, which is the empire of the world." [8] On the basis of this conviction, Seward dedicated himself to urging Americans to "contest for the ultimate empire of the ocean." [9]

Asia, the Ultimate Objective

When Seward spoke of dominating world markets, he knew precisely where the success of that policy would be determined. Empire, he believed, was tending westward, as illustrated in this bit of verse: [10]

> The Eastern Nations sink, their glory ends,
> And empire rises where the sun descends.

Asia was for Seward the "new theatre of human activity," and commerce was the "great agent of this movement." So convinced was he of this that he derogated the fears of Lewis Cass of Michigan and others that European powers, especially

---

of America. The map . . . thus gives to America the central and commanding position to which she is entitled, as the continent whose commerce and commercial relations are already controlling among them" (*New York Journal of Commerce*, Nov. 17, 1866). For an interesting discussion of the nascent geopolitics of the time, see Charles Vevier, "American Continentalism: An Idea of Expansion, 1845–1910," *American Historical Review*, LXV (Jan., 1960), 323–35.

[8] *Cong. Globe*, 32d Cong., 2d sess., Jan. 26, 1853, App., p. 127. Thoughts of commerce were never far from Seward's mind even when the subject seemed far removed. In a speech to the Senate on the Hungarian revolution, in which he spoke on behalf of a resolution declaring the opposition of the American government to unjust and unrepresentative governments in Europe, he remarked that "the commerce of Hungary is, however, an interest to be secured by us; and inconsiderable as it must be under a despotism, it would expand under a republic" (*ibid.*, 32d Cong., 1st sess., March 9, 1852, p. 244).

[9] *Ibid.*, 32d Cong., 1st sess., April 27, 1852, p. 1200.

[10] Seward, *Works*, IV, 166.

Great Britain, were bent on the recolonization of Latin America. When Cass submitted a resolution to the Senate that would reaffirm the Monroe Doctrine's noncolonization provisions, Seward professed not to know what the uproar was all about. He could find no threat from any European power in the Western hemisphere. He told his fellow Senators they were looking in the wrong place for threats to America. The contest for empire, he said, was to be found "not on the American lakes, nor on the Atlantic coast, nor on the Caribbean seas, nor on the Mediterranean, nor on the Baltic, nor on the Atlantic ocean, but on the Pacific ocean, and its islands and continents." The rivals and competitors of the United States were to be found "on those continents and seas in the East where the prize which you are contending with them for is to be found." And so Seward exhorted Americans to achieve their destiny of dominating the markets of Asia, for if they succeeded, the United States was certain to become "the greatest of existing states, greater than any that has ever existed." [11] That greatness was assured if the United States could extend its power "to the Pacific ocean and grasp the great commerce of the east." [12]

Along with the commercial benefits, Seward expected great political and moral consequences. One of his most persistent beliefs was that the United States had a mission to bring about the regeneration of Asia. In 1848, in an address before the Young Catholic Friends' Society of Baltimore, he spoke of the necessity for the United States to establish freedom of

[11] *Cong. Globe*, 32d Cong., 2d sess., July 29, 1852, pp. 1975–76; Jan. 26, 1853, App., p. 127; July 29, 1852, pp. 1857–58. Seward reverted to a metaphor he had used earlier on the slavery issue, claiming that the westward trend of empire was a "higher law, a law of Providence" (Madison, Wis., Sept. 12, 1860, Seward, *Works*, IV, 319).

[12] Seward, *Works*, V, 320.

the seas, "without which no nation in modern times can be great," and to secure the markets of Europe, Africa, China, and the "eastern Indies." Once this was done, the United States would "furnish a political alembic which, receiving the exhausted civilization of Asia and the ripening civilization of western Europe, and commingling them together . . . would disclose the secret of the ultimate regeneration and reunion of human society throughout the world." [13] Over twenty years later, Seward was still stressing this mixture of the material and the mystical. Traveling around the world in 1870, he stopped at the American consulate in Hong Kong and made a brief speech to the staff. He held out to them the "bright and glorious prospect" of the "regeneration of civilization in the East." The United States, he assured them, "have assumed the leadership in this great work." Nor did he leave any doubt about what he thought the means of this great transformation would be. Although he paid tribute to the work of the missionaries, he doubted that Christianity was capable of regenerating Asia because it required "some intellectual and social advancement which can only be effected through international commerce, . . . that commerce to come across the American continent and the Pacific Ocean." [14]

Seward's Views Supported

Many influential people in the United States, in and out of official circles, agreed with Seward that commercial domination and the control of the Pacific were important, perhaps crucial, objectives. The prestigious *New York Journal of Commerce* emphasized the central importance of foreign markets for the economic well-being of the United States. As the Civil War was drawing to a close, it reminded its readers that "commerce with foreign countries is necessary to our

[13] *Ibid.*, III, 113.   [14] Seward, *Travels*, pp. 255–56.

national life and vigor, and the nation will insist upon it." The *Journal* did not think it was possible to "shut ourselves up from the outside world, and grow rich by a mutual exchange of products." It derided those who thought that domestic trade would suffice by comparing them to the "two boys in their father's attic . . . making ten dollars apiece by swapping jackknives with each other." [15] The *Army and Navy Journal* spoke of "that Eastern commerce which presents itself to the mercantile imagination with Oriental magnitude of proportion." [16] The National Board of Trade, in its first annual meeting, expressed confidence that the "trade of the Pacific is yet in its infancy." [17] Rear Admiral David Dixon Porter, Commandant of the Naval Academy at Annapolis, friend of William Seward and sometime special agent for the State Department, was of the opinion that "whatever nation has had control of the East India trade has governed the commerce of the world." [18] And finally, the San Francisco Chamber of Commerce, while introducing the sobering note that "there is not much in the history or present condition of [the Chinese] empire to warrant expectation of great commercial advantage soon to accrue," nevertheless claimed that it was "certain that a trade would gradually develop the resources of that secluded empire," and eventually bring great riches to California. [19]

[15] Jan. 17, 1865.   [16] June 29, 1867, p. 709.

[17] *Proceedings of the First Annual Meeting, December, 1868* (Boston, 1869), p. 201.

[18] Porter's views appear in the draft of an article, "On the Present and Future Progress of America," which can be found under date of February 11, 1868 (Letterbooks, Porter Family Papers, Library of Congress). Porter submitted it to the *Army and Navy Journal,* but it was never published (*ibid.,* D. D. Porter to Editor, Feb. 18, 1868).

[19] *Report of the Special Committee of the San Francisco Chamber of Commerce,* Sept. 11, 1866, encl. in D. Macgowan to Seward, Sept. 17, 1866, NA M179, R244.

Opinions such as these from influential quarters, which fell in so neatly with Seward's own convictions, lent important support to his efforts to extend American influence and commerce into Asia. They could hardly have failed to encourage the man who had predicted as early as 1854 that the future progress of the United States would be "through the Manillas [*sic*], and along the Indian coast, and beyond the Persian gulf, to the far-off Mozambique." [20]

Rivals for Commercial Hegemony

Seward did not believe that it would be an easy task for the United States to gain control of world markets. He was fully aware that competition with the European contenders would be brisk. Fortunately for the United States, he thought, it would be "a competition depending not on armies nor even on wealth, but directly on invention and industry." On this basis, Seward was confident that Americans would be equal to the challenge.[21] Despite this sanguine view of the prospects, he was fearful that if the United States did not move energetically in Asia to extend its commerce, it would be shut out and the trade would "fall into the hands of other maritime powers." [22]

Those other maritime powers with whom Seward thought the United States must contest the commercial supremacy of

[20] Seward, *Works*, IV, 166.
[21] *Cong. Globe*, 32d Cong., 1st sess., April 27, 1852, p. 201. Shortly after the fall of Richmond, commercial circles were already preparing to take up the struggle. *The New York Journal of Commerce*, for example, announced that "the grand conquest we have to make is not over English armies, but over English commerce, wealth, industry. We have before us the opportunity of taking over the first position among the maritime and commercial nations" (April 7, 1865).
[22] *Cong. Globe*, 34th Cong., 1st and 2d sess., Aug. 12, 1856, p. 2058.

the globe—France, Russia, and Great Britain—were not equally dangerous.[23] France he did not rate as much of a threat; Russia and England seemed to him much more formidable, and Russia he considered a future rival, not a present one. He did not expect Russia and the United States "to come into rivalry and conflict" soon, even though the American Minister to Russia, Cassius M. Clay, thought otherwise.[24] Clay pointed out that Russia was continually expanding her Asiatic trade, and at the same time expanding her territories, "making 'points d'appui' " for further political and commercial advances. He urged Seward to seek naval and military strong points in the seas bordering Japan and China, from which future American commerce might be protected.[25] But Seward was not greatly perturbed. He did expect a challenge from Russia eventually, because he foresaw that both England and France were "temporary" and "ephemeral" powers in Europe, "while the Russian empire is an obstinate and portentous reality." He was convinced, with the "first Napoleon . . . that Europe must be soon either republican or Cossack," and he suspected it would eventually be the latter.[26]

For the time being, the major rival and obstacle was England. Seward left no doubt about that. Everywhere he looked he saw England in advance of the United States, for "wherever western commerce has gained an entrance to the continent of Asia, there that flag is seen waving." [27] The world's commerce, he said, "is practically divided" between

[23] Ibid., 32d Cong., 1st sess., July 29, 1852, p. 1976.
[24] Seward to Clay, May 6, 1861, For. Rel. (1861), Pt. 1, p. 293.
[25] April 17, 1868, ibid. (1868), Pt. 1, pp. 468–69. For an interesting discussion of Clay's views on Russia, see Albert Parry, "Cassius Clay's Glimpse into the Future," Russian Review, II (Spring, 1943), 52–67.
[26] Cong. Globe, 34th Cong., 1st sess., Jan. 31, 1856, p. 79.
[27] Ibid., 32d Cong., 1st sess., July 29, 1852, p. 1976.

the United States and England, yet the bulk of it remained in British hands, a condition which gave him no joy or respite.[28] Seward unceasingly called upon the Senate to come to the aid of American merchants who, he said, were begging the government to take action in counteracting their chief competitor.[29]

However much Seward may have feared the British, he could not at times suppress his admiration for their success, and saw them as a model to be followed. Look at England, he implored Americans, "completing a vast web of ocean steam navigation, based on postage and commerce, that will connect all the European ports in the West Indies, all the ports of Asia and Oceania, with her great commercial capital. Thus the world is to become a great commercial system, ramified by a thousand nerves projecting from the one head at London." [30] Undoubtedly, Seward meant this both as a tribute to British enterprise and as a paradigm to be emulated. It is, in fact, nothing less than a précis of Seward's program for American commercial expansion, even to the extent of seeing New York City as the successor to London as the nerve center of a world-wide commercial empire. Almost twenty years later, Seward was still thinking along the same lines. Now out of office, he was inclined to be more mellow and generous toward Britain, but his comments remain instructive. They show his continued appreciation of British methods and objectives, and also what he had hoped to accomplish while Secretary of State. "Wise old England!" he exclaimed. "How she fortifies her island Realm, and yet all the while develops and improves the energies of her people, while she does not hesitate to undertake the police regulation of the world! She

[28] *Ibid.*, Aug. 14, 1852, p. 916.   [29] *Ibid.*, April 27, 1852, p. 1201.
[30] *Ibid.*

knows, moreover, when and where and how to establish the necessary police stations." [31]

Seward Prepares America for a Global Role

Recognizing that the United States faced a long and uphill fight, Seward proposed a number of programs designed to prepare the nation for the assumption of leadership in commercial expansion. Among them were such domestic programs as aid to farmers, the transcontinental railroad and telegraph, surveys of the Pacific and Arctic Oceans, and subsidies to shipping companies and international carriers.

The fear that the loss of California and the Pacific coast would doom the commercial empire was in great measure responsible for Seward's eagerness to bind that region to the United States by modern means of transportation and communication. He was convinced that the "commercial, social, political movements of the world" were "in the direction of California," and he wished, at all costs, to hold on to California, "which bounds at once the empire and the Continent." [32] Seward's concern for the maintenance of an entrepôt on the Pacific led him, as pointed out earlier, to vote for the admission of California even if it came in as a slave state.

The railroad and the telegraph were, in Seward's mind, "indispensable agencies in perfecting the integrity of the Nation and in attaining its destiny." [33] He fought relentlessly

---

[31] Seward, *Travels*, p. 472.

[32] *Cong. Globe*, 31st Cong., 1st sess., March 11, 1850, App., pp. 261–62.

[33] Seward to the Pacific Rail Road Convention, Oct. [8], 1849, Seward Papers. Two decades later, Seward was still stressing the importance of railroads for commercial expansion. He told the New York Chamber of Commerce that the "extension of our inland railroads 4,000 miles in a single year cannot fail to develop inland commerce,

for a route that would give the United States one continuous line of communication, having the "Atlantic Ocean & Europe on one end and the Pacific Ocean & Asia on the other." [34] Such a route was needed to command the Asiatic trade, and it would have the undeniable advantage of not being shared with any other power, and thus could not be exposed to foreign control or interference.[35]

The transcontinental railroad, it was hoped, would become the major carrier of the world's goods from West to East, because it would be "the shortest route for merchandise" from England and the continent to China, India, Australia and South America by way of New York and San Francisco.[36] Seward's confidence in the vital role of the railroad led him to assert in 1869 that "San Francisco is firmly established as the Constantinople of American empire." [37]

Seward was fully aware that the competition with Britain would be at its most strenuous on the seas and oceans of the world, and most particularly on the Pacific. For this reason, the condition of the American merchant marine was of special interest to him. He warned the Senate that "no nation was ever highly prosperous, really great, or even truly independent, whose foreign communications and traffic were conducted by other states." He called their attention to other great empires,

the most reliable basis for all foreign trade and navigation" (draft of remarks to New York Chamber of Commerce reception, March, 1870, Seward Papers).

[34] Seward to S. B. Ruggles, Nov. 6, 1852, Seward Papers, Library of Congress.

[35] *Cong. Globe*, 32d Cong., 2d sess., Feb. 8, 1853, App., p. 146.

[36] *The Commercial and Financial Chronicle*, June 1, 1867.

[37] Seward, *Works*, V, 573. For a discussion of the significance of railroads in the shaping of American foreign policy in the post-Civil War era, see Howard B. Schonberger, *Transportation to the Seaboard, the "Communication Revolution" and American Foreign Policy, 1860–1900* (Westport, Conn., 1971).

"Tyre, and Egypt, and Venice, and the Netherlands, and Great Britain," which, by "becoming the merchants, became thereby the masters of the world." He argued successfully for subsidies to the ill-fated Collins steamship line, which was in competition with the Cunard line on the Atlantic, casting his argument in familiar form as he told the Senate that it was incumbent upon the American government to undertake this responsibility if it was to compete for the "ultimate empire of the ocean." He tried to get support for a line of steamers from New York to Hamburg so that it would "enable us to take control of a trade which at present we only divide with foreigners at great disadvantage to ourselves." The Senate, he said, must decide whether "we shall secure the commercial ascendancy of the world or shall suffer it to pass from our grasp." [38]

On the other side of the continent, Seward urged the charting of the Pacific and Arctic Oceans.[39] He stressed its necessity because "we are now a Power of the Pacific ocean. . . . If we look north or south, east or west, we are practically the only real Power there is that dwells upon the Pacific ocean. . . . The trade of the Pacific ocean is the trade and commerce of the world." [40] The shortage of marine facilities on

[38] *Cong. Globe*, 32d Cong., 1st sess., April 27, 1852, p. 1200; March 23, 1852, p. 826; March 1, 1852, p. 657.

[39] *Ibid.*, Aug. 2, 1852, p. 1935. Seward introduced a bill to survey "Behring's Straits, and also such parts of the China Sea, Straits of Gaspar, and Java Sea as lie directly in the route of vessels proceeding to and from China" (*ibid.*, pp. 1973, 2041).

[40] *Ibid.*, 34th Cong., 1st and 2d sess., Aug. 12, 1856, p. 2058. Seward's advocacy of a naval powder magazine at Mare Island, Calif., is hard to square with his view that the United States was the only power in the Pacific. He urged the magazine because "if there is any place in the world we want a powder magazine, I am very sure it is on the Pacific side of the continent, for that is the only place where we are exposed to any enemy" (*ibid.*, Aug. 15, 1856, p. 2130).

the Pacific coast disturbed Seward, especially the absence of dry docks for the repair of merchant vessels. He demanded that the construction of one be undertaken immediately. In the meantime he suggested that the United States Navy make its facilities available for this purpose. Failure to do so, he argued, would be injurious to American commerce in the Pacific regions and to "our navigation to China" as well.[41]

Seward did not ignore agricultural matters in his concern for American supremacy in the world's marketplace. His eagerness to make it easier for settlers to acquire land was based on the idea that farmers would supply food cheaply to industrial workers (brought over under the liberal immigration laws he favored), who would in turn produce the manufactured commodities for trade.[42] Ever present in Seward's mind was the fear that a failure to maintain agricultural parity with Great Britain, Russia, and other European nations would shut out the United States from foreign markets; in fact, those countries might "even ultimately undersell us in our own."[43]

If we bear in mind that when Seward spoke of the American empire he meant commercial supremacy, we can better understand his supposed insatiable desire for territorial expansion. Commercial hegemony did not require vast stretches of territory. Indeed, too rapid an extension of the national domain would probably have hindered rather than advanced

---

[41] *Ibid.*, 31st Cong., 1st sess., Sept. 28, 1850, p. 2057.

[42] *Ibid.*, 31st Cong., 2d sess., Feb. 27, 1851, p. 740.

[43] Seward, *Works*, III, 181. There is an excellent discussion of agrarian influences on American foreign policy during Seward's tenure as Secretary of State in William Appleman Williams, *The Roots of the Modern American Empire: A Study of the Growth and Shaping of Social Consciousness in a Marketplace Society* (New York, 1969), pp. 107–71.

Seward's real goal. The domestic controversy it would undoubtedly have provoked would have absorbed a great deal of the energy and time he would have preferred to devote to the prosecution of his programs. Doubtless, this was a consideration in his leisurely approach to the acquisition of Mexico and Canada. So far as Mexico was concerned, he was prepared to wait as long as a century. He manifested no such patience in his efforts to realize the commercial empire.

The recognition that for Seward empire was not territory but commerce removes much of the confusion and ambiguity surrounding his expansionism. Perhaps he did not define his terms as precisely as he might have, but he did describe accurately enough what his real objective was: "To what end has this expansion tended from the beginning? Whither does it now tend, if not to commerce on the islands and continents which lie between us and the setting sun?" [44] Seward advocated just enough expansion to make possible the attainment of that end.

The programs Seward proposed to achieve the American empire were neither vague nor ambiguous. They were coherent, consistent, and integrated, and their implementation he believed to be well within the capabilities of the nation. The empire was predicated upon a strong and stable society, without internal division or conflict; a flourishing agricultural and industrial economy, operated by a work force replenished by a steady stream of immigrant labor; a national government prepared to come to the aid of the merchant, the industrialist, and the farmer, and provide the needed support for the competition they were certain to meet from abroad; a global network of communications and shipping; equality of opportunity in Asia among the commercial nations of the world;

[44] Cong. Globe, 33d Cong., 1st sess., June 29, 1854, p. 1566.

and finally, the establishment of New York City as the financial center of the empire. Thus, with a powerful economy outproducing and outselling the world, naval and coaling stations at strategic points on the globe, and domination of the monetary systems of the world, the United States would be in truth the greatest of nations. Eventually, political domination would follow the economic as a matter of course. Expansion would be a function of commercial hegemony: "Commerce is the god of boundaries, and no man now living can foretell his ultimate decree." [45]

Such was the imperial vision of William Seward. His energies in the post–Civil War period were devoted to making it a reality.

[45] *Ibid.*, 31st Cong., 1st sess., March 11, 1850, App., p. 262.

CHAPTER III

Wiring an Empire:
The Intercontinental Telegraph

The attainment of Seward's version of a commercial empire was predicated in part on the unification of the world's markets into a global network whose direction and control would be situated in the United States. He hoped to achieve this unification by establishing an intercontinental telegraphic communications network and instituting international monetary reform. In both these endeavors he was fortunate to have the cooperation and assistance of two remarkable men, Perry McDonough Collins and Samuel Bulkley Ruggles. Indeed, these men largely conceived the extraordinary and ambitious projects that Seward then enthusiastically adopted, because they conveniently fitted into his own imperial ideas. He gave these projects his unqualified approval and lent the full support of his office to their implementation. In the end, neither undertaking would be successful, but that does not detract from Seward's boldness and foresight as he undertook to breathe life into the American economic empire through them.

Perry McDonough Collins and the Overland Line

Like Seward and Ruggles, Collins was a New Yorker, but unlike them, he had sought his fortune outside the state. His early career resembled that of the typical man on the make in the United States in the middle of the nineteenth century, as he wandered from law to politics to merchandising and ultimately to banking and land speculation. After having traveled in the South for a time, he went West and ended up in California.[1] In Sonora he first became interested in the possibilities of the telegraph, after he had invested in the Tuolumne Telegraph Company, which operated a line from Stockton to the gold fields of Columbia, California. There he became involved in the American-Russian Commercial Company, an American concern then doing business in the Russian territory that was later to be Alaska, and which had hopes of expanding its operations into the Pacific islands and Asia.

Also like Seward, Collins was a man of large-scale vision and monumental projects. He quickly became convinced that the Amur region in eastern Russia was "the destined channel by which American commercial enterprise was to penetrate the obscure depths of Northern Asia, and open a new world

---

[1] Biographical data on Collins is sparse. The best account by far is in *Siberian Journey, Down the Amur to the Pacific, 1856–1857: A New Edition of a Voyage Down the Amoor by Perry McDonough Collins,* edited, with an Introduction by Charles Vevier (Madison, Wis., 1962), pp. 10–13, 19–21. My account of Collins' life draws heavily on Vevier. There is also an invaluable bibliography on pp. 357–62. A briefer account may be found in Charles Vevier, "The Collins Overland Line and American Continentalism," *Pacific Historical Review,* XXVIII (Aug., 1959), 237–53. Vevier sees Collins as a "rough-hewn geopolitician" and an exponent of what he calls "American continentalism," a concept he spells out more fully in his "American Continentalism: An Idea of Expansion, 1845–1910," *American Historical Review,* LXV (Jan., 1960), 323–35. For a very short treatment of Collins that does not materially differ from Vevier's, see Eldon Griffin, *Clippers and Consuls: American Consular and Commercial Relations with Eastern Asia, 1845–1860* (Ann Arbor, Mich., 1938), pp. 340–42.

to trade and civilization." [2] In 1856 he successfully sold this idea to Secretary of State William Marcy and had himself appointed United States Commercial Agent for the Amur River.

Collins immediately left for Russia, where in April, 1856, he began a journey down the entire length of the Amur River, a distance of some 2,690 miles—"from St. Petersburg to Kamchatka"—which lasted the better part of two years.[3] As Charles Vevier has pointed out, he was the "second American to cross the Ural Mountains and was the first foreigner to descend the Amur to its mouth." [4] The trip confirmed his assessment of the region's commercial possibilities, which after some fanciful mathematical calculations, he computed to be in the neighborhood of twenty million dollars annually.[5] Here was a theme that appealed to his promoter instincts, and he played it incessantly as he sought support for a global overland telegraph system.

In Collins' view, the chief obstacle to tapping the source of this great wealth was the lack of communications with the Amur region. Recalling his earlier experience in California, he hit upon the idea of a telegraph line that would not only

[2] Vevier, *Siberian Journey*, p. 45.
[3] P. McD. Collins to Seward, April 16, 1861, NA M179, R180.
[4] "Collins Overland Line," pp. 239–40.
[5] Collins to Lewis Cass, March 6, 1858, NA T111, T2 (Consular Dispatches, Amoor River). The fanciful character of the estimate is obvious when it is compared with the fact that the Statistical Office of the Consular Bureau estimated that in 1858 American trade with the Amur region amounted to only one million dollars (H. C. McLaughlin to G. J. Abbott, Superintendent, Statistical Office, Jan. 17, 1861, *ibid.*). Despite this, McLaughlin refers to the "almost fabulous commercial resources" and the "vast and lucrative commerce" of the region. As will be seen later, hard reality was not allowed to obtrude on the visions of a glorious future.

connect the United States with Russia, but that would also continue overland around the world and bring the whole of the globe into practically instantaneous communication with the United States. The ultimate objective was to control the commerce of Asia, if not the whole of international trade. As he wrote later to Seward, his voyage had convinced him that the commerce then going to Europe from northern and central Asia could be rerouted by steamship by way of the Amur to the ports on the Pacific coast. This reversal of trade would be facilitated by a telegraph line connecting Europe with the United States across Asia, with lines to China and Japan. Such a telegraph would compel London "to communicate through New York and San Francisco in order to conduct the commerce of Europe with Japan and China." In this way the United States would exercise control over European trade with the Far East. Collins believed that the "chief agent in subjecting the vast commerce of Asia to our rule" would be the Russian-American telegraph, or as it was later more commonly called, the Collins Overland Line.[6]

Before Collnis could convince the Buchanan administration to underwrite the project, the election of 1860 brought a change in government and brought in William Seward as Secretary of State. In him Collins found not only a sympathetic audience but, what is more, one who could grasp the implications of the Collins line and support it with vigor and tenacity.

Preparing the Way Abroad

After a few anxious months in which Seward unaccountably offered the post to two others, Collins was reappointed as Commercial Agent on the Amur River. The first order of

[6] Jan. 4, 1869, *ibid.*

business was to get the necessary grants from Russia and England to build portions of the line on their territories and possessions. The projected route of the intercontinental telegraph was from St. Petersburg to St. Louis, Missouri, by way of the Amur River, East Cape, Bering Strait, Prince of Wales Cape, Sitka, Vancouver, B.C., Astoria, and San Francisco—a distance of some 14,000 miles, all of it overland except for the Bering Strait. The Russians had assumed the responsibility for building that portion of the route from St. Petersburg to Nikolayevsk, at the mouth of the Amur, just across the Tatar Strait from Sakhalin Island, and Collins was to take it from there. In his annual report for 1861, Collins informed Seward that Russia was making "considerable progress" on its end of the intercontinental telegraph, and anticipated that by the spring of 1862 it would have reached Omsk in western Siberia, approximately 2,500 miles east of St. Petersburg. Another line was being constructed westward from the Amur to meet it, but at that time the two lines were still 5,000 miles apart.[7]

In this report Collins continued to express unbounded confidence in the commercial potential of the area. The climate, he said, was most advantageous for the growing of cereals. All manner of crops could be raised, including fruit, corn, wheat, rye, buckwheat, and barley. He mentioned the feasibility of using Bactrian camels in the mining districts of Nevada, a commodity he thought might become "an important branch of Amoor commerce." Collins was particularly anxious to put to rest the canard that the climate was in-

---

[7] "Report for the Year Ending December 31, 1861," *ibid.* For a full discussion of the curious affair of Collins' reappointment see my doctoral dissertation, "William Henry Seward and the Foundations of the American Empire" (Rutgers University, 1972), pp. 61–66.

salubrious for the "European races" and asserted that a "more patent error was never indulged in." His most enthusiastic comments were saved for the benefits that would accrue to American commerce and expansion. He linked Russia and Japan, claiming that the "two countries are well suited for an exchange of commodities, of which our enterprising merchants will not long remain idle spectators," and closed with a rousing peroration:

Her people require and desire the products of our shops and looms, our engines, machinery and implements. We desire their raw materials; the exchange under like circumstances has always proved vastly profitable to commerce. Imagine five to ten millions of people with whom such an exchange can be made and it needs no prophet to foretell the profitable results.[8]

Fired by this glowing report, Seward began to exert the considerable influence of his office on behalf of the Overland line. That he could spare so much time for the project despite the precarious military situation at home and the delicate diplomatic complications with Britain is clear evidence of how highly he regarded it. In this effort he enlisted the aid of Senator Milton S. Latham of California and Simon Cameron, who had recently replaced Cassius M. Clay as Minister to Russia. Later he would call upon the valuable services of his old friend Samuel B. Ruggles of New York.

In the Senate, Latham had taken up one of Seward's favorite projects, the subsidization of a mail steamship line from San Fransisco to China, by way of Hawaii and Japan. His argument in support of it had the Seward touch: "Senators! we are the only people of pure Caucasian origin, at *home* on the shores of the vast Pacific ocean; we alone possess

[8] "Report for the Year Ending December 31, 1861."

a Pacific empire, and we are bound to extend its power and influence morally, if not physically, not only on this continent but on the coast of Asia." To those who argued that the existing trade with China and Japan did not warrant the expenditure, Latham replied that this trade was not an accurate index of the profitability of the line because "trade itself begets trade." This spirit animated Latham's introduction of a bill to appropriate $100,000 for the survey of a route for the Collins line from San Francisco to the Amur River.[9] The bill was reported out by the Committee on Military Affairs. Latham had written the recommendation, stressing the commercial benefits of the line and, significantly, adding an argument that had not before been emphasized. Latham claimed that American merchants, "driven from time-honored and beaten paths" by the war, needed "new avenues for expansion and extension of trade." [10] The Civil War was turning the attention of the builders of commercial empire more and more toward Asia.

In June, 1862, Seward, Latham, and Collins conferred on the drafting of a memorandum to Simon Cameron. The memorandum itself was drafted by Latham, submitted to Seward for revision and dispatched that same day to the American Minister in Russia. As modified by Seward, it called Cameron's attention to Collins' work, explained that Collins was "zealously and effectively engaged in advancing the enterprise" and said that its completion "will doubtless be effective in enlarging the commerce between the countries and between the two continents." Cameron was instructed to extend any assistance that he properly could "in favor of this great enter-

[9] *Cong. Globe*, 37th Cong., 2d sess., April 10, 1862, p. 1600; Feb. 17, 1862, p. 841.
[10] 37th Cong., 2d sess., Senate Committee Report No. 13.

prise" and to keep in touch with Collins when he arrived in Russia.[11]

Collins reached St. Petersburg in early September, 1862, to apply for a grant, and although Cameron assured him that he foresaw no difficulty, the negotiations proved lengthy.[12] While awaiting the outcome, Collins presented Seward with a proposal that must rank as one of his more fanciful. According to Collins, the Governor General of Siberia had suggested to him the possibility of sending an agent to the United States in order to recruit 5,000 Americans "of Sclavic [sic] origin" for resettlement along the Ussuri River and the coast of Tartary. They were to be given "special privileges, a section of country to themselves, all expenses paid, rations for two years, land, cattle, houses, sheep, farming implements, and freedom from local or other taxation." Collins thought the plan "sagacious," and told Seward it would give Russia "a population touched by American quickness, agricultural and mechanical ideals, and who would with the axe, the saw, the plow, and that other implement not exactly agricultural or mechanical, the rifle, fence strongly and surely against the more Southern Manchoos and the jealous Coreans." [13] Nothing came of the idea, but it remains an interesting if bizarre notion that the American frontier experience could be transferred abroad with beneficial results to the host country.

The long delay in obtaining a grant from Russia was caused principally by Russian insistence that the Collins line be run directly across the Pacific from the mouth of the Amur River

[11] Collins to Seward, June 9, 1862, NA T111, T2; Memorandum, Latham to Department of State, June 9, 1862, *ibid.*; Seward to Cameron, June 9, 1862, NA M77, R136 (Diplomatic Instructions, Russia).
[12] Collins to Abbott, June 28, 1862, NA T111, T2; Cameron to Seward, Sept. 9, 1862, NA M35, R19 (Diplomatic Dispatches, Russia).
[13] Oct. 31, 1862, NA T111, T2.

to Russian America, a route that would entail 600 miles of submarine cable. Collins preferred to run the line across the Bering Strait and then along the coast of eastern Siberia to Okhotsk and thence to Nikolayevsk on the mouth of the Amur, a route requiring less than 100 miles of undersea cable.[14] The disagreement was resolved in favor of the American plan, and Cassius M. Clay, now back in Russia as United States Minister, was formally notified on June 16, 1863, that a grant had been made to Collins. Clay said it was a "liberal" one; Seward expressed his "sincere satisfaction" and belief that the act showed the wisdom of the Emperor and that it manifested the friendly attitude of Russia toward the United States.[15]

The basic clauses of the agreement established the right of the company (yet to be formed) to build a line along the route proposed by Collins and to build stations and roads for surveys and repairs; provided for the use of armed Russian men to protect the line and stations at company expense; ruled that "all workmen and a part of the men in service along the line" were to be Russian subjects (it was suggested that as many as possible ought to be married men with their families because this would be "better and more convenient" for the company, as well as the men); imposed a limit of five years for the construction of the line and thirty-three years for the exclusive right of way, contingent on starting within two years of the grant. Not granted was a proposal by Collins that villages be built using Russian convicts and exiles as settlers ("inconvenient," as the Russians delicately put it). Also, no

[14] Melinkoff to Collins, Nov. 30, 1862, enclosed in Collins to Seward, Jan. 20, 1863, *ibid.*

[15] Clay to Seward, June 17, 1863, NA M35, R20; Seward to Clay, July 13, 1863, NA M77, R136; F. W. Seward to Collins, July 15, 1863, NA Record Group 59 (Consular Instructions, Amoor River).

right of sovereignty was granted, nor (perhaps with the fate of the American Indian in mind), any authority to "subordinate the Natives" on the frontiers, nor full title to the land, except for tax-free use. Government dispatches were to be given priority over private communications and the tariffs were not to exceed those prevailing in Russia. The Imperial Government offered Collins an indirect subsidy of only $100,000 because "the mercantile intercourse of Russia with America is not very considerable." Furthermore, since the "principal benefits" of the line would be reaped by the United States, England, and France, the Russians suggested that Collins seek his subsidy from them. They pointed out that the 900,000 rubles which they were spending to build the connecting line was a sufficient subsidy. Collins was not altogether happy with the Russian refusal of a subsidy and he requested a revision of this portion of the grant.[16]

Without waiting for a reply, Collins left for London to apply for authorization to run the line over England's territory in British Columbia down to the fortieth parallel, the boundary with the United States. He also planned to ask for a subsidy of £20,000 a year for thirty-three years. He again called upon Seward's "friendly offices," and asked him to write to the American Minister to England, Charles F. Adams, asking Adams to support the project. Seward proceeded to do so. Collins also indicated he would go to France, because that country held the "third rank commercially" and its trade with the United States was large enough to justify her interest in the scheme.[17]

[16] Melinkoff to Collins, June 4, 1863, encl. in Collins to Seward, June 18, 1863, NA T111, T2; Collins to Seward, June 25, 1863, *ibid.*; F. W. Seward to Collins, July 28, 1863, NA RG 59 (Amoor River).

[17] Feb. 20 and June 25, 1863, NA T111, T2; Seward to C. F. Adams, July 13, 1863, *For. Rel.* (1863), Pt. 1, p. 311.

By August, 1863, Collins was in London, where the negotiations proved almost as lengthy as those in Russia. The delay stemmed in part from a jurisdictional dispute between the home government and Hudson's Bay Company. In December, after this conflict had been resolved, Collins presented his plan to Lord Palmerston and the Duke of Newcastle. Neither had any strenuous objection and Collins thought the Duke "constantly courteous and favorably disposed." The grant, made in February, was similar in many respects to the Russian, giving Collins the right to build a telegraph line, stations, and other required installations through the "British Dominions in the North Pacific and connecting Russian America with the United States." While use of the land was granted, the soil itself remained in possession of the Crown. Supplies and material needed by the company would be admitted duty free. Government messages were to be given precedence and the government could "take possession of the telegraph for its own purposes in case of emergency, subject of course, to reasonable compensation." The company was given until January, 1870, to complete the line; regrettably, from Collins' viewpoint, no subsidy was given.[18]

Now that the Russian and British grants had been secured, Collins thought "the most difficult part of the undertaking" had been completed.[19] In truth, however, his problems were only beginning. The subsidy had yet to be obtained from the United States Congress, and after that there remained the stupendous challenge of building the vast intercontinental telegraph itself.

[18] Collins to F. W. Seward, Dec. 30, 1863, NA T111, T2; Collins to Seward, Feb. 8, 12, 1864, *ibid.*
[19] Collins to Seward, Feb. 12, 1864, *ibid.*

Seward and Ruggles Join Forces

The major task now facing Seward and Collins was to pry a subsidy for the intercontinental telegraph out of a Congress beset with finding the money to finance a civil war. Seward had been instrumental in Collins' success until this time and Collins was suitably appreciative. From London he had written the Secretary that "an entirely new channel of commerce for our merchants and a very wide field for American enterprise generally will be opened" by the overland telegraph. But, he said, it could not have been possible "without generous and highly advantageous assistance from the Department of State since the present Secretary came into office." He was hopeful that the "attention and publicity given to this new commercial world, by the Department of State and myself so fully and frequently will awaken our merchants to its truly valuable future." [20]

Up to this point, Seward's contribution, although significant, had been largely indirect, and had consisted of talking up the project among American diplomats abroad and urging them to smooth Collins' way whenever and wherever they could.[21] Now Seward's campaign would have to be more direct; it would involve the Congress, which would be called upon to subsidize the project, in addition to American mer-

[20] Aug. 18, 1863, *ibid.*

[21] For example, the following to the American Consul at Leghorn, Italy: "The Department has long had its attention directed to the development of the commerce of the United States with the Russian Possessions. . . . You do not seem to be aware how much has been done and is now doing for the development of the American trade with Asia through the Amoor by Mr. Collins, an active and intelligent Commercial Agent" (F. W. Seward to J. Stevens, May 22, 1862, NA RG 59 [Consular Instructions, Leghorn, Italy]).

chants and commercial men, whose influence he hoped would persuade Congress to support the Collins line. To run this campaign he turned to one of his closest friends, Samuel Bulkley Ruggles of New York City. Ruggles had been interested in railroad and telegraph projects for many years and, just as importantly, was one of the more influential members of the New York Chamber of Commerce, a position from which he could effectively publicize the Collins line.[22]

Collins, no mean publicist himself, had already undertaken to "place the importance of North Eastern Asia fully and prominently before our Mercantile and Commercial world" in an article in *Hunt's Merchants' Magazine*. The collaboration of Ruggles and Collins undoubtedly started in the early stages of the Amur project, for Collins wrote the State Department in 1861 that he had been assured of the opportunity by the New York Chamber of Commerce "of presenting to many of the first commercial men of New York a full exposition of [the Amur region] and the benefits that American commerce may derive therefrom." Ruggles, soon to be chairman of the Chamber's Committee on Telegraphic Communication, must surely have had knowledge of Collins and his work. Just about then, too, Collins began to pass out information on the Amur region to members of Congress, including those from New York.[23]

The Collins line needed all the help it could get in Congress. A bill introduced in the House by John Cochrane of New York, on February 18, 1861, failed to get any action, owing perhaps to the lateness of the session and the impending

[22] The partnership between Ruggles and Seward is important for an understanding of Seward's policies. This relationship is reserved for fuller treatment in Chapter IV.

[23] Collins to F. W. Seward, Sept. 18, 1861, NA T111, T2.

crisis. It asked for $50,000 to make a survey of the Northern Pacific and Bering Strait for the purpose of "telegraphic communications between the mouth of the Amoor River in Asia, and the confines of the Russian possessions in America." [24] Senator Latham's 1862 bill also had languished, although he had supported it with a strong speech which emphasized the advantages of the intercontinental telegraph for the Asiatic trade.[25]

Collins refused to be daunted, and once more he appealed to Congress. His third memorial, on April 12, 1864, was referred to the Senate's Commerce Committee, chaired by Zachariah Chandler. This time the wheels began to turn. On April 14, Chandler wrote to Seward that he would be "glad to receive from you such information upon the subject as may be in the possession of the Department, together with your views upon the expediency of granting the prayer of the memorialist." [26]

Seward, who recognized an opportunity when he saw one, immediately set to work. As one of his first moves he called Ruggles to Washington to confer on the matter.[27] There the

[24] *Cong. Globe*, 36th Cong., 2d sess., Feb. 18, 1861, p. 230.

[25] In his speech, Latham provided a striking metaphor: "We hold the ball of the earth in our hand and wind upon it a net work of living and thinking wire, till the whole is held together and bound with the same wishes, projects and interests." If the Collins line were built, those "wishes, projects and interests" would clearly be American. 37th Cong., 2d sess., Senate Committee Report No. 13.

[26] "Memorial of Perry McDonough Collins . . . ," in *Papers Relating to the Intercontinental Telegraph* (Washington, D.C., 1864), pp. 7–10.

[27] George Templeton Strong, "Diary," New York Public Library (microfilm copy), entry for May 1, 1864: "Mr. SBR came in at dinner from Washington. Seward had sent for him to advise about a Report—or something—as to a proposed line of telegraphic communication with Europe by way of Behring's Straits & Asia."

strategy was laid out and promptly put into action. Upon his return to New York two weeks later, Ruggles presented a resolution to the Chamber of Commerce calling on Congress to give "speedy and favorable consideration and support" to the Overland line. It was unanimously adopted and submitted to Congress.[28] Ruggles sent copies of the resolution to Collins, who passed them on to Seward with the hope that they would have "their legitimate influence upon a proposition which must if carried out add greatly to our own commercial prosperity." [29] Assistant Secretary Frederick W. Seward (Seward's son) replied that "the Department has read these papers with eminent satisfaction and congratulates you upon the conspicuous prospects of the great enterprise." [30] Collins himself was not idle. He saw to it that favorable notices of his plan found their way into the leading newspapers, including the *New York Tribune*.[31]

While this public relations campaign was underway, Seward, in response to Senator Chandler's query, assembled a number of documents in support of the Collins line. The most important of these was a letter to the Chairman of the Commerce Committee, in which Seward argued at length for the plan, stressing its significance for the commercial future of the United States. The document not only reveals a good deal about Seward's ideas, but also demonstrates the close partnership between Seward and Ruggles. For Ruggles had done more than merely "advise about a Report"; he had

[28] "Intercontinental Telegraph," New York Chamber of Commerce, *Annual Reports and Proceedings*, May 5, 1864, (New York Public Library).

[29] May 26, 1864, NA T111, T2.

[30] May 28, 1864, NA RG 59 (Amoor River).

[31] Collins to Seward, May 25 ,1864; F. W. Seward to Ruggles, June 13, 1864, NA T111, T2.

actively collaborated with Seward in writing it. How much of Ruggles' deft hand the final version contained can be seen by comparing the preliminary draft of the letter, in the Seward Papers at the University of Rochester, and the final version transmitted to Chandler.[32]

The "Communication" shows Ruggles' great experience in preparing reports: it is shorter, better organized, makes its points more effectively and uses less flamboyant language than Seward's draft. The original draft, however, being pure Seward, is a better index of his opinions on the significance of the intercontinental telegraph than Ruggles' revision. In the "Communication," Seward takes a great deal more of the credit for the concept. In the draft he speaks only of having "encouraged" Collins, but in the "Communication," although conceding that the project was "truly" Collins', he nevertheless asserts that while Collins was "engaged in maturing and developing it . . . he had been acting under the instruction and with the approbation of the Department."[33]

The "Communication" goes briskly to the point and seeks to answer two fundamental questions about the Collins line: its feasability and whether its utility would justify the subsidy. For our purposes the question of its utility is more significant, because the answer to it would more clearly demonstrate Seward's objectives. He begins with the claim

[32] The full title is "Communication of Hon. William H. Seward, Secretary of State, upon the subject of an Intercontinental Telegraph, connecting the Eastern and Western Hemispheres, by way of Behring's Straits, in reply to Hon. Z. Chandler, Chairman of the Committee on Commerce of the US Senate, to which was Referred the Memorial of Perry McDonough Collins," in *Papers Relating to the Intercontinental Telegraph*, pp. 11–25. In the following discussion, it will be referred to simply as "Communication."

[33] Draft, p. 2; "Communication," p. 23.

that the telegraph is as indispensable as the steam engine in commercial and political affairs. He establishes a clear connection between foreign and domestic commerce by observing that "the nation that enjoys the most prosperous foreign commerce exhibits the greatest industrial activity and domestic happiness within its own borders." If telegraphic communication were to be combined with maritime communication, "new and stronger reciprocity would be exhibited, not only in commercial centers, but in every recess of the land." The intercontinental telegraph would connect the commercial cities of the United States with the markets of Asia, Europe, and the Middle East. Given such a development, Seward found it difficult to "overestimate the direct effect of this new application of the national energy" on the economic progress of the United States, but he was confident it would be accompanied by a practically limitless "increase of national influence" and the consequent extension "throughout the world [of] American ideas and principles of public and private economy, politics, morals, philosophy and religion." He was especially optimistic about its beneficial impact on the Pacific coast of the United States.[34]

Although the "Communication" presents in compact form many of the ideas which Seward had expressed before, it is a much pruned, formal document that does not really convey the spirit and verve found in the draft, which contains views and opinions either entirely eliminated or considerably modified by Ruggles' editing. For example, Seward places much greater stress on the importance of Asiatic commerce in the draft than appears in the "Communication." He admits he is "seduced" by the prospect that within a generation trade on the Pacific Ocean would exceed that on the Atlantic, and is

[34] "Communication," pp. 17, 18, 21–22.

emphatic in his assertion that the Collins line would stimulate American commerce with Japan and China. He foresees the day when the trade centers of the United States will be connected with Europe, China, India, Japan, and Africa, achieving peacefully a commercial victory greater than Holland and Great Britain had done "by tedious and exhaustive conquests." He speaks of the Pacific Ocean as the "basis of renewed civilization" following the vast increase of commerce in both directions, a commerce that would be almost entirely controlled by Americans. The Collins telegraph is indispensable to these ends, for "when we shall have this new connection we shall no longer be strangers in the East." [35]

Seward, fully aware that not everyone shared his view, did concede that to many his speculations on the commercial benefits of the intercontinental telegraph would appear imaginative. Still, he could claim that the benefits were slowly but perceptibly becoming realities. In Asiatic Russia, for instance, the Emperor had directed that English be taught to prepare his subjects for "full, free, and intelligent intercourse with the American people." A vast movement of peoples was underway, "a great . . . migration from all parts of Russia and China and Japan to the Eastern shores of the Pacific Ocean," a migration that would ultimately create "a commerce which would [be] probably purely American." [36]

Seward's decision to ask Ruggles to refine the soaring rhetoric of his draft into a more sober document, suitable for presentation to a Congress which was not in the mood for flights of fancy, proved wise. The Commerce Committee adopted Seward's "Communication" as its report, and it may well have been because of Ruggles' revisions that Congress proved so receptive to the Collins scheme.

[35] Draft, pp. 18–20, 23, 26.   [36] *Ibid.*, pp. 24, 21.

On June 9 a bill to support the Collins line was introduced in the Senate, sponsored by Senator Chandler. It gave to Collins, "his associates and assignees," the right to build a telegraph line from the terminus of the transcontinental telegraph north through the United States to the Canadian boundary. In addition, the Secretary of War was "authorized and instructed" to dispatch a vessel to survey a route in the northern Pacific and to "assist" in laying the cable, transporting material, and giving any other assistance which would "secure a successful promotion of the enterprise." If the line was completed within five years, the company was to have a ten-year monopoly on government messages, for which it was to be paid $50,000 a year. If the total revenue of government business annually exceeded $100,000, the company was to return the excess to the government. Despite some talk of improper influence, the bill was approved by the Senate, 36–3, but without the subsidy so desired by Seward. After an uneventful passage through the House, President Lincoln signed it into law on July 1, 1864.[37]

The Chinese and Latin American Extensions

The idea of a telegraph line that would run from St. Petersburg, Russia, all the way to St. Louis, Missouri, was indeed a brilliant one. But it was only a part of the great intercontinental telegraph system that Collins had envisioned. Two other lines were projected to complete the system. One line was intended to connect the major coastal cities of China; the other was to link all countries on the continents of the western hemisphere by running a telegraph down the east coast of Mexico, Central America and South America, and up the

[37] *Cong. Globe*, 38th Cong., 1st sess., June 9, 1864, p. 2818; June 21, 1864, p. 3126.

west coast. The Chinese line would join the Collins line at the Amur; the Latin American line would be linked with the transcontinental line in the United States. The truly extraordinary idea was to link the three continents with one continuous telegraph line, entirely overland, except for the short underwater cable across the Bering Strait. The purpose was to "bring the commerce of the whole world upon the 'Russian Extension Line.' " [38]

A little more than a week after Seward had sent his "Communication" to the Senate in support of the Collins line, he received a letter from Collins announcing that he had organized, a month earlier, the East India Telegraph Company, whose objective was to "unite the great commercial cities of China with the Russian Line upon the Amoor." [39] The prospectus of the company pointed to the absence of a telegraph line in China despite "the great increase of its trade with all commercial nations." [40] On the assumption that the Overland line to the Amur (not yet approved by Congress) was "*assured* of completion," the company planned to construct a telegraph line designed to connect Canton, Macao, Hong Kong, Amoy, Foochow, Ningpo, Shanghai, Nanking, and Peking and thence to the Amur. Potential investors were assured that the Chinese were "particularly favorable to the American People and government." The officers of the East

[38] Western Union, *Statement of the Origin, Organization and Progress of the Russian-American Telegraph Western Union Extension, Collins Overland Line* (Rochester, N.Y., 1866), p. 16.

[39] May 25, 1864, NA T111, T2.

[40] *Prospectus of the East India Telegraph Company*, encl. in *ibid.*, p. 3. Collins was one of the directors of the company. See N. Mickles to Seward, Jan. 23, 1867, NA M179, R250. In addition, he was also a director of the Western Union Telegraph Company and managing director of the Collins Overland Line. All this while, of course, he was still Commercial Agent for the United States at the Amur River.

India Telegraph Company alluded to the long interest of the "mercantile community" of New York in the international telegraph (one again senses the work of Ruggles). They concluded that "the immense population of the cities named, and their immense trade with all the great commercial nations," would render the proposed line "one of the most remunerative of any in the world, relying *only* for its business upon the needs of those engaged in mercantile pursuits," and held up the prospect of "over FOUR HUNDRED AND TWENTY MILLIONS" of customers yearning for Western merchandise.[41]

The news seemed to have escaped Seward's immediate attention, and Collins merely received a reply from the pen of the Assistant Secretary commending him for "the zealous energy of the prosecution of your great enterprise." [42] Collins, in a display of that "zealous energy," then wrote to Cassius M. Clay and asked him if he would not bring the new project to Seward's attention. This letter is a significant one, for it reveals the fundamental purpose of the Overland line. Telegraph communication with China, said Collins, "has always been one of the leading inducements in the construction of the overland telegraph to Europe." The China trade, he said, "is of gigantic proportions now" and the future would be even brighter if the Chinese extension were built. Clay immediately informed Seward that "our American friends" were "very anxious" to build the Chinese extension and he suggested that Seward instruct Anson Burlingame, United States Minister to China, to make an effort to get a charter from the Chinese.[43] This time the news reached Seward, who quickly replied that he had "lost no time" in instructing

[41] *Ibid.*, pp. 4, 6.   [42] May 26, 1864, NA RG 59 (Amoor River).
[43] Oct. 28, 1864, NA M35, R20; Nov. 14, 1864, *ibid.*

Burlingame to get to work on the project.[44] And, indeed, that very day Seward forwarded all the relevant documents to Burlingame and urged him to do all he could to "facilitate the work." [45] It proved a tedious business, however, although Collins sought to persuade the Russians to prod the Chinese into action. The Russians said they could do little, claiming that the chief problem was Chinese fear of the Mongols, and that conciliation in the form of "palm oil" might have to be resorted to.[46]

While negotiations proceeded along their oleaginous way, the East India Company and its project were being promoted at home. The pages of *The Telegrapher* were often the forum for grandiose claims of untold riches to come. The Chinese telegraph was seen as the beneficiary of the Atlantic cable, which would render it "of increased and assured value to the commerce of the treaty powers." In the familiar language of the huckster, it was presented as "one of the grandest and most moneymaking enterprises now dawning upon the world." True, the company had until now "remained silent," but that was because it was "quietly perfecting its arrangements." Investors could take heart in the firm conviction that American interests in China were "not inconsiderable, as may be judged by references to the many merchants whose interests lie in that country." [47]

Collins, leaving no possible avenue of support unexplored, made an effort to get the assistance of shipping companies with interests in Asian commerce. In a confidential circular (written from the offices of Western Union) to the directors

[44] Dec. 13, 1864, NA M77, R136.
[45] Dec. 13, 1864, NA M77, R38 (Diplomatic Instructions, China).
[46] Collins to Seward, May 10, 1865, NA T111, T2.
[47] *The Telegrapher*, Aug. 15, 1866, p. 184; Jan. 2, 1867, p. 98.

of the Pacific Mail Steamship Company, he forecast the "rich pecuniary reward" that would "attend your participation in the enterprise." The Chinese extension, he asserted, "would prove more profitable than any telegraph line of equal extent in the world. Looking at the actual commerce of China as it now exists, there can be no reasonable doubt of this." [48]

The East India Company, meanwhile, grew impatient over the protracted negotiations. On January 17, 1867, N. Mickles, the vice president, wrote Seward to ask what news he had from Burlingame regarding rumors that an award had been made before he had left China for the United States. Seward replied that he had heard nothing but would certainly look into it, and promptly sent to Burlingame, now in Washington, a copy of Mickles' letter with the comment that "no despatch of the nature indicated has been received from you." [49]

When Burlingame did not act with the promptness expected of him, Mickles wrote to J. E. Stuart, a Congressman from New York, explaining the project to him and soliciting his intervention with Seward. Mickles called Stuart's attention to the already "vast trade" between China and the United States, a trade that was increasing at a pace which entitled an enterprise such as the East India Telegraph Company, "conceived in the interest of that commerce," to the "consideration of the government." Stuart, with the compliance usually shown by New York congressmen when solicited by commercial and mercantile interests at home, forwarded Mickles' letter to Seward and urged him to do what he could for the company. Seward, for his part, sent both letters on to Burlingame advising him that while he should not commit the

[48] Jan. 12, 1867, NA M179, R250.
[49] Jan. 17, 1867, NA M179, R250; Seward to Mickles, Jan. 21, 1867, NA M40, R62; Seward to Burlingame, Jan. 21, 1867, NA M77, R38.

government to this project in preference to others, he should use his good offices to promote "the object sought." [50]

Burlingame answered that he was doing all he could and he assured Seward that from the beginning of his mission he had impressed upon the Chinese the importance of the telegraph and railroad and had "tried in every way to secure the right to build them." But he had encountered great difficulty in obtaining a formal agreement because he could not overcome Chinese objections to the telegraph. The Chinese were under the unfortunate impression that the electric lines would "interrupt the 'fung-shue' or streams of good luck passing over the country." Besides, he pointed out, any grant to the United States would also be given to all other countries in accordance with the most-favored nation clause, and that "the first to occupy the ground will have the advantage." He did not think it likely that this would be an American company and had consequently refused to advise Americans to risk money on the project. Seward expressed regret over Burlingame's failure and the hostility of the Chinese to the telegraph, but he hoped that in time they would abandon their superstitions and prejudices. He also thought that "efforts should be made to hasten their enlightenment" and urged Burlingame to undertake the task.[51]

Perseverance finally paid off. A grant was obtained from China, much to the delight of the *Philadelphia Ledger*, which felt that the line "should certainly be of advantage to American interests" in China, and of *The Telegrapher*, which was certain that the "pecuniary success" of the project could not be doubted and prophesied that "American enterprise and

[50] March 15, 1867, encl. in J. E. Stuart to Seward, March 18, 1867, NA M179, R254; Seward to Stuart, March 30, 1867, NA M40, R62; Seward to Burlingame, April 5, 1867, NA M77, R38.

[51] Burlingame to Seward, May 22, 1867. *For. Rel.* (1867), Pt. 1, pp. 483–84; Seward to Burlingame, September 20, 1867, NA M77, R39.

capital, will, doubtless, greatly strengthen American interests and influence" in China.[52] But the grant had come too late for any of the work to be undertaken before Seward left office.

Two months after urging the Chinese extension on Seward, the indefatigable Collins came forward with yet another proposal—the Latin American telegraph line. On July 30, 1864, less than a month after President Lincoln had signed the Overland bill, Collins wrote to the Secretary introducing the plan and presenting a Mr. M. A. Zabriskie, "who has been engaged in telegraph enterprises for many years," to further explain it. The objective was to encircle the continent below the United States with a telegraph line, tie this in with lines in the United States, which in turn would be connected with the Collins Overland Line and the Chinese Extension, thus "concentrating the globe upon our overland lines." [53]

The first step, according to Collins, would be to start on the east coast of Brazil, run a line straight across South America to the Pacific coast, and then continue on to Panama. Zabriskie was to go to Brazil and obtain a grant there, and then visit all the other Latin American countries for the same purpose. Collins was suitably apologetic for once again asking much, but he felt justified because he knew Seward's deep interest "in promoting telegraph communication throughout the civilized world." He requested that Seward inform American diplomats throughout Latin America of the project and ask them to "further" it.[54]

[52] July 25, 1868, p. 392. *Ledger* remarks quoted there. See also May 30, 1868, p. 329; Nov. 14, 1868, p. 95, for similar comments.

[53] July 30, 1864, NA T111, T2.

[54] *Ibid.* For his assistance, Zabriskie received Western Union stock from Collins at bargain prices. It was probably from the shares Collins had been given to spread around where they would do the most good. See Vevier, "Collins Overland Line," p. 247.

Seward, with his customary enthusiasm for such enterprises, set to work with little delay. On August 18, he issued a circular addressed to American diplomats in Latin America. In it he called their attention to the Collins Overland Line and its objective of linking Europe and America by way of Asia. He rehearsed the history of Collins' efforts to promote the line. Seward then outlined the first phase of the Latin American telegraph and "authorized and requested" the diplomats to let the governments to which they were accredited know that the Collins proposal was "regarded with favor by the Government of the United States" and that he would be "pleased to learn that like favor had been extended by the States of Latin America." [55] Collins thanked Seward for "this very favorable and highly important state paper," and announced that he would now expedite the negotiations so as to dispense with the preliminaries as quickly as possible, although he was expecting some unavoidable delay. On May 10, 1865, Collins reported that the United States Minister to Brazil, James Watson Webb, had presented the plan to the Brazilian government and was confident of a favorable verdict.[56]

[55] "To the Diplomatic Officers of the United States in Latin America," Aug. 18, 1864, NA M77, R28.

[56] Collins to F. W. Seward, Aug. 25, 1864, NA T111, T2; May 10, 1865, *ibid*. The Brazilian project got bogged down over charges that Webb would not support the telegraph line unless he received a little "palm oil." The irascible Minister to Brazil enlivened the dispute by suggesting that the project was a scheme to enrich Seward's nephew, Clarence, a partner in the law firm of Blatchford, Seward, and Griswold of New York City. Webb went so far as to claim that Clarence had really written the Circular of August 18, 1864. Seward rejected the charge with some asperity. See Blatchford, Seward, and Griswold to Seward, Aug. 16, 1865, NA M179, R254; Seward to Webb, Sept. 25, 1865, NA M77, R24 (Diplomatic Instructions, Brazil); Zabriskie to President Andrew Johnson, April 25, 1867, Andrew Johnson Papers (Library of Congress); Seward to Webb, May 30, June 1, 1867, NA M77, R24.

There was, however, one very large proviso in the ambitious plans for the Chinese and Latin American telegraph lines. Both depended for their existence on the successful completion of the Collins Overland Line to the Amur. If that line failed, then the whole complex structure would fail with it.

The End of the Overland Intercontinental Telegraph

Not long after President Lincoln had signed the Collins bill into law, work got underway. By October, *The Telegrapher* reported that an expedition of at least seven vessels was outfitting in New York.[57] Collins, meanwhile, had sold his interest in the project to Western Union for $100,000 and stock in the new company, now officially designated the Western Union Extension. He wrote Seward that he was leaving with Hiram Sibley, president of Western Union, for St. Petersburg on September 21 to clear up some points about the grant.[58] His arrival in Russia was noted by the *Journal of Commerce* with the comment that "the growth of commerce in the East, resulting from the steady encroachment of the European powers, to say nothing of the American whaling fleet in the Pacific and Ockhotsk [*sic*] Sea, gives to this enterprise an importance which augments from year to year." [59]

By November 21, 1865, a line had been strung from New Westminster, British Columbia, to Finster's River. A work party was in Siberia building toward the Bering Strait. A survey was being made of the Strait by a United States naval vessel to determine a suitable path for the undersea cable. Optimism was rising and Collins wrote to Seward that the work was not as "difficult as many predicted." [60]

[57] Oct. 31, 1864, p. 9.   [58] Nov. 21, 1865, NA T111, T2.
[59] Dec. 23, 1864.   [60] Nov. 21, 1865, NA T111, T2.

This favorable view, which permeated the official reports of Collins and Western Union, was sometimes accompanied by hints of trouble, but these hints were always buried under promises of untold wealth to come. In an address to the Travelers' Club in New York City in December, 1865, following his return from Russia, Collins did admit to some problems, but he was certain no real difficulties would be encountered. "We may break a wire and loose [*sic*] a day or a few days, but this is not to defeat the telegraph. . . . We know no such word as fail." This misplaced optimism regarding the construction of the line proved as unfounded as the earlier predictions of the fabulous business it would bring when completed. But Collins, not one to dwell on gloomy news, hastened to tell the assembled merchants and businessmen, in a nice figure of speech, of the "slumbering millions . . . who await our magnetic touch" and of Asia, "where commerce in vast proportions will be made quick." He promised them that "half the population of the whole world will be made tributary to us" and that the "commerce of the world will find its path across this continent." [61]

But as the Collins line inched its way painfully up the rugged coast of Western Canada toward Russian America, an event a continent away blasted the hopes of Collins and Seward for the intercontinental telegraph. On July 27, 1866, the *Great Eastern* reached Heart's Content, Newfoundland; Cyrus W. Field had at long last completed the laying of the Atlantic cable. He jubilantly announced the news to Seward two days later, along with expressions of gratitude for the Secretary's "services in the Senate of the United States" in the 1850's. [62] On August 26, commercial traffic between the

[61] "Speech Before the Travelers' Club and Other Societies," Dec., 1865, in Western Union, *Statement of the Origin*, pp. 144, 153, 165.
[62] July 29, 1866, NA M179, R242.

United States and Europe opened. The first message transmitted proved to be, in effect, the death notice for the Collins
line. As the *Cincinnati Gazette* observed: "In the present
state of things it would be certain folly to spend any more
upon it." [63]

Although it is true that the Atlantic cable gave the *coup de
grâce* to the Collins line (it was manifestly uneconomical and
inconvenient to send messages overland some 14,000 miles
when they could be sent directly to Europe, less than a third
of the distance), this was by no means the sole reason for its
demise. Work on the line had not been progressing nearly as
well as many had claimed, including Western Union itself,
and doubtless it would have been abandoned in any event as
too costly. News of the difficulties was masked behind a
stream of sanguine public statements which gave assurances
that "everything was progressing finely." [64] All the while,
however, Western Union was quietly preparing to abandon
the project. On January 3, 1867, the directors of the company
notified Seward of their doubts that the line could be worked
for "commercial business with the expectations of its proving
remunerative to stockholders." [65] The following month Sibley
and Collins were authorized to go to Washington and talk
with Seward about the possibility of the government acquiring the line. This failed, and on March 25, the company
officially notified Seward that it was halting work.[66] Of
course, it denied that lack of capital or construction problems

[63] Quoted in *New York Journal of Commerce*, Sept. 27, 1866.

[64] *The Telegrapher*, Jan 2, 1866, p. 24. See also Jan. 2, 1865, p. 27;
July 31, 1865, p. 129; Sept. 25, 1865, p. 164; Dec. 1, 1865, p. 1; Feb. 15,
1866, pp. 53–54; April 2, 1866, pp. 99–100.

[65] O. H. Palmer to Seward, Jan. 3, 1867, NA M179, R250.

[66] Resolution of Western Union Telegraph Company, February 27,
1867, NA M179, R252; William Orton to Seward, March 25, 1867,
NA M179, R254.

were responsible for the suspension; rather, the whole blame was placed on the Atlantic cable.[67]

Despite efforts by Western Union to keep the news of the suspension covered up for a time while it unloaded its stock, word leaked out and was greeted with stunned disbelief that soon turned to anger and recrimination. *The Telegrapher*, which had given unrestrained support to the project, but now certain that it had been gulled, turned on the company. It accused Western Union of "gross mismanagement, and such a disregard of the plainest dictates of common foresight and prudence, that the inevitable collapse of the whole scheme has long been predicted by those best acquainted with the facts in the case." Probably feeling that it had been one of those who had not been "best acquainted with the facts," it charged the company with misleading the public, through "occasional paragraphs in the newspapers," into believing that the scheme had been a success, and further claimed that it had engaged in "sharp practices." [68]

Though these charges might be dismissed as simple outrage at having been taken in, there is enough evidence to lend the color of truth to them. The project had been plagued by delays, bad weather, poor choice of route in British Columbia, and overall mismanagement. That Western Union, when it became evident the end was near, sought to unload the losses on its stockholders, did not serve to quiet suspicions.[69]

[67] Orton to Seward, March 25, 1867, NA M179, R254.

[68] March 15, 1867, pp. 158–59.

[69] See the reports of Col. Charles S. Bulkley in Western Union, *Statement of the Origin*, pp. 116–26; Robert Luther Thompson, *Wiring a Continent: The History of the Telegraph Industry in the United States, 1832–1866* (Princeton, N.J., 1947), pp. 435–36, for the questionable financial dealings; see *The Telegrapher*, March 15, 1867, p. 158, for the poor choice of route.

But beyond this, there was the wholly fanciful expectation of great financial reward from the operation of the line. When the Collins line was put forth by Western Union, it tried to attract investors with grandiose predictions of profits. It predicted that with two wires in operation, one thousand messages a day could be transmitted. By working the line "uninterruptedly night and day" and charging twenty-five dollars a message, the lines would gross $25,000 a day, $750,000 a month, and $9,000,000 a year. Figuring operating costs at $1,125,000 a year, a tidy profit certainly seemed possible.[70] The fantasy becomes obvious when these projections are compared to the actual income from the Atlantic cable in its first two years of operation. During that time, while working only six hours per day, it sent 63,985 messages and had a daily average income of only $3,000. Its net profit for the period was $2,400,000.[71]

Western Union pointed to these unfulfilled expectations in its letter of suspension. They had been certain when Collins first presented his plan that the "immense trade of the East would meet us with their business." But these hopes "proved illusory" and they "could not properly employ the capital entrusted to us except under the promise of reasonable return from its investment."[72]

But it should not have been necessary to wait for the completion of the Atlantic cable to realize that the "immense trade of the East" was not there. All that was needed was to have read the reports of the Vice Commercial Agent on the Amur, H. G. O. Chase. All the time Seward, Collins, and

[70] Western Union, *Statement of the Origin*, p. 16.
[71] Alvin E. Harlow, *Old Wires and New Waves: The History of the Telegraph, Telephone and Wireless* (New York, 1936), p. 297.
[72] William Orton to Seward, March 25, 1867, NA M179, R254.

Ruggles labored to bring the Overland line to completion, Chase was reporting with monotonous regularity that trade in the area was "insignificant." He was convinced that a "desirable or growing trade in this country" was not likely in the "near future" and that many foreign businessmen were determined to "withdraw from it as soon as possible" for "no general advance in these matters has taken place." [73] For the last quarter of 1865, no American ships arrived or departed at Nikolayevsk. In February, 1867, at the time when the project was being abandoned, Chase reported that "the general character of the trade has not materially changed" and that "exports abroad from this port with the exception of furs, are still so insignificant as not to be recorded in the Gov't statistics." Chase left his post in September, 1867, bitterly complaining about uncooperative Russian officials and pessimistic about the future. His successor, H. W. Hiller, reported no American ships arriving at the Amur in the last quarter of 1868.[74]

[73] H. G. O. Chase to F. W. Seward, March 30, 1864, NA T111, T2. Regarding shipping in the Amur region, Griffin says that from 1856, when the first vessel arrived, to 1860, perhaps twenty-three or twenty-five merchant ships had called at Nikolayevsk, the main port. He calls the trade "not impressive" (Griffin, *Clippers and Consuls*, pp. 343–46). Even so, he says, the "tendency was . . . to import more goods than could be absorbed" (*ibid.*, p. 345).

[74] H. G. O. Chase to F. W. Seward, Jan. 6, 1866, NA T111, T2. See also Dispatch of April 13, 1866, *ibid;* H. G. O. Chase to Seward, Feb. 1, 1867, *ibid;* H. Hiller to Seward, Dec. 31, 1868, *ibid.* In 1870, Cyrus W. Field, hoping to emulate his triumph on the Atlantic, campaigned for a cable across the Pacific by way of Hawaii and Midway. He could get little financial support, however, because many felt the commercial return would not be sufficient. The cable was not laid until the beginning of the twentieth century when conditions seemed more propitious following the acquisition of the Philippines (see Harlow, *Old Wires and New Waves*, p. 298).

These unencouraging reports seem not to have received close scrutiny at the State Department. But it is likely that even if they had been read more carefully than they apparently were, they would not have changed any minds. Belief in the inexhaustible trade of the Orient was one of the assumptions of the era. Policy makers and businessmen were prepared to act on these beliefs rather than on any objective evaluation of reality.

Seward, at any rate, was not dismayed, although he expressed "profound disappointment" at the failure of the Collins line. Rather, he said, "I abate no jot of my former estimates of the importance of the Intercontinental Pacific Telegraph." [75] Collins, as well, was not ready to abandon the idea, although much of the opprobrium for the failure fell upon him.[76] In his letter of resignation to Seward, he recapitulated the history of the intercontinental telegraph. His vision still as bright as ever, he was convinced that he had not been mistaken about the importance of Asia to American commerce. He placed the blame for the failure on "others to whom I had to entrust its construction." He said the acquisition of Alaska had only confirmed his view of American "power and commerce on the Pacific," and he had no doubt "that commerce, considerations of national securities [sic], and enterprise" would subject "the vast commerce of Asia to our rule." Then "London will have to communicate through New York and San Francisco in order to conduct the commerce of Europe with Japan and China" and that "vast com-

[75] Seward to Western Union Telegraph Co., March 28, 1867, NA M40, R62.

[76] *The Telegrapher* characterized him as "a perfect maelstrom for the funds of his friends and supporters, and the less capitalists have to do with his wild and impracticable projects the better off they will be pecuniarily" (June 26, 1869, p. 352).

merce would become so engrafted upon our commerce and people that in the future we would not only command but control the European trade of the East and reap therefrom what by position and progress is our legitimate right." And to show that he was by no means deflected from this view, he announced that he was forming a new company to complete the line. He closed with thanks to Seward for his "constant support and generous confidence." [77]

Seward replied that he had "read with deep interest" Collins' "observations . . . upon the subject of Asiatic commerce" and said he was pleased to hear that Collins intended to resume the work. He assured Collins that the "information which you have given me upon this important subject is so valuable, and your remarks in that connection so clear, full, and forcible that, with the President's permission, I shall submit a copy of your communication to the Congress of the United States." [78]

Failure in one area, however, had been matched by success in another. The Atlantic cable was in operation, and even if Asiatic trade was disappointing, there was still that other aspect of the telegraph which Collins had alluded to: the control of European trade with the Orient. Accordingly, Seward wired his congratulations to Western Union on the completion of the cable: "I regard it as a tributary to an expansion of our national commerce and ultimately of our political institutions both of which I think important forces in the progress of civilization." [79]

Thus, the effort to unify the markets of the world by means

[77] Jan. 4, 1869, NA T111, T2.

[78] Jan. 12, 1869, NA RG 59 (Amoor River).

[79] Seward to Western Union Telegraph Co., March 28, 1867, NA M40, R62.

of the intercontinental telegraph had failed. But there remained another way to achieve this objective. If Seward
could not get to Europe through Asia, perhaps he could get
to Asia through Europe.

CHAPTER IV

The Monetary Basis of Empire:
Unification of the World's Coinage

The year 1867 was one of mixed blessings for William Seward. His disappointment over the failure of the Collins Overland Line was offset by the purchase of Alaska, and he had renewed hope that the objectives that were to have been achieved by the intercontinental telegraph might yet be reached by other means. A single standard of world coinage might unify the international marketplace under American hegemony as effectively as the telegraph.

Like the intercontinental telegraph, unification of the world's coins was a bold and imaginative idea which owed much to a figure who has not yet been fully appreciated by historians. Thanks to Charles Vevier, Perry McDonough Collins has received a measure of scholarly recognition. Not so Samuel Bulkley Ruggles. Despite a solid biography of him, he has generally been seen as a man of narrow interests; his influence on Seward and his contribution to Seward's version of commercial empire have gone unrecognized. For Seward and Ruggles formed a political partnership, and if more often than not Ruggles was the silent partner, his ideas found their voice in Seward. The monetary conference at Paris in 1867 was only one of their joint ventures. But before taking up that episode, a closer look at the Ruggles-Seward combine might contribute to an understanding of Seward's objectives.[1]

Samuel Bulkley Ruggles

There was a more than superficial resemblance between Perry McDonough Collins and Samuel Bulkley Ruggles. Both were intimately involved with Seward in projects of global scope and significance; both were men of broad vision and bold imagination; and both were, like Seward himself, "speculators" in empire. Still, there was a difference, subtle and intangible, but nonetheless real, that makes it far easier to imagine Seward and Ruggles as a team than Seward and Collins. It is not that Collins was a charlatan, but there was an indefinable air of the pitchman and the huckster about him. However much Seward may have agreed with Collins' plans, it is hard to think that a man of Seward's probity and sobriety could have been very comfortable with him. Next to Collins,

[1] The biography is D. G. Brinton Thompson, *Ruggles of New York: A Life of Samuel B. Ruggles* (New York, 1946). Two more recent works in the economic history of the post-Civil War United States deal in part with Ruggles. Allen Weinstein (*Prelude to Populism: Origins of the Silver Issue, 1867–1878* [New Haven, 1970, p. 259] calls him "the earliest post–Civil War American gold standard advocate." Walter T. K. Nugent (*Money and American Society, 1865–1880* [New York, 1968, p. 73]) discusses the Paris monetary conference from the standpoint of its relationship to domestic monetary concerns. Nugent sees Ruggles as a somewhat ineffectual figure. His characterization of Ruggles as "one of that spectacular breed of grand promotors . . . who blazed paths as bright as comets, and after left works that were no more permanent" is more colorful than accurate. W. A. Williams (*Roots of the Modern American Empire*, p. 162) says that Ruggles "sounded as though he had studied with William Seward." They did indeed often sound alike, but a more accurate evaluation of the relationship would be that they went to the same school, studied together, and that occasionally Seward cribbed from Ruggles.

Ruggles appears as a practical man of affairs, an investor in solid enterprises with whom Seward could and did have much in common, and to whom he could entrust sensitive and complex undertakings with confidence.[2]

Ruggles was a capitalist on the make, a rising entrepreneur, one of a type common in the United States before the Civil War. He seemed to have a hand in every venture that promised a profit. He was at one time or another, and sometimes simultaneously, a land speculator and city planner in New York City (he created Lexington Avenue, Gramercy Park, and Irving Place); an advocate of internal improvements, especially canals and railroads (he was president of the board of Erie Canal commissioners, one of the commissioners of the Union Pacific Railroad, and cofounder and member of the board of the Erie Railroad); an investor in foreign enterprises (he was a cofounder of the Panama Railroad Company and one of its directors); a financier (he was a cofounder of the Bank of Commerce in New York City and on its board of directors until 1852); a powerful figure in the economic and political life of New York (he was a member of the New York Chamber of Commerce). And if this were not enough, he was considered a wizard in statistical analysis and finance, a monometallist and a life-long advocate of international monetary reform.[3] Ruggles, in short, was an important figure in New York political and economic life at the very time that Seward was a rising political star. It would have been surprising if they had not seen that each had something to contribute to the other and decided to join forces.

[2] Despite the significance of Ruggles' relationship with Seward, he does not appear at all in Bancroft's *Life of Seward*. Van Deusen's *Seward* contains only a passing reference to him.

[3] Thompson, *Ruggles,* pp. 26–110.

William Seward and Samuel B. Ruggles

The partnership of William Seward and Samuel Ruggles went back at least as far as the 1830's when Seward was governor of New York, and probably farther back than that, since Ruggles considered himself "one of the oldest" of Seward's friends.[4] During the early years of their friendship, Ruggles had aroused Seward's interest in internal improvements, especially railroads.[5] When Seward went to the Senate, Ruggles continued to advise him. Occasionally, his contributions were more substantial than mere advice. For example, in 1852 Seward wrote Ruggles that he planned to make a speech on the transcontinental railroad and asked him for "books & papers" on the subject because "I am nothing in such matters without you." [6] He also asked for any speeches Ruggles had made about the railroad, and requested ideas from him because "while your hand is in you can touch that subject more epigramatically than I." [7]

Ruggles shared Seward's views on the necessity for an American commercial empire. In 1848, Seward gave a speech on the "True Greatness of Our Country," in which he spoke of the "irresistible attraction" of the United States for the commerce of Europe and Africa . . . the rising insular communities in the Southern ocean, as well as the trade of the

[4] S. B. Ruggles to Seward, Dec. 25, 1865, Seward Papers.

[5] See Ruggles to Seward, Dec. 17, 1838, Ruggles Papers (New York Public Library).

[6] Nov. 6, 1852, Seward Papers (Library of Congress).

[7] June 18, 1854, April 12, 1859. Seward Papers (Library of Congress). See also entry for Jan. 4, 1861, in the "Diary" of George Templeton Strong (Microfilm copy, New York Public Library), for a suggestion that Ruggles wrote one of Seward's speeches in the Senate on the Pacific Railroad bill.

populous regions of China and the eastern Indies." [8] Ruggles congratulated Seward on the speech and told him that "the Great American Future was never before so brightly revealed, or so magnificently depicted." [9] Seward was highly pleased, although he did not think it merited such extravagant praise. He thought it lacked the "silken tones" he had heard at Ruggles' lectures in Union Square. Seward modestly admitted that he did not treat such subjects very well. "But I will maintain," he went on, "that if you would but divide the labor of discussing them equally with me now, as you were wont, we two could shore up the destinies of this great nation as well as any one man in the country can do." In 1849 Seward, forecasting the role Ruggles would later play, told him, "I shall insist on dragging you up from your elegant repose into new and bolder and higher service than you have as yet extended to the country." [10]

Seward and Ruggles thought as much alike as any two individuals can. They held similar views on most issues and especially on the future role of the United States in the world. Seward made good his promise to thrust Ruggles into "new and bolder and higher service" when he called on him for indispensable aid in the campaign for the Collins telegraph. It was not long thereafter that Seward would need him again.

Seward and the Role of New York in the New Empire

Implicit in any plan to unify the markets of the world, whether by telegraph or monetary unification, was the as-

[8] Seward, *Works*, III, 12–13.

[9] Ruggles to Seward, Dec. 29, 1848, Ruggles Papers (New York Public Library).

[10] Seward to Ruggles, Jan. 9, 1849, Seward Papers (Library of Congress). For Ruggles' views on commercial empire see S. B. Ruggles, *American Commerce and American Union* (New York, 1856), pp. 11–13, 33.

sumption that the capital of this network would be New York City. We have already seen that Collins fully expected the intercontinental telegraph to transfer the commercial capital of the world from London to New York. This was Seward's thinking as well, and had been for many years. As far back as 1837, he had expected New York to be the center of an American commercial empire. In a speech delivered during the gubernatorial campaign that year, he contemplated the relationship "between his own humble action and the destiny of the country." His own generation, he said, could "see only the nucleus of the great capital which is to establish the commercial balance between the New World and the Old." The Hudson River, he proclaimed, was the "true and proper seat of commerce and empire." [11] Later, in the Senate, he was an eloquent and effective spokesman for New York. Although he often debated with his Southern colleagues against localism and in favor of nationalism, he still could not forbear to recognize the claims of the State to which, "by birth and gratitude," he belonged. New York, "with less than two hundred miles of internal navigation connected with the ocean, has . . . secured the commerce of the continent, and is steadily advancing to the command of the commerce of the world." [12] Seward opposed the establishment of a branch of the United States Mint in California, insisting that it more properly belonged in New York City. The commerce of the world was concentrating at New York and it was there that coin was to be used as the "medium of exchange of the pro- ductions of all countries and climes." [13] He pointed to the net-

[11] Seward, *Works*, III, 312, 333.

[12] *Cong. Globe*, 31st Cong., 1st sess., March 11, 1850, App. p. 269.

[13] *Ibid.*, May 24, 1850, p. 330. This idea was shared by David Dixon Porter, one of Seward's intimates. In Porter's view, if the East India trade "could be once diverted from its present course and directed to New York, Wall Street would become the great monetary centre

work of canals and railroads that would eventually tie New York with the Pacific and, of course, extend its domination to the Orient as well as Europe.[14] "All honor, then, to the merchants of New York!" he cried, for "they are the true builders of the power and greatness of the state." The merchants build this power "by building canals and railroads, to increase the freedom of inland trade, and swell to its utmost limits foreign commerce." [15]

A speech that Seward made at Oswego, New York, in November, 1856, provides a clear indication of what lay behind his interest in expansion. The ostensible subject of his address was the political crisis in the United States and the problem of slavery extension. But in the course of his remarks he observed that "our commercial and political systems must be extended somewhere, or else the growth of the cities and towns of Western New York must be arrested." There was no prospect for additional growth, as he saw it, unless "new and distant regions" were made "tributary to them for manufactures and for commerce." [16]

Thus, Seward was receptive to plans that would contribute to his lifelong goal of making New York the commercial and financial hub of the new empire. By concentrating the control of the world's financial and monetary resources in the hands of New York merchants and bankers, that goal would practi-

---

and Downing Street would occupy but a secondary place in the estimation of the world" (D. D. Porter to Mr. Church, Feb. 18, 1868, Porter Family Papers [Library of Congress]).

[14] *Ibid.*, April 29, 1850, p. 304.   [15] Seward, *Works*, III, 324.

[16] William H. Seward, *Immigrant White Free Labor, or Imported Black African Slave Labor* (Washington, D.C., 1857). This speech, in which Seward called for the creation of a new political party on the basis of "the political equality of all white men," is not included in the five-volume collected *Works*.

cally be assured. The conference on world monetary reform at Paris in 1867, held in conjunction with the Universal Exposition, offered Seward his opportunity, and naturally he turned to Ruggles for the major share of the work.

Preparing for the Conference

Even before the Paris monetary conference, Seward had tapped his old friend for important services. In 1863, Ruggles had been the United States representative at the Berlin Statistical Congress. How much Seward relied on Ruggles can be seen in George Templeton Strong's comment that Ruggles tried to beg off serving at this "very imposing commercial synod" by pleading pressing business affairs, but that Seward would accept no excuses and mailed him his commission anyway. Ruggles reluctantly accepted because Seward thought him the "very best man in the country for the job." [17]

As the American delegate to the Berlin Statistical Congress in 1863, Ruggles first proposed equalizing the gold content and value of the British pound sterling and American half-eagle with a new twenty-five-franc gold piece to be coined by the French.[18] Afterward, when a "senseless clamor" broke out in the United States over "Frenchifying" American money, Ruggles wanted it made plain that the idea "did not in any way originate with the Government of France." He insisted that the objective of international monetary unity was "far more American than European in its origin." [19] Nothing

[17] George Templeton Strong, "Diary," entries for Aug. 17, 18, 1863 (New York Public Library).

[18] Ruggles to Seward, Sept. 14, 1863, NA M37, R22 (Special Agents), pp. 6-7.

[19] S. B. Ruggles, *Supplementary Report on the International Monetary Conference at Paris, 1867*, April 8, 1870; Ruggles, Speech at Banquet for the Chinese Embassy, June 22, 1868, both in *ibid.*

came of this proposal, however, and it was not until the Monetary Conference that Ruggles' suggestion was finally acted upon.

In March, 1865, the French government invited the United States to participate in the Universal Exposition to be held in Paris in 1867. Seward quickly accepted, and he appointed an advisory committee of ten citizens of New York, one of whom was Ruggles, to prepare for American participation.[20] Ruggles set to work with customary zeal, even offering to save Seward "some needless expenditure of precious time" by composing a "suitable Executive notice of the worldwide subject of Uniform *weights and measures*." The recommendations would "occupy comparatively little room in the Message," he assured Seward. "I am very sure, that the worldwide topic of a uniform *coin* . . . can be made deeply interesting to every spot on the globe where *money* has any value." The United States, he urged, "ought to be not only forward, but conspicuous, in these movements." [21]

So, even before the United States government had taken any official action, Ruggles was laying the groundwork. He publicized the exposition to the New York Chamber of Com-

[20] Francois Henri-Louis de Geofroy to Seward, March 27, 1865, Senate Executive Document No. 5, 39th Cong., 2d sess.

[21] Ruggles to Seward, unofficial and private, Nov. 21, 1865, Seward Papers. Ruggles' offer was not accepted and no reference to coins, weights, or measures appears in President Johnson's Message in December, 1865. Ruggles was not the sole influence on Seward's views of weights, measures, and coins. J. Q. Adams was one of Seward's idols, and he was much taken with Adams' economic ideas, especially in regard to the vital importance of international commerce (see William H. Seward, *Life and Public Services of John Quincy Adams, Sixth President of the United States, with the eulogy Delivered Before the Legislature of New York* [Auburn, N.Y., 1849]). Bancroft says it was ghost-written by J. M. Austin, a clergyman (*Life*, I, 201).

merce, which appointed him to a special committee on the Universal Exposition.[22] From this vantage point, Ruggles proceeded to gather as much support from influential people as he could. As he told Seward, it seemed "desirable, without delay to unite all the Chambers of Commerce and Boards of Trade of the *whole country as a body*, in the work of cooperating with the Government." As evidence of his efforts he sent Seward copies of the Resolution and Report adopted by the New York Chamber of Commerce which, he predicted, would "soon be reechoed by their kindred associations between the two oceans." With pardonable pride he informed Seward that "it required some little effort to elevate the tone of public opinion, both in and out of Congress, to the dignity of the occasion." [23] Nor did Ruggles neglect the press. The *New York Journal of Commerce* carried an editorial which claimed that civilization would be considerably advanced if the chief trading nations would adopt a "common system by which to compute all the exchange of commerce." [24] All the while, Ruggles traveled about the country rounding up manufacturers, businessmen, financiers, anyone of influence he could buttonhole to serve as unpaid commissioners for the United States at the exposition.[25]

The results of Ruggles' lobbying in Congress soon became apparent. Representative John A. Kasson of Iowa, Chairman

[22] New York Chamber of Commerce, *Annual Reports and Proceedings*, Jan. 4, 12; Feb. 1; March 1, 1866 (New York Public Library).

[23] Ruggles to Seward, Feb. 3, 1866, Seward Papers. A note in Seward's handwriting reads, "I think he has executed the work admirably." More formally he told Ruggles that "your proceedings seem to have been wisely conceived" (Seward to Ruggles, Feb. 3, 1866, *ibid.* [letterpress copy]).

[24] Feb. 9, 1866.

[25] Ruggles to Frederick William Seward, Aug. 10, 1866, Seward Papers.

of the House Committee on Coinage, Weights, and Measures, issued a report advocating United States participation in an international conference on coinage, even at the cost of "some sacrifice of national *amour propre* for the general good." He called for the appointment of a special commission to investigate the question of coinage reform. In the House he spoke in support of the committee's report, saying that "there is no one subject that can come before an international or other congress that has more important relations to the commercial and social intercourse of the world than this one." [26]

Kasson's call was seconded by the influential *Commercial and Financial Chronicle* of New York, which saw in the idea special significance for international trade. The paper referred its readers to the monetary convention signed by France, Belgium, Italy and Switzerland in December, 1865. It predicted that the agreement would result in a "natural increase in the trade of the countries embraced in the new Monetary Union," and called the convention a characteristic product of "that progress which has long been going on to unite nations into a single commonwealth for commercial purposes." The *Chronicle* hoped that the United States would quickly join the movement for monetary reform and that with the passage of Congressman Kasson's bill "the introduction of this coinage would seem to be well timed." [27]

In the meanwhile, Seward had appointed N. M. Beckwith, an American living in Paris, Commissioner General to oversee preparations there prior to official American participation in the exposition. The French approached Beckwith informally to see if he would sound out Seward's attitude toward Amer-

[26] House Report No. 62, 39th Cong., 1st sess. (1866); *Cong. Globe*, 39th Cong., 1st sess., May 17, 1866, p. 2654.

[27] Oct. 6, 1866.

ican participation in an international monetary conference. Beckwith, in turn, wrote to Seward who not only responded favorably, but also announced the appointment of a special commissioner to engage in preliminary discussions with the French. Not surprisingly, it turned out to be Ruggles.[28]

This was still at the informal level, however. Seward was not approached formally until January, 1867, when Jules Berthemy, the French Minister to the United States, inquired whether the United States was willing to subscribe to the monetary convention of December 23, 1865, or if it might not prefer to "take part in an international conference at which might be discussed the means of arriving at a more extended monetary understanding." [29] After first getting the favorable opinion of the Secretary of the Treasury, who said the value of monetary unification was "too patent to require arguments in its support," Seward informed Berthemy that the United States "has repeatedly manifested its interest in the question of international unification of monetary standards" and that "it only remains to be decided how the desired result may be brought about." Seward agreed that the opening of the Universal Exposition in Paris would be a splendid opportunity.[30] On May 27, Berthemy issued a formal invitation to the conference, scheduled to begin in Paris on June 17, and asked Seward for the name of the delegate from the United States. Seward promptly accepted, and named Samuel B. Ruggles, who was in fact already in Paris, and who was, in the words

[28] June 29, 1866, Sen. Exec. Doc. No. 5, 39th Cong., 1st sess.; Seward to Beckwith, Oct. 4, 1866, *ibid*.

[29] M. Berthemy to Seward, Jan. 4, 1867, *For. Rel.* (1867), Pt. 1, p. 296.

[30] Seward to H. McCulloch, Jan. 30. 1867, NA M40, R62; H. McCulloch to Seward, Feb. 7, 1867, NA M179, R251; Seward to Berthemy, Feb. 13, 1867, *For. Rel.* (1867) Pt. 1, p. 297.

of Seward, "familiar with the views of this government." [31] Ruggles was indeed familiar with the government's views, and a brief review of them will tell us a great deal about what he tried to do at the conference.

The American Objectives

As United States representative in Paris, Ruggles' objectives combined elements of chauvinism and a strong desire to assure America's predominance in the world's commercial and financial dealings with his own predilection for monometallism. The fundamental difficulty with America's role in international trade, as Ruggles saw it, was that the basic gold coin of the United States weighed $3\frac{1}{2}$ percent more than its French counterpart and $2\frac{1}{16}$ more than the British coin. Ruggles, a staunch advocate of the gold standard, blamed the disparity on the United States' bimetal currency system, which required fixing relative values for gold and silver.[32]

The consequences of this imbalance were vividly portrayed by Ruggles. Owing to their differential weight and value, American coins did not circulate in other countries; no sooner did they arrive in Europe than they were melted down into

[31] M. Berthemy to Seward, May 27, 1867, *For. Rel.* (1867), Pt. 1, p. 298; Seward to Berthemy, May 29, 1867, *ibid.*, p. 299. See also Seward to Ruggles, May 29, 1867, and Seward to General John A. Dix, May 29, 1867, *ibid.*, pp. 299–300. W. A. Williams (*Roots of the Modern American Empire*, p. 167) says that Ruggles was appointed as a result of "strong pressure from the New York State Chamber of Commerce, as well as the support of Kasson and Sherman." As the foregoing has sought to demonstrate, Ruggles was Seward's obvious and logical choice, and would almost certainly have been appointed without pressure from any quarter.

[32] Ruggles, *Supplementary Report*, April 8, 1870, NA M37, T22, p. 51.

the coins of other nations. This lamentable practice occurred at the expense of the American shipper and was an insult "to our cherished republican emblems." [33] To Ruggles it was pitiful indeed to see the eagle, the "imperial bird, the very type of the great Republic, crossing the ocean, and touching the continent only to descend into the melting pots of the mints of Paris and London." [34] What is more, many American merchants, to avoid the added cost of recoining, shipped bars of gold instead, which Ruggles deemed "only one grade higher in civilization than the ingots or bullion of semi-barbarous communities." [35]

If, however, the world's coinage could somehow be made uniform, this disparity would vanish and the benefits for American commerce would be incalculable. Ruggles reminded Seward that once before, in the days of the Roman Empire, the world had enjoyed the advantages of a common coin, but had lost it when the Empire fell. Now a new imperial power, with its "continental and interoceanic position on the globe" and with the "pre-eminent and distinguishing advantage of having two outlets for their coin—one leading westward across the Pacific to Asia, the other eastward across the Atlantic to Europe," had the opportunity to reestablish a common coin as "uniform and as circumambient as the atmosphere of the world." [36]

Such an agreement would not only eliminate "needless recoinage, brokerage, and exchange," Ruggles told Seward, but more important the dollar "would become practically, if not

---

[33] *Ibid.*

[34] Ruggles, Speech at Banquet honoring Chinese Embassy, June 22, 1868, *ibid.*

[35] Ruggles, *Supplementary Report*, April 8, 1870, *ibid.*, p. 52.

[36] Ruggles to Seward, May 30, 1867, *For. Rel.* (1867), Pt. 1, p. 301.

nominally the monetary unit, and the actual denomination in which money contracts embracing different countries or distant quarters of the globe would or might be payable." [37] Then Ruggles offered an observation which recalled predictions Seward had made several times in the past, and which probably reflected, at least partially, Seward's interest in the monetary conference. According to Ruggles, the "more important and higher issue would be . . . between the dollar, decimally divided, and the sovereign, (or pound sterling) not decimally divided but more inconveniently divided in shillings, pence and farthings." And in that contest, he anticipated the victory of the American dollar over a standard that had "hitherto maintained an undue predominance in the money payments of the world." [38]

The Franco-American Entente

The next step in obtaining these objectives was to get French concurrence in the plan Ruggles had first proposed at the Berlin Statistical Congress in 1863: the adoption of the franc as the standard coin, the minting of a new twenty-five-franc gold piece, and the pegging of the American dollar and the British sovereign to it. Even before the official invitation had been received, Ruggles had left for Paris, presumably in his capacity as United States Commissioner on the International Exposition. His mission had other objectives, however. Ruggles arrived in Paris on March 23, 1867, and was soon involved in preliminary discussions with the French government on the nature and goals of the forthcoming monetary

[37] July 18, 1867, *ibid.*, pp. 347–48.

[38] Ruggles to Senator John Sherman, Dec. 30, 1867, in John Sherman, *Recollections of Forty Years in the House, Senate and Cabinet* (2 vols.; Chicago, 1895), I, 510.

conference. He opened these discussions on May 5, with Etienne de Parieu, vice-president of the Council of State, by proposing that the United States would adjust its gold dollar to conform to the shape, weight, and fineness of the five-franc gold piece if France would coin a twenty-five-franc piece that would be the equivalent of the United States half-eagle, i.e., five dollars. De Parieu was agreeable, and said that if Ruggles put the proposal in writing, he, de Parieu, would "induce the action that might be in my power with respect to fixing the opening and the course of the announced international conference." (De Parieu would be chairman of the conference at its substantive meetings.) He would also bring the matter to the attention of Emperor Napoleon III, who had manifested interest in coinage reform. Ruggles replied that he was not prepared to engage in formal diplomatic negotiations and would have to discuss the proposal with General John A. Dix, the United States Minister to France. He did so, and apparently received authorization to continue, because he soon had an interview with the Emperor himself on the forthcoming conference.[39]

Thus Ruggles and the French were actively collaborating on the agenda and strategy of the conference, with Ruggles taking the initiative. As we shall later see, this Franco-American entente did not sit well with the British.

Before Ruggles' audience with Napoleon III took place, however, reinforcements arrived in Europe to strengthen his hand and to lend more weight, if any was needed, to the American position on monetary reform. On April 10, a little more than two weeks after Ruggles had arrived in Paris,

[39] M. de Parieu to Ruggles, May 7, 1867, *For. Rel.* (1867), Pt. 1, p. 350; Ruggles to M. de Parieu, May 9, 1867; Ruggles to Seward, May 30, 1867, *ibid.*, pp. 300–301.

Senator John Sherman of Ohio, Chairman of the Senate Finance Committee, left New York for Europe on a three-month vacation, with, according to his *Recollections*, "no plan, route or business, except to go where I drifted with such companions as I met." [40] One of his fortuitous encounters was with Congressman John A. Kasson, himself a firm advocate of a uniform coinage, who was going to Europe to negotiate postal conventions with Britain, France, Prussia, and Belgium. Their conversations doubtless turned to the forthcoming conference, and Sherman probably took some of Kasson's views with him to Paris.[41]

As luck would have it, Sherman drifted into Paris at the very moment Ruggles was there, and the two were soon corresponding. On May 17, Ruggles wrote Sherman for his opinion on the adoption of the French five-franc coin as the basic unit in international exchange and whether Congress would go along with the scheme. The following day Sherman replied that while he could not say with certainty what the Congressional attitude would be, he did assure Ruggles that

[40] John Sherman, *Recollections*, I, 396.

[41] Edward Younger, *John A. Kasson, Politics and Diplomacy from Lincoln to McKinley* (Iowa City, 1955), pp. 223–27. It seems rather too fortuitous that these men were traveling on the same ship for Europe at the very moment that Ruggles was in Paris to discuss international monetary questions. But just how much they had to do with those negotiations is not clear. Kasson's biographer is no help. He merely says that from May to August Kasson "hurried back and forth between London, Paris and Brussels, negotiating, sightseeing, socializing, and writing long letters to his sisters" (Younger, *Kasson*, p. 224). Nugent (*Money and American Society*, p. 78) may be right when he says that "simple coincidence" cannot explain why two men with such obvious interest in the money question "happened to journey to Paris at the crucial moment." Sherman, we know, did have something to do with the conference; Kasson's role remains tantalizingly obscure.

the subject had "excited the attention of several important commercial bodies in the United States" and that in his view the climate was now so favorable that he was confident Congress would approve any useful means of providing the American businessman with a "uniform standard of value and exchange." And most important for the conference, Sherman supported the Franco-American position on the five-franc coin. If this position was adopted, he said, "France will surely abandon the impossible effort of making two standards of value. Gold coins will answer all the purposes of European commerce." He closed with the observation that the "tendency of the age is to break down all needless restrictions upon social and commercial intercourse" and suggested that this "result would be of greater value than the usual employments of diplomatists and statesmen." [42]

Armed with these good tidings, Ruggles went to talk to Louis Napoleon, who received him cordially and appeared to be mightily impressed with his views and the Sherman letter. Ruggles reported the proceedings to the State Department, which expressed pleasure at the "auspicious augury" that an agreement would eventually be reached on the coinage question, supported Sherman's position, and advised Ruggles that "concurrence by this government in any reasonable plan" was practically a certainty.[43]

There seems to be little doubt that Ruggles was the motive force behind the conference, and that he was operating with

[42] May 17, 1867, *For. Rel.* (1867), Pt. 1, p. 378; May 18, 1867, *ibid.,* pp. 379–80. Both Ruggles and Sherman were advocates of the gold standard. For the relationship between the monetary conference and the "money question" in the United States, see Nugent, *Money and American Society,* pp. 67–90.

[43] Frederick W. Seward to Ruggles, June 21, 1867, *For. Rel.* (1867), Pt. 1, pp. 303–304.

the full knowledge and support of Seward. This can be seen in Ruggles' justifiably confident assertion to Seward that the "matter of a *uniform coin* has been so rapidly advanced by the efforts of the representatives of the United States at Paris, that Monsr. prime minister Rouher has set in motion, as you see, another 'international conference' which if not strictly *diplomatic* in its *personnel* is sufficiently authoritative & representative." [44] Ruggles expressed himself even more emphatically later, telling Seward that "it is but due to the history of the unification of money to state that the earnest and active agitation . . . on the part of the United States, exerted its full share of influence in leading the movement of France to adopt the decisive measure of inviting in diplomatic form an authoritative 'conference' of delegates." [45]

The conference itself was anticlimactic, for the Franco-American entente carried all before it, with one notable exception. The British attitude was lukewarm at best, and their delegation soon made it known that they did not like what was going on. This was not encouraging to Ruggles, since without their agreement all would be in vain. The British reluctance to support the Franco-American proposal was the first hint that the grand design might not get off the drawing board.

[44] Ruggles to Seward, personal and private, June 3, 1867, Seward Papers. This letter provides additional support for the view that Ruggles and Sherman conferred in Paris. Ruggles says that he was hoping to get a treaty between the United States and France on the parity of gold coins "tho Sen. Sherman & Gen'l Dix do not think it expedient."

[45] July 18, 1867, *For. Rel.* (1867), Pt. 1, p. 346. The Franco-American "entente" on coinage unification belies Van Deusen's observation that Seward was "unwilling to participate in conferences designed to produce joint agreement with other powers" (*Seward*, p. 514). The

The Conference and Its Results

The International Monetary Conference opened in Paris as scheduled on June 17, 1867. Nineteen nations (or twenty, depending on whether Sweden and Norway counted as one or two countries) were present. All except the United States were European; there were no representatives from Latin America, Asia, Australia, or the West and East Indies. Ruggles noted this and was not pleased by the delegates' apparent lack of interest in these areas.[46] The delegates were not empowered to make binding commitments, but only to discuss the difficulties in the way of a uniform coinage and to make recommendations that would be the basis for agreements and treaties.

The major questions before the conference were essentially those already discussed by Ruggles and the French.

(1) Should an entirely new international monetary system be developed, or should each nation retain its own distinctive system but modify it to meet the new conditions?

(2) Should a single standard of coinage or a double standard be adopted?

(3) What should be the basic unit upon which all coins would be based? [47]

Paris Monetary Conference is not discussed in this otherwise fine biography.

[46] Ruggles, *Report on the International Monetary Conference*, Nov. 7, 1867. *For. Rel.* (1867), Pt. 1, p. 361. Possibly their absence could be explained by the fact that many of these areas were on the silver standard and might have jeopardized the work of the gold monemetallists at the conference. On this point, see Nugent, *Money and American Society*, pp. 84–85.

[47] *Official Reports of the Proceedings of the International Monetary Conference*, 2d Sitting, June 19, 1867, *For. Rel.* (1867), Pt. 1, p. 309.

Throughout the discussions, Ruggles clung tenaciously to the position he had already staked out for the United States. He urged the retention of the current monetary systems of each state, but insisted that the American dollar and the British pound sterling be brought into parity with the French franc. The United States was willing to "make this sacrifice," but he warned the delegates that this self-abnegation would not long continue; it was "now or never." His position carried the day, and the conference voted unanimously against the adoption of an entirely new system of international coinage.[48]

On the question of a single or double standard, Ruggles was equally insistent. Indeed, his determination to secure the adoption of an international gold standard led him to make a curious assertion: the United States was on a single standard, he said. He conceded that the double standard "exists legislatively in the United States," but "it is virtually abolished in practice." Hence, he concluded that the United States had "the gold standard alone." The impact of this dubious reasoning is hard to judge, but the conference dutifully adopted the gold standard for international trade.[49]

The final question concerned the selection of the basic monetary unit for international coinage. Ruggles, as expected, argued for the adoption of the five-franc coin, provided that a twenty-five-franc piece be minted that would be equal in weight and value to the American half-eagle and the British sovereign. Easy convertibility of coinage was absolutely essential to the American position; without it the other points were academic. The French delegation, in accordance with

[48] *Ibid.*, pp. 313–14.
[49] *Ibid.*, 4th Sitting, June 21, 1867, p. 325; 3d Sitting, June 20, 1867, p. 320.

the scenario already drawn up, fully agreed with the American proposal. They saw little, if any, difficulty in maintaining their end of the bargain.[50]

At this point the British delegation, heretofore mostly silent observers, began to interject a few caveats. The Master of the Royal Mint, Thomas Graham, called the delegates' attention to England's "delicate and exceptional situation"; he wanted it clearly understood that his government considered the entire proceedings only "theoretical." He was there, he said, merely to listen and could not consider the recommendations as binding. This was not a welcome piece of news to Ruggles or the French; they could not see the conference founder on the rock of British exceptionalism. Prince Jerome, Louis Napoleon's son, now serving as president of the conference, testily reminded the British that the delegates had not been convened for "speculative studies" and he urged the conference to get on with its business. Jerome's little lecture neither intimidated nor impressed the British, who were beginning to catch the drift of the Franco-American proposals and did not like what they saw. If the five-franc coin were adopted as the basic unit, Graham remarked, then "all accounts in England must be kept in dollars." Consequently, when the vote was taken, the British delegation voted against it. They were joined by the Swedish delegation, but to no avail. The vote in favor of the five-franc coin was an overwhelming 13-2.[51]

Nor were the British enthusiastic about Ruggles' other favorite idea—the introduction of the twenty-five-franc coin. They saw little reason to reduce the value of the pound to meet the value of the new coin and began to suspect, only too

[50] *Ibid.*, 6th Sitting, June 28, 1867, pp. 33–34.
[51] *Ibid.*, pp. 332–34.

accurately, Ruggles' ultimate objective. One of the British delegates, Ribus Wilson, cryptically observed that "England could not but appreciate the intention with which it has been proposed to introduce the twenty-five-franc piece." [52]

The fears of Great Britain notwithstanding, the conference at its close on July 6, adopted five recommendations which the delegates were to take back to their governments:

(1) A single monetary standard (gold)
(2) The coins of the several states to be of equal weight and diameter
(3) Coins to be of equal fineness of gold
(4) The basic unit to be the weight of the present five-franc gold coin and its multiples
(5) The coins to bear the insignia, designs, and mottos of the individual countries and to be legal tender for all public and private payments.[53]

In his official report, submitted to Seward on November 7, Ruggles sought to clarify the work of the conference and to explain its significance. The United States, he wrote, "cannot wisely or rightfully remain in continental isolation." [54] The effort at coinage reform "illustrates the power of oceans not to divide but to unite the continents in a common 'solidarity.' " [55] In his view the adoption of the gold standard was "the cardinal, if not the all-important" feature of the plan, because he expected gold production in the United States to increase rapidly in the next fifteen years and add at least $900 million to the world's supply. With coinage reform making it easier for American gold coins to circulate, this

[52] *Ibid.*, pp. 334–35.
[53] Ruggles, *Report*, Nov. 7, 1867, NA M37, T22, p. 1.
[54] *Ibid.*, p. 7.
[55] Ruggles to Seward, Nov. 11, 1867, *For. Rel.* (1867), Pt. 1, p. 364.

enormous increase would make the United States one of the dominant commercial nations in the world. For this reason, Ruggles told Seward, he had insisted that unification be "now or never." [56]

Ruggles recurred to his favorite analogy—the Roman Empire during the Augustan Age—when coinage was "directly or indirectly subject to the central authority." The collapse of the Empire had brought monetary chaos which had continued into the modern era. For this fragmented condition there was only one solution: "The disintegrated political and monetary world must be reintegrated." [57] And what nation in the nineteenth century was better situated to play the imperial role than the United States, which could "alone accomplish this mission?" [58]

In his discussion of the results of the conference, Ruggles touched upon a theme which up to then he had only hinted at—the significance of coinage reform for Asiatic trade. While he conceded that the "future development of the trade and power of the two Americas on the Pacific, an ocean as yet almost unoccupied, would open a field of view quite too large for exploration on the present occasion," he nevertheless expressed surprise that so little notice had been taken at the conference of "that populous quarter of the globe in estimating the world-wide advantages of a common money." Although the "pagan Asiatics did not quite understand money matters," he believed that the coins of China and Japan could be readily assimilated to the proposed twenty-five-franc piece, and that "in due time, at least, a portion of eastern Asia may be brought within a world-embracing and world-protecting

[56] Ruggles, *Report*, Nov. 7, 1867, NA M37, T22, p. 7.
[57] *Ibid.*, p. 8.
[58] Ruggles to Seward, July 18, 1867, *For. Rel.* (1867), Pt. 1, p. 349.

belt of monetary unification." This was of special importance, he informed Seward, because the gold from the fields of Nevada and California was now finding its way directly to China across the Pacific instead of taking its previously circuitous route to Panama, across the Atlantic, through the Mediterranean and Red Seas and the Indian Ocean. The role of the intercontinental telegraph in this development was apparent in Ruggles' comment that this direct route "in connection with the land and ocean telegraphs" would result in great economy. And then, making the clinching point, he assured Seward that the "inexorable law of cheapness will soon render permanent this strange geographical inversion, by which the money of the Pacific slope of the western world is sent westward to find the markets of the east." [59]

The prospects of a lucrative Asiatic trade usually inspired Ruggles to indulge in the high-flown rhetoric that has caused some to dismiss his comments as no more than windy talk. A good example of his rhetoric is his speech at the banquet honoring a delegation of Chinese who were visiting the United States in 1868 in the company of Anson Burlingame. Raising a toast to "MONEY! the undisputed Monarch of the World," Ruggles urged the Chinese to join in the movement for monetary reform and so "carry the uniform coin to the very wall of China." He predicted a rosy future for American money, "those golden tokens of Power" which bore the representation of the "classic eagle coming down from antiquity, the historically established symbol of imperial sovereignty." Soon that "American eagle and its subdivisions would have the same value and the same currency at New York and Pekin—at London and Paris—at Valparaiso and Archangel—on the

[59] Ruggles, *Report*, Nov. 7, 1867, NA M37, T22, pp. 2–8.

Alps and the Andes—on all the lands and all the seas of our terraqueous globe." [60]

The absolute seriousness behind this kind of rhetoric emerges in a letter from Ruggles to Senator Sherman. In the letter, Ruggles predicted the ultimate victory of the American dollar in the coming struggle with the British pound sterling. He said the British at the conference had been grim and uneasy because they had "virtually admitted" to Ruggles that the struggle was inevitable.[61] If their fears needed any confirmation, it could have been found in a supplementary report Ruggles issued several years later. There he forecast that the dollar, "standing midway between the 'pound' and the 'franc,'" as a consequence of monetary unification, "would be greatly facilitated in becoming the common money of account in all the nations." [62]

The Failure of Monetary Reform

Late in November, 1867, Ruggles presented his report in person to President Andrew Johnson, who, as George Templeton Strong waspishly commented, "did not seem quite to understand the matter." [63] For a time it appeared that the recommendations of the conference would be quickly enacted. Berthemy had written to Seward on August 28 urging speedy American approval, thereby setting an example which he said would "certainly be followed by other states." Seward

[60] Ruggles, Speech at Banquet honoring Chinese Embassy, June 22, 1868, NA M37, T22.

[61] Dec. 30, 1867, in Sherman, *Recollections*, p. 410.

[62] Ruggles, *Supplementary Report*, April 8, 1870, NA M37, T22, p. 26.

[63] George Templeton Strong, "Diary," entry for Nov. 27, 1867 (New York Public Library).

answered that "the matter will receive attentive consideration" and promised Berthemy that the views of the various
branches of the American government would be communi-
cated to him "at the earliest practicable period." [64]

He received the prompt support of Secretary of the Treasury McCulloch, who "heartily" congratulated the work of
the conference and assured Seward that the results had his
"cordial concurrence." [65] The French showed their determination by striking off sample copies of the proposed new
twenty-five-franc gold coin and sent a few to President Johnson and Seward. Seward took the opportunity to confirm
what must have been fairly obvious by asserting that the
"sentiments of the President of the United States and my own
upon this interesting subject have already been correctly
interpreted to you by our representative Mr. Samuel B.
Ruggles." [66] Senator Sherman lent the weight of his considerable influence by reporting out of the Senate Finance
Committee a bill which incorporated most of Ruggles' recommendations and a great many of his arguments as well. Sherman expressed confidence that the other nations at the conference would act favorably on the recommendations and said
that "upon Congress now rests the fate of a measure . . . that
will shed unfading glory upon the age of its adoption." [67]

Unfortunately for the plans of Seward, Ruggles, and Sherman, Congress showed little inclination to act speedily.

[64] M. Berthemy to Seward, Aug. 28, 1867; Seward to Berthemy,
Sept. 16, 1867, *For. Rel.* (1867), Pt. 1, p. 356.

[65] Sept. 26, 1867, NA M179, R264.

[66] V. Dumas to President Johnson, Nov. 5, 1867; Seward to V. Dumas, Nov. 27, 1867, *For. Rel.* (1867), Pt. 1, p. 360.

[67] John Sherman, *Selected Speeches and Reports on Finance and
Taxation, from 1859 to 1878* (New York, 1879), pp. 179–87. The quotation is from p. 187.

Sherman's bill was tabled and never again reached the floor of the Senate. In vain did commercial organizations such as the National Board of Trade urge upon the Congress "the desireableness of efforts to secure uniformity of coinage among the commercial nations of the world." [68] The lethargy of France and England did not help supporters of the measure. Despite their previous assurances, the French decided it was unwise to abandon the double standard, and the twenty-five-franc gold piece was never coined. Great Britain would not reduce the gold content of the pound sterling by the requisite two-pence to bring it in line with the half-eagle and the abortive new French coin.[69]

So ended Seward's second attempt to unify the world's markets under the leadership of the United States. The plans for establishing the intercontinental telegraph and unifying the world's coins were extraordinary and imaginative approaches to the achievement of a commercial empire. Though

[68] National Board of Trade, *Proceedings of the Second Annual Meeting, Richmond, Virginia, December, 1869* (Boston, 1870), p. 15.

[69] On the reactions of France and England, see Nugent, *Money and American Society*, pp. 111–18. Nugent says that the British "were puzzled over the diplomatic ramifications of the conference, especially the willingness of the United States to ally itself with France, even if that meant reducing the content of the dollar by three and a half percent" (p. 112). The puzzlement is not hard to explain. By concentrating on the domestic question, Nugent misses the significance of the conference for Seward's commercial empire. The British, however, knew full well what Ruggles was after by his close cooperation with the French. They knew, and Ruggles knew they knew, that with his proposals the United States hoped to replace England as the chief commercial nation in the world, an ambition that Seward, as well, had long cherished. For subsequent efforts at international coinage reform, see Nugent, *Money and American Society*, pp. 251–59. For Ruggles' continued activity on the question, see Thompson, *Ruggles*, pp. 153–62.

they were not conceived by Seward, he quickly grasped their significance and he worked diligently to bring them to fruition. They were two very different yet complementary means to an end he had long sought, for they were consonant with ideas he had himself expressed on many occasions. Along with the triumphs, Seward knew many disappointments as Secretary of State, but it is doubtful that any were more difficult for him to accept than the failures of the Collins Overland Line and the monetary conference of 1867.

CHAPTER V

Way Stations of Empire: Alaska, the West Indies, the Panama Canal

The intercontinental telegraph and monetary reform were important elements in William Seward's conception of empire, but more than filaments of steel and bands of gold were required if that empire was to be held together. For the empire was a commercial one, and commerce meant trade, which in turn meant shipping. Shipping in the post–Civil War era meant the replacement of sails with steam; and that meant coaling stations. Suitable places must be found at which trans-oceanic merchantmen could fuel up with coal and take on supplies for the long haul to Asia and the South Pacific.

In the four years following the war, Seward was greatly occupied with seeking out those places on the trade routes from New York and San Francisco to the Orient which would facilitate the growth of American commerce. His major efforts were concentrated on Alaska, the West Indies, and the Isthmus of Panama. All of these efforts have been of interest to historians, but mainly in terms of Seward's "expansionism." This discussion will not be concerned with the minutiae of diplomacy, which have been adequately dealt with elsewhere, but with fitting Seward's attempts at territorial acquisition into his concept of commercial empire. In addition, it will be concerned with the methods Seward used to advance his projects, with the kinds of support he sought, and the motives and objectives of those whose support he needed.

Alaska

The purchase of Alaska has received perhaps more attention from historians than any other of Seward's activities except for his Civil War diplomacy. Little can be added about the purchase itself that is not already known. What does require further discussion, however, is Seward's motive for the purchase. This was not a troublesome matter for earlier commentators. Thomas A. Bailey dismissed the question rather abruptly with the comment that "Seward acted to satisfy his own insatiable passion for territorial expansion." [1] This view was supported by Victor J. Farrar, who, in the standard work on the purchase, asserted that Seward bought Alaska as the consequence of a "megalomania of expansionism." [2] Tyler Dennett has written that "the purchase of Alaska was less a commercial than a political venture." [3] More recently, Joseph G. Whelan has repeated the assertion that Seward's major ob-

[1] "Why the United States Purchased Alaska," *Pacific Historical Review*, III (March, 1934), 40. Bailey adds two other reasons: "to improve the strategic position of the United States in the Pacific, and . . . to revive the decaying popularity of the State Department, which was sharing the opprobrium being heaped upon the head of Johnson."

[2] *The Annexation of Russian America to the United States* (Washington, D.C., 1937), pp. 113–14. Farrar rightly dismisses Russian-American friendship as Seward's major motive for the purchase (*ibid.*, pp. 109–10).

[3] "Seward's Far Eastern Policy," *American Historical Review*, XXVIII (Oct., 1922), 61. This is surprising since Dennett correctly divines the basis of Seward's policy in Asia (*ibid.*, p. 46). Richard W. Van Alstyne (*Rising American Empire*, pp. 176–77) correctly points up the relationship of Alaska to the economic thrust into Asia.

jective was territorial. After citing and disposing of such factors as economic potential, international politics, British designs, and Russian-American friendship as not going to "the heart of the matter," Whelan found the main impetus "simply this: Seward was an ardent expansionist; his mind had been conditioned by an expansionist philosophy." [4]

Aside from their factual deficiencies these assertions suffer from circular reasoning. In essence, their argument goes something like this: Seward's dedication to unlimited expansionism compelled him to seek territorial possessions; Seward's search for territorial possessions proves his dedication to unlimited territorial expansionism. The available evidence, however, makes clear that his interest in Alaska derived not from a conditioned reflex but from a desire for an entrepôt in the Northwest for the trade of the Pacific and Asia.[5] Alaska was not just another piece of real estate to add to the national domain; it was an integral part of his plan of a commercial empire.

The difficulty in establishing with complete certainty Seward's motives for the purchase of Alaska lies in the paucity of evidence in the official records.[6] Seward said very lit-

---

[4] "William Seward, Expansionist," pp. 122–23. Whelan's discussion of the purchase follows closely Frank A. Golder, "The Purchase of Alaska," *American Historical Review*, XXV (April, 1920), 411–25. Golder says the reason Seward bought Alaska "is not quite . . . clear" and attributes it finally to Seward's hope that "it would bring him once more into popular favor" (*ibid.*, pp. 424–25).

[5] Interestingly, Bailey claims that the popular demand for Alaska was based on a sophisticated knowledge of its economic importance rather than on a recrudescence of Manifest Destiny (Bailey, "Why the United States Purchased Alaska," pp. 43–49). Seward, it would seem, was not privy to this knowledge, a position that can be maintained only by failing to ask where the public got its information.

[6] See Farrar, *Annexation of Russian America*, pp. 105–106; Whelan, "William Seward, Expansionist," p. 101.

tle, officially or unofficially, on the subject while he was Secretary. However, this lack of data can be overcome by noting Seward's attitude toward Alaska before the purchase, by seeking the views of the friends, colleagues, and supporters who managed Seward's campaign for public support of the purchase, and by examining Seward's views after he left office.

Seward was fully aware of the commercial importance of Russian America when he was in the Senate, for in 1852 he introduced a bill to provide for a naval survey of the Bering Strait and the North Pacific with precisely that importance in mind.[7] Russian America was the linchpin of the Collins Overland Line. Seward most certainly knew of the reports on the economic resources of the region sent back by the Western Union men in the field. Thus, his interest was not sudden, nor should it have been unexpected.[8]

The great obstacle to the purchase in Congress would likely come, Seward feared, from President Andrew Johnson's enemies, who because of heated domestic issues might seize the opportunity to embarrass his Secretary of State.[9] It was largely for this reason that Seward was eager to present the purchase as a selfless act of generosity toward Russia, a nation that had presumably befriended the United States during the war.[10]

[7] *Cong. Globe,* 32d Cong., 1st sess., Aug. 2, 1852, p. 1973.

[8] Vevier, "Collins Overland Line," pp. 251–53.

[9] See Donald Marquand Dozer, "Anti-Expansionism During the Johnson Administration," *Pacific Historical Review,* XII (Sept., 1943) 259–60, for newspaper opinion on this point.

[10] "Notes informally submitted to the Chairman of the Senate Foreign Relations Committee," NA RG 59, State Department Report Books, IX, 485–88. In this document, Seward emphasizes Russia's "demonstration of sympathy and solicitude for the stability of the Union" during the Civil War (*ibid.,* p. 485). Significantly, Seward does not use this justification anywhere else. Farrar, who does not

To avert what he felt might be a serious threat to the purchase, Seward promoted a publicity campaign to educate the people on the desirability of Alaska. He orchestrated the campaign with the consummate skill he had already displayed on a smaller scale in his advocacy of the Collins line. The strategy was to furnish copious data to eager journalists, plant favorable stories in the leading journals, and circulate enthusiastic letters from prominent spokesmen, associates, and friends. By examining the arguments advanced in this campaign, it will be possible to draw some conclusions regarding Seward's motives.[11]

---

find Seward's reason persuasive, falls back on the equally dubious justification of "land-grabbing" (*Annexation of Russian America*, pp. 110–14). This does not mean, of course, that others did not accept Russian friendship as a plausible reason. *The Journal of Commerce* (March 24, 1866) anticipated the "not absolutely improbable idea" of a Russo-American "alliance" in the Pacific against England and France. The visit of a party headed by Assistant Secretary of the Navy Gustavus V. Fox to Russia in 1866 caused the *Army and Navy Journal* (Oct. 6, 1866) to comment that the "good feeling toward our people and Government" by the Russians "has neither precedent nor parallel in the history of nations." At least part of the public was thus favorably disposed toward Russia and the purchase. See, on this point, Richard E. Welch, Jr., "American Public Opinion and the Purchase of Russian America," *American Slavic and East European Review*, XVII (Dec., 1958), 493; and Bailey, "Why the United States Purchased Alaska," pp. 39–40. Bailey agrees with Farrar that Russian friendship was not a crucial factor in Seward's decision.

[11] Welch ("American Public Opinion," p. 482) argues that Seward's "educational campaign" has been "overemphasized" by historians, that the press was not "bribed" or "controlled" by Seward, and that he did not spend "vast sums" to subsidize newspapers. All this to show that Seward's influence "was not conclusive" in the passage of the treaty. These arguments may be conceded without surrendering the point to be made here. Welch, having admitted that Seward "planted" information and made available letters and scientific reports, says it is "relatively unimportant" whether the press "obtained these opinions

The treaty with Russia for the purchase of Alaska having been concluded at the end of March, Seward anticipated strong opposition in the Senate and therefore sought to buttress his position as effectively as he could. Among the first to supply Seward with arguments was Perry McDonough Collins, whose Overland line was already near collapse. On April 4, 1867, five days after the treaty was made public, he wrote to Seward in order to correct "erroneous statements in the press" regarding the value of Russian America. He recalled that in his efforts to find a suitable route for the telegraph, he had acquired a great deal of knowledge about the area. He reminded Seward of the large timber forests, the gold deposits, the abundant game and fish to be found there. But its greatest significance lay in the increasing commerce on the Pacific. Alaska, he said, is "just what we want there . . . in order to give us the supremacy of that great Ocean." He expected that the huge population of Asia would be "great customers" for everything from fish to ice, and would produce a commerce that "in the hands of Americans would soon grow to wonderful proportions." Seward found Collins' letter so persuasive that he had copies printed and distributed.[12] Other correspondents struck a similar note on the Alaska purchase, and many of their letters, as well, found their way into public print.[13]

and reasons from prepared releases or original research." But it is important here since the kind of information released (and Welch admits that "all the information so distributed was favorable to the purchase") is crucial in determining what Seward thought significant about Alaska. The "prepared releases" reveal his ideas, and so they must be considered if we are to find out what those ideas were.

[12] April 4, 1867, NA M179, R255. On the printing, see the marginal note in Seward's handwriting on the original.

[13] Among them: W. W. Miller to G. Gibbs, Sept. 2, 1867, NA M179, R264; E. Conkling to Seward, Oct. 26, 1867, *ibid.*, R266; E.

Not content with merely circulating favorable correspondence, Seward took a more direct role in advertising the attractions of Alaska. In this connection, he made use of his well-placed friends and associates. One of the most important of these was Henry J. Raymond, the editor of the *New York Times*. Raymond's paper served as such a significant conduit for Seward that it became in effect a quasi-official organ of the State Department.[14] The day after the purchase was announced, the *Times* reported the treaty under the bold head: "BRIGHT PROSPECTS FOR OUR JAPAN AND CHINA TRADE," and assured its readers that the acquisition would "influence in our favor the vast trade of the Pacific." The following day, Raymond wrote that the "main importance of this acquisition grows out of its bearing upon the future trade with Japan, China and the other countries of Eastern Asia." [15] To make certain that the *Times* was in accord with the Secretary's views, Raymond wired his reporter in Washington to interview Seward about the treaty.[16] Seward cooperated by giving Raymond a copy of Collins' letter and providing details which enabled the *Times* to comment editorially that "the commercial value of the Aleutian Islands

---

McCook to Seward, Aug. 22, 1867, *For. Rel.* (1868), Pt. 2, pp. 301–302; Jos. S. Wilson to Seward, Aug. 6, 1867, NA M179, R262; E. Hamilton to Seward, April 4, 1867, *ibid.*, R255; J. Clancy Jones to Seward, Dec. 14, 1867, *ibid.*, R268; E. Evans to Seward, Aug. 18, 1868, Seward Papers.

[14] Note, for example, Seward's request to Thurlow Weed to "be prepared and have Raymond prepared when the news transpires, to speak in regard" to the purchase of the Danish West Indies (Seward to Weed, Oct. 30, 1867 [Confidential], Seward Papers).

[15] *New York Times*, March 31, 1867; April 1, 1867.

[16] Raymond to L. L. Crounse, April 2, 1867, Seward Papers. It is interesting that a telegram to a *New York Times* reporter should be found in Seward's private papers.

is of prime consequence to our opening of Oriental trade." The *Times* continued to emphasize the significance of the purchase for commerce, and on April 11 announced that the "Japan and China route is open." On June 17, Raymond replied to the skeptics who protested that if Russia could not do anything with Alaska neither could the United States. Alaska, he said, because of "its geography, its climate and its products, can only be of use to a great commercial nation. . . . There is no sort of equal comparison between our commercial marine and [Russia's] on the [Pacific]."[17]

This theme was echoed in other newspapers. For example, the *Philadelphia North American and Gazette* was convinced that "American commerce in the Pacific must and undoubtedly will be very benefited by the change."[18] In fact, one of the major points made by those newspapers that supported the purchase was its commercial significance for Asia and the Pacific.[19]

[17] *New York Times*, April 11, June 17, 1867. The same idea in almost the same language appeared in the *Army and Navy Journal* (Nov. 16, 1867): "The situation of that region is, at the outset, such as to make it valuable only to a great commercial nation. Russia has had no commerce worth speaking of during four-fifths of the time that she has held Russian America, and her commercial navy even now is all out of proportion to the population and wealth of the empire. On the other hand, our Navy and merchant marine are very powerful, and whatever advantage could be got out of the country they can secure."

[18] April 12, 1867, in House Executive Document No. 177, 40th Congress, 2d sess., p. 38.

[19] Welch concludes that his analysis of editorial opinion in forty-eight newspapers around the country showed that the reason most often advanced was "the probability that we should derive great economic benefits from the purchase." Those economic benefits were most often connected with the Pacific Ocean and the Asiatic trade (Welch, "American Public Opinion," *passim*).

While Seward was managing the newspaper end of the campaign, he was also marshaling his close associates to share the burden of proselytizing for Alaska. It must be assumed that they consulted with him and that their arguments in its favor could not have differed widely from his. Captain Gustavus V. Fox, former Assistant Secretary of the Navy, who had made a goodwill trip to Russia for the State Department the year before, busied himself writing articles for newspapers in the New England area and also getting "many leading men to telegraph . . . New England's Senators" to support the treaty.[20]

Another important figure in the campaign was John Van Schaick Pruyn, father of Robert, the former United States Minister to Japan, and of Erastus, current consul at Caracas, Venezuela. He also reported to Seward that he had "written several Senators urging confirmation of the Russian American treaty." He forwarded a clipping from the *Argus* of Albany containing an article he had written. It prophesied that "the day is coming when the commerce of the Pacific will rival that of the Atlantic and be almost entirely under our control," a favorite Seward theme. He promised another article the next day.[21]

The *eminence grise* of the campaign was Robert J. Walker who, it seems, was being paid by the Russian Minister to the United States, Baron von Stoeckl, to shepherd the treaty through the Senate.[22] He was surely one of the most active

[20] G. V. Fox to Seward, April 8, 1867 (Private), Seward Papers. Fox also urged the acquisition of "whatever part of the isthmus [of Panama] is feasible for a ship canal."

[21] John V. L. Pruyn to Seward, April 8, 1867 (Personal), Seward Papers.

[22] Walker's role has been analyzed in Richard H. Luthin, "The Sale of Alaska," in Morgan B. Sherwood, ed., *Alaska and Its History*

supporters of Seward's purchase and frequently conferred with him about it. He believed that "the theatre of our greatest triumphs is to be the Pacific, where we will soon have no formidable rival." The result would be "political and commercial control of the world." [23] The language as well as the sentiment is almost pure Seward.

There were rumors that Seward had expended large sums of Departmental funds in propagandizing the purchase, a charge he denied categorically.[24] The available evidence suggests that, if any funds were used, they were not the Department's. Seward had no difficulty in persuading people to undertake chores for him. Many were willing, indeed eager, to join in his projects. Sometimes help was thrust upon him. A case in point is Lloyd Pearsall Smith, editor of the newly founded *Lippincott's Magazine*. While the treaty was still being debated in Congress, Smith wrote to the Department to announce that his magazine was planning an article on Alaska for an early issue and he felt that it "should harmonize with the views of the Department." He requested a meeting with Seward, as a result of which he was given a supply of maps and other data on Alaska for his early use. The article was submitted to Seward in advance of publication, and he read it "with much interest." [25] Well he might, for it described the

(Seattle, 1967), pp. 233–51. The vexing conundrum of who, if anyone, got what, if anything, from whom, has received extensive analysis without definitive answers in William A. Dunning, "Paying for Alaska," *Political Science Quarterly*, XXVIII (Sept., 1912), 385–98, and in Whelan, "William Seward, Expansionist," pp. 114–22.

[23] Walker to Seward, July 2, 1868, Andrew Johnson Papers (Library of Congress).

[24] House Report No. 35, 40th Cong., 3d sess. (1869).

[25] Logan P. Smith to F. W. Seward, Dec. 28, 1867; Smith to Seward, Jan. 3, 1868, NA M179, R270.

climate, people, and economic resources of Alaska in very favorable terms and asserted that the area was important for the "maintenance of the great commerce of the Pacific, which the rapid succession of events is developing in our hands, and in our hands almost alone." [26] It was the view that had already appeared, phrased somewhat differently, in the *Times*, in Pruyn's article for the Albany *Argus*, and in other similar efforts.

Later that year, a lengthy article in *Lippincott's*, giving in great detail the advantage of Alaska commercially, concluded that "in a few years we will control the Pacific coast as effectually and certainly as we control the Atlantic: already the trade of the Northern Pacific is in our hands." [27] When, early in 1869, Smith wrote to ask Seward if he could be of further use, he called the Secretary's attention to the two articles on Alaska and modestly suggested that they "were not without influence in promoting the policy of the Department." He generously offered the pages of his magazine once more to "communicate anything unofficially to the public" regarding the rumored purchase of Cuba.[28]

From other quarters, as well, came offers of assistance. The Reverend William M. Martin, Assistant Secretary of Home Missions of the Presbyterian Church and a self-described "resident of the Pacific" for many years, was enthusiastic over the purchase of Alaska. He wrote Seward asking for data that he might use "to rouse the representative men in all our commercial centres." At the moment he was planning to speak

[26] "Alaska—What Is It Worth?", *Lippincott's Magazine*, I (Feb., 1868), 191.

[27] "Scientific Expedition to Alaska," *Lippincott's Magazine*, I (Nov. 1868), 484, 485.

[28] Jan. 20, 1869, Seward Papers.

at the Historical Society of Brooklyn, before men "of the largest intelligence and commercial influence." [29] The following month at Utica, New York, he stoutly defended Seward's purchase with the argument that the "great commercial problem was to barter the trade of Western Europe with that of Eastern Asia." [30]

A group of influential New York merchants, financiers, and businessmen expressed their appreciation of the Alaska purchase early in 1868 by presenting Seward with a painting by the contemporary artist, Emanuel Leutze, commemorating the signing of the treaty. These men, who were to be very prominent in another of Seward's ventures, expressed "their high sense of the commercial, social, and political importance of the territorial acquisition," and forecast that the Northern Pacific would prove to be "the destined theatre, for many coming ages, of the expanding trade and power of the American Republic." [31]

But what did Seward himself have to say about the purchase of Alaska? There is, unfortunately, very little on the public record that can be directly attributed to him; he simply preferred to let others speak for him, perhaps because he did not wish to jeopardize the treaty by having the stigma of Johnson's conflict with Congress rub off on it. Seward's one comment was the oblique observation that "energetic commercial movements already made on the Pacific coast indicate a high

[29] Jan. 3, 1868, *ibid*.

[30] O. B. Matteson to Seward, Feb. 12, 1868, Seward Papers, enclosing clipping from Utica newspaper.

[31] Peter Cooper, A. T. Stewart, Hamilton Fish, Moses Taylor, Marshall O. Roberts, F. A. Conkling, William E. Dodge *et al.* to Seward, Jan. 6, 1868, Seward Papers. Leutze's best known painting is his "Washington Crossing the Delaware."

appreciation of this acquisition." [32] Alaska's relationship to
Asia was obviously uppermost in Seward's mind a little more
than a month after the purchase, when, speaking to a group
of Japanese commissioners in the United States to buy naval
vessels and arms, he called their attention to a globe of the
world, indicating "the position and outlines of Japan," and
told them, "we have been buying territory not far from
Japan." [33]

After he had left office, however, Seward made a visit to
the Northwest and Alaska in the late summer of 1869. In
three speeches there he gave a full account of the importance
of the purchase as he saw it. His emphasis was almost exclusively on the commercial benefits, especially regarding Asiatic
trade. By virtue of the purchase, he said, "Japan, China, and
Australia, are . . . commercially bound to the American
Pacific coast." At Salem, Oregon, he announced that he had
"realized, if indeed I did not discover, in those territories a
new, peculiar, and magnificent field of commerce and empire." He pronounced Puget Sound "as a base of future

[32] Seward to Alexander Asboth, Oct. 30, 1867, NA M77, R10 (Instructions, Argentina). Seward's consistency is nowhere better illustrated than in this passage in President Johnson's fourth annual message to Congress: "A more thorough and systematic survey of the
North Pacific Ocean is advised in view of our recent acquisitions, our
expanding commerce and the increasing intercourse between the Pacific States and Asia" (Seward's draft, Dec. 9, 1868, Seward Papers).
This was sixteen years after Seward had called for a similar survey
when in the Senate.

[33] Notes from Japanese Legation, NA M163, R1, quoting a story in
the *National Intelligencer* (Washington, D.C.), May 2, 1867. Frederick Seward quoted his father as saying that Alaska "would give a foothold for commercial and naval operations accessible from the Pacific
states" (Frederick W. Seward, *Reminiscences of a Wartime Statesman
and Diplomat* (New York, 1916), p. 360.

empire" and exclaimed that "the extension of American invention and enterprise into Japan, China, Australia, and India as
worthy of consideration equally with international commerce
between the United States and the countries of Western
Europe." [34]

But the Alaska purchase was not an isolated, fortuitous
event. On the very day the announcement of the purchase
was made public, Seward spoke with John Bigelow, a personal
friend and former Minister to France. Bigelow recorded in
his diary on March 30, 1867, that Seward had "intimated that
this was part of a system of negotiations which he was con-
ducting, he thought to a successful issue." [35] Alaska, therefore,
was not merely one more item in a shopping list of territories
meant to satisfy an insatiable craving for expansion. It was,
rather, along with the West Indies and the isthmian canal, part
of a vision whose ultimate aim was American commercial
supremacy.

The West Indies

The significance of the West Indies in Seward's plans for a
commercial empire has been obscured by a wrong assumption.
The idea that Seward's primary objective was to secure a
naval base there for strategic purposes was originally put
forth by his son, Frederick William, who wrote that during
the Civil War his father "had found the government laboring
under great disadvantages from the lack of advanced naval
outposts in the West Indies and the North Pacific. So, at the
close of hostilities, he commenced his endeavors to obtain a

[34] Seward, *Works*, V, 571, 574, 577–78. The speeches were at Sitka,
Alaska, Victoria, B.C., and Salem, Oregon.
[35] *Retrospections of an Active Life* (5 vols.; Garden City, N.Y.,
1913), IV, 53.

foothold in each quarter." [36] This theme was picked up by historians and reiterated as the basis for Seward's attempted purchase of a coaling station in the West Indies. Albert K. Weinberg, for example, subsumes his comments on Seward's interest in the Caribbean under the heading of "Self-Defense." [37] Halvdan Koht says "there can be no doubt" that Seward's policies "were of a purely defensive character." [38] Frederick Merk has written that Seward wanted islands there because "he felt the need for outposts of American defense." [39] Finally, this thesis is the basis for Whelan's discussion of Seward's Caribbean policy.[40]

The shortcoming of these evaluations lies in their exclusionary nature. That Seward was interested in a naval base for strategic purposes has a basis in fact, but it was not his sole interest, nor even his major one. The truth of the matter is that in Seward's mind, as in the minds of many in his era, naval objectives were hardly distinguishable from commercial objectives. For example, one of the chief items in support of the idea that Seward's aim was strictly strategic was his instruction to Charles Francis Adams, United States Minister to Great Britain, on April 25, 1866, citing the indispensability of coaling stations "under our own flag for naval observation

[36] *Reminiscences of a Wartime Statesman*, p. 360.

[37] *Manifest Destiny*, pp. 392–93.

[38] "The Origins of Seward's Plan to Purchase the Danish West Indies," *American Historical Review*, L (July, 1944), 762.

[39] *Manifest Destiny and Mission*, p. 229.

[40] "William H. Seward, Expansionist," pp. 95–101. Full treatment of the day-by-day diplomacy in the West Indies can be found in Charles C. Tansill, *The Purchase of the Danish West Indies* (Gloucester, Mass., 1966), pp. 1–153; Charles C. Tansill, *The United States and Santo Domingo, 1798–1873* (Baltimore, 1938), pp. 213–337; Rayford W. Logan, *The Diplomatic Relations of the United States with Haiti, 1776–1891* (Chapel Hill, 1941), pp. 296–303, 322–32, 325–29, 338–40.

and police and for defensive war." But later in that communication and generally overlooked, Seward pointed out the
need "for the protection of our widely spread commerce
when we are at peace with ourselves." [41] Another document
frequently cited is President's Johnson's third annual message
to Congress in December, 1867, which contains a lengthy
disquisition on the need for naval bases in the West Indies.
This portion of the message was drafted by Seward and has
been pointed out as his "strategic conception" for national
defense. Yet a close reading of it reveals no fewer than three
references to commerce: to the islands' considerable commercial value, to the exclusion of the United States from trade
there by European possessors, and to their use by Confederate
raiders in preying on Northern shipping during the war.[42]
Clearly, the separation of strategic necessity from commercial
advantage is not an easy one.

The argument that Seward's interest in purchasing coaling
stations was primarily military is further weakened by the
absence of a proximate threat from any foreign power then
holding possessions in the area.[43] This obvious weakness was
pointed out by *Hunt's Merchant's Magazine* in commenting
on Seward's arguments in Johnson's message. The editor observed that, as a defensive bastion, the West Indies were
hardly in the same category as Gilbraltar, that England did
not rely on the Isles of Man and Wight, and that France did
not covet the islands of Guernsey and Jersey for self-defense.
Moreover, what was the urgency? *Hunt's* pointed out that

[41] April 25, 1866, NA M77, R79.

[42] Whelan, "William H. Seward, Expansionist," p. 250, n. 6; Seward's draft of third annual message, Dec. 3, 1867, Seward Papers.

[43] Koht's argument that Seward's main concern was strategic is
largely conjectural. No evidence is presented that Seward acted on
that assumption (Koht, "Origins of Seward's Plan," pp. 762–67).

the Mexican crisis with France had passed peacefully, Britain showed no great hostility, the United States had emerged from the Civil War with a powerful battle-tested army, and the country was not planning any aggression. Why was "immediate action" necessary?[44] Secretary of the Navy Gideon Welles, although no unreconstructed opponent of coaling stations, failed to see the value of the West Indies for strategic purposes. He thought a naval station might have had some value during the war but did not think "we should experience such want again." Besides, in the event of war with Britain, France, or Spain, we could simply sail in "and seize one of these islands." [45]

We begin to approach a little nearer to Seward's actual views if we note the comments of Rear Admiral David Dixon Porter, his confidant and agent, who had been involved in the West Indies since 1846 and who had been advising Seward about them since 1865.[46] Porter was sent to the Dominican Republic in the winter of 1866 along with Frederick W. Seward, to report to the Secretary on the islands' worth. In his report, after discussing the military merits of the Bay and

[44] *Hunt's Merchant's Magazine*, LVIII (Jan., 1868), 17–18.

[45] Welles, *Diary*, III, 95–96. Welles, who thought Seward "crazy on the subject of obtaining territory" (*ibid.*, p. 103), nevertheless advocated the acquisition of naval stations when he thought it necessary. It was he who ordered the Navy to search for Midway Island and take possession of it. He also favored acquiring the Bay of Fonseca and other points (see Welles to Rear Admiral Thatcher, Comm. North Pacific Squadron, May 28, 1867, Welles Papers (Library of Congress); Welles to Seward, April 20, 1866, NA M179, R237; Welles to Seward, July 27, 1866, Welles Papers (Library of Congress); Senate Exec. Doc. No. 79, 40th Cong., 2d sess.; Senate Committee Report No. 194, 40th Cong., 3d sess.).

[46] Olive Risley Seward, "A Diplomatic Episode," *Scribner's Magazine*, II (Nov., 1887), 586; Tansill, *Santo Domingo*, pp. 127–29.

Peninsula of Samaná, Porter expatiated on the aid they would give "to commercial enterprise" and then went on to observe that Samaná Bay "occupies a most important position in reference to the trade of the Gulf of Mexico and the interoceanic routes across Central America." [47] When Seward later asked him for his view on St. Thomas in the Danish West Indies, Porter approved its purchase as a naval and commercial station because it lay "right in the track of all vessels from Europe, Brazil, East Indies, and the Pacific Ocean, bound to the West India Islands or to the United States. . . . The distinguishing characteristics of St. Thomas are its advantages as a place of trade." [48] Porter, who believed along with Seward that the index of a nation's power is its commercial prosperity, expected the Far Eastern trade to be "diverted from its present course and pass on to our great metropolis New York." [49] In this event, a coaling station in the West Indies would serve a useful function.

[47] Porter to Seward, Feb. 7, 1867. Porter Family Papers (Library of Congress). An amusing sidelight might perhaps be mentioned here. Porter had included in his report some gratuitous comments on the inhabitants of the island who "showed the tendency of the African race to run to seed when left to provide for themselves." But, he thought, with the "good example set them by the 'white folks,' for whom they have the highest respect, they could be made a more serviceable population." When the document was being prepared for submission to Congress, these observations were eliminated because Porter feared they "might be quoted to my prejudice by some of those in the Senate who may have darkey on the brain!" (Porter to Seward, Jan. 21, 1868, Seward Papers).

[48] Porter to Seward, Nov. 6, 1867, NA T350, R8 (Dispatches, St. Thomas).

[49] Porter to Editor, *Army and Navy Journal*, Feb. 11, 1868, Porter Family Papers (Library of Congress). For one who put so much stock in coaling stations, Porter was curiously reluctant to abandon sail for steam in the navy. In the 1870's and 1880's, when his influence was

Porter is a key figure for another reason. He lamented the decline of the merchant marine following the Civil War and urged its prompt rebuilding, as might be expected given his views. But he also shared a commonly held position on the function of the navy. He wrote Seward that "when our commerce has once more been reestablished, we must devote some portion of our intelligence to its protection. A commercial nation requires an efficient navy." He suggested that the number of naval vessels should be proportionate to the size of the merchant marine: so many tons of military vessels to so many tons of commercial vessels.[50] The idea that the true function of a navy is the protection of commerce was typical of the time. It can be seen in a letter from George Frederick Seward, nephew of William H. and United States consul at Shanghai, to J. Ross Browne, United States Minister to Japan in 1868, in which he advised the establishment of a coaling station at Midway Island in the Pacific. He said this would affect favorably the navy and the Pacific Mail Steam Ship Company, and so "promote that commerce for which in great part both of these exist." [51] This was also the view of

greatest in the Navy Department, he insisted that the fleet use sail in preference to coal wherever possible (see Harold and Margaret Sprout, *The Rise of American Naval Power, 1776–1918* [Princeton, N.J., 1944], pp. 167–68, 177–80, 195–96).

[50] These ideas appear in an article Porter prepared for the *Army and Navy Journal*, Feb. 18, 1868 (Porter Family Papers [Library of Congress]). Porter has been ill served by his biographers. Paul Lewis (*Yankee Admiral: A Biography of David Dixon Porter* [New York, 1968]), concentrates heavily on Porter's Civil War service and ignores his diplomatic ventures, his ideas on commercial expansion, and his significance in shaping postwar Navy policy. James R. Soley (*Admiral Porter* [New York, 1903]), is equally unsatisfactory.

[51] Oct. 28, 1868, encl. in G. F. Seward to W. H. Seward, Nov. 20, 1868, NA M112, R9 (Consular Dispatches, Shanghai).

the San Francisco Chamber of Commerce, which said that all other great commercial powers "each have naval stations, which secures for their mercantile marine a degree of protection which we, no less than they, may find desirable." [52]

Corroborating evidence that Seward's basic reason for purchasing coaling stations was commercial can be found in a book whose author presented himself as having been at first opposed to such purchases and then, persuaded of their true value, becoming an ardent advocate. James Parton, who has been described as "a fire-eating Republican radical," seems to have been privy to much of Seward's thinking, for his book, *The Danish Islands, Are We Honor Bound to Pay for Them?*, contains material he probably could not have obtained except from Seward or someone close to him.[53] Parton argued that the Danish West Indies were important because "every American ship which trades with South America, on either side of it, or with California, Oregon, and Alaska; every whaling ship that makes its way to and from the fishing-grounds of the Pacific, passes by or among them for shelter and supplies." [54]

Although eventually Frederick W. Seward in his *Reminiscences* would claim that his father wanted outposts in the West Indies for strategic purposes, he told a somewhat different story in a series of magazine articles in 1894. The

[52] *Report of the Special Committee of the San Francisco Chamber of Commerce*, Sept. 11, 1866, encl. in D. MacGowan to Seward, Sept. 17, 1866, NA M179, R244. MacGowan was an agent for the East India Telegraph Company, discussed in Chapter III.

[53] James Parton, *The Danish Islands, Are We Honor Bound to Pay for Them?* (Boston, 1869), p. 62. The characterization is by Eric L. McKitrick in *Andrew Johnson and Reconstruction* (Chicago, 1964), p. 376.

[54] Parton, *The Danish Islands*, p. 62.

articles consisted of extracts from a journal he kept while on a cruise to the West Indies in January, 1866, with his father. In them he says that Seward commented on Samaná Bay to the effect that "there are in the world a few isolated points whose possession enables the power that holds them to control trade, and to direct naval and military operations with especial advantage." The order of priorities roughly approximates the true nature of Seward's interests in the region, and is closer to the truth than his son's later comments.[55]

The campaign to assure public acceptance of the 1867 treaty purchasing St. Thomas and St. John in the Danish West Indies was prosecuted with Seward's customary efficiency and zeal, and supported by those who stood to profit most from their acquisition. The chief New York organizer was apparently Samuel S. Cox. In December, 1867, he reported to Seward on the status of the campaign. The New York City Common Council had adopted a motion which stressed the importance of the islands "both as regards commerce and increased military and naval facilities cannot be overestimated." The Board of Aldermen went on record; they considered "the recent acquisition of the island of St. Thomas as a movement in the direction of American interest and destiny abroad." Cox promised that more New York City memorials were on the way. He also sent Seward an article on the subject written by a friend, which he proposed to to publish, and asked Seward after he had read it if he "might

[55] Frederick W. Seward, "Seward's West Indian Cruise," *Godey's Magazine*, CXXVIII–CXXIX (April–Nov., 1894). The quotation is in the July issue (p. 7). The discrepancy may be accounted for by the fact that his *Reminiscences* were published in 1916, the second year of World War I and the year the United States purchased the Virgin Islands from Denmark. His revised evaluation of Seward's objectives may have been influenced by these events.

indicate either to your son, or to myself, when I see you, what it were best to omit, & what to dilate upon. I do not know whether you would desire its publication; or if so, in what form, whether pamphlet or in a newspaper." [56]

In addition, Colonel C. M. Zulick, of Philadelphia, presented similar resolutions to the Corn Exchange of that city. The Baltimore Common Council would not meet until January, but he promised "there will be a handsomely drawn memorial from the Mayor & others." [57] Doubtless, such bodies were far more interested in the commercial aspects of the purchase than in its strategic or military side.

Another advocate of the purchase was H. N. Congar, former United States Consul at Hong Kong, who wrote Seward on the stationery of the New Jersey Department of State. He enclosed an article from the *Trenton Daily True American* written by Judge David Narr, who had been United States Commercial Agent at St. Thomas during the Polk administration. According to Congar, Narr's acquaintance "with the whole subject, and with the real necessities of our own commerce, would I think make him useful in the explanation of the real merits of this acquisition." And so he was. Narr's article explained the great significance of St. Thomas to "a commercial people"; he described it as the "entrepôt of West India and South American commerce" and said he believed "it will tend greatly to the commercial interests of the country." [58]

The *Army and Navy Journal*, a semi-official organ of the military forces of the United States, might have been ex-

---

[56] Dec. 17, 1867 (Private), NA M179, R269.

[57] C. M. Zulick to S. S. Cox, Dec. 14, 1867, encl. in *ibid*.

[58] Dec. 20, 1867, *ibid*., enclosing article from the *Trenton Daily True American*.

pected to stress the military aspects of St. Thomas. Indeed, it approved the purchase because with it "we buy a position," but it was also a "point of great national and commercial advantages." The theme of combining military and commercial objectives was a familiar one at the time. The *Journal* stressed this aspect of the purchase by reprinting an extract from the *London Morning Star*. Commenting on President Johnson's third annual message, the *Star* pointed out the strategic advantages of St. Thomas, but then went on to say: "The active and most powerful influence will be exerted by the superior commercial activity of the Americans. . . . Although the obtaining of war-ports has been the leading idea of the late acquisition, the intense business activity of the Americans will doubtless soon convert the new colony into a commercial centre, where they will amass all the rich produce of the neighboring islands before launching it upon the markets of the world." [59]

Most important, Seward himself revealed how he regarded a coaling station in the West Indies in a communication to Charles Sumner, Chairman of the Senate's Foreign Relations Committee. Arguing in favor of the treaty's approval, Seward said: "It is assumed that when St. Thomas and St. John are brought under the jurisdiction of the United States they will constitute a halfway station for our national commerce with South America and the Pacific coast, an entrepôt for our trade with the tropical regions and a relay for our squadrons of war or apprehended disturbance of general peace." [60]

But Seward was destined to be frustrated. Natural disaster in the islands, added to the Senate's lack of interest in them, led the Senate to reject the purchase of the Danish West

[59] Nov. 9, 1867, p. 89; Jan. 4, 1868, p. 312.
[60] Jan. 18, 1868, Seward Papers.

Indies. Seward's efforts to acquire Samaná Bay in the Dominican Republic and the Mole-Saint-Nicholas in Haiti also failed. Not until the twentieth century would his objectives in the Caribbean be fulfilled.

James Parton, who echoed Seward, stressed the importance of the islands as halfway stations for the commerce of the Pacific coast. "The Darien Canal," he wrote, "which is likely to be our next great project, will throw into the family of nations all the States of the Pacific shore, will bring Valparaiso within twelve days sail of New York, and will open to our commerce ten thousand miles of inhabited coast. . . . We must have a port in the West Indies, if only to aid in executing this undertaking." [61]

An isthmian canal was indeed Seward's "next great project." It was the logical next step on the road to establishing the commercial supremacy of the United States.

The Panama Canal

Seward's interest in getting a treaty from Colombia for a canal through the Isthmus of Panama shows that he expected to achieve the American commercial empire through diplomacy and by closely working with those whose interests would be benefited in a direct way by its achievement. We have seen Seward's relationship with the New York commercial community in such projects as the Paris Monetary Conference, the Alaska purchase, and the Danish West Indies venture. Here it is carried to its ultimate development, and serves to illustrate how symbiotic this relationship was and how tightly woven was the network of diplomacy and commercial enterprise in the Seward era.

As was true of the other projects, Seward's interest in a

[61] Parton, *The Danish Islands*, p. 62.

short cut through Central America that would link East and West was of long standing. In 1852 he told the Senate that "our Panama route to China has a decided advantage over that of the Isthmus of Suez." In 1856 he proposed an amendment to a bill for a powder magazine in California that would have provided $10,000 to "make such exploration and verification of several surveys already made of a ship canal near the Isthmus of Darien to connect the waters of the Pacific with the Atlantic." [62]

During the Civil War, little time and less means were available to carry forward any plans for an isthmian canal. But with the close of hostilities, Seward's interest was rekindled, the more so when it was thought that Great Britain had similar designs.[63] The pace picked up when Rear Admiral Charles H. Davis submitted a report in response to a Senate resolution of March 19, 1866, asking the relative merits of the various canal routes. The report favored a canal across the Isthmus of Panama, and resulted in an appropriation of $40,000 for a survey of the recommended route.[64]

On the very day of the Senate resolution, Seward was responding to a memorandum from Estorijo Salgar, Colombian Minister to the United States, in which the Colombian government proposed an American survey of the isthmus and promised preferential treatment to United States citizens if construction of a canal were undertaken. Seward unhesitatingly accepted the offer, but an inexplicable silence descended upon

[62] *Cong. Globe,* 32d Cong., 1st sess., July 29, 1852, p. 1976; 34th Cong,. 1st and 2d sess., Aug. 15, 1856, p. 2130.

[63] Burton to Seward, Feb. 2, 1866 and Feb. 6, 1866, *For. Rel.* (1866), Pt. 1, pp. 507–10. See Seward's letter to the United States Coast Survey expressing a "lively interest in the Isthmian transit routes" (Seward to Capt. P. C. West, Nov. 30, 1865, NA M40, R60).

[64] Senate Exec. Doc. No. 62, 39th Cong., 1st sess.

the previously voluble Colombians, and try as he might Seward could get nothing further out of them.[65]

Colombia's reticence compelled Seward to hedge his bet by negotiating the Dickinson-Ayon treaty with Nicaragua for a canal through that country.[66] But his heart was set on Panama, an unrequited yearning further enhanced by the deluge of propaganda showered upon him by Dr. Edward Cullen, an Irish physician, who claimed to have found an easy passage through the Isthmus of Darien, and who urged Seward to move quickly to obtain the necessary rights from Colombia lest some European country get them first. Seward found Cullen's views "suggestive and instructive." [67]

The real difficulty was not Seward's tergiversation but the lack of a firm commitment from American financial and commercial circles assuring the building of a canal if the treaty were secured. Seward explained the problem to Peter J. Sullivan, United States Minister to Colombia, on March 2, 1868, at the time Seward was authorizing him, on the basis of Cullen's

[65] Salgar to Seward, March 16, 1866; Seward to Salgar, March 19, 1866 and Nov. 23, 1866, *For. Rel.* (1866), Pt. 1, pp. 597–98; Seward to President Johnson, Feb. 4, 1867, NA RG59, Report Books, IX, 102–106.

[66] For text of treaty, see Senate Exec. Doc. No. 47, 48th Cong., 2d sess., pp. 779–86.

[67] Charles Francis Adams to Seward, Feb. 9, 1867, NA M30, R89 (Dispatches, Great Britain), encl. Cullen's letter; Seward to Charles Francis Adams, Feb. 25, 1867, NA M77, R80; W. B. West to Seward, April 26, 1867, NA T199, R5 (Consular Dispatches, Dublin); West to Seward, July 25, 1867, *ibid.*; F. W. Seward to West, Nov. 29, 1867, NA RG59 (Consular Instructions, Dublin); Seward to Sullivan, Sept. 5, 1867, NA M77, R45 (Instructions, Colombia). Cullen's credentials were somewhat dubious. Gerstle Mack calls him "a liar of the first water" (*The Land Divided: A History of the Panama Canal and Other Isthmian Canal Projects* [New York, 1944], p. 249). There is a brief sketch of Cullen in E. Taylor Parks, *Colombia and the United States, 1765–1934* (Durham, N.C., 1935), pp. 333–34.

enthusiasm, to negotiate a convention for the building of a "ship canal through the Isthmus." The problem, he said, stemmed from the fact that "the feasibility of the construction of the proposed ship canal at reasonable cost is not yet established in the popular mind, or even in the financial circles of the nation." Since the government was not likely to undertake the actual work of construction itself, the project would have to be left to individuals or corporations. The government might provide some aid through subsidy or other means, but it would not be feasible at present to build the canal with federal funds. Unfortunately, it was "equally impossible in view of the present condition of commercial affairs and mercantile credit to procure at the moment the subscription of capital necessary for the great enterprise we have in view." He was hopeful, though, that "statesmen and capitalists throughout the world" would become "greatly enlightened" within the next three years.[68]

The cause of Seward's pessimism was a letter he had received a few days earlier from a committee of businessmen he had brought together in the hope they might finance the canal. The committe, chaired by Cornelius K. Garrison, informed Seward that they had fully considered the importance of the canal to world commerce and, more particularly, its significance for American trade. They regretted, however, that they had been "forced to the conclusion that no association of American capitalists can safely undertake the enterprise," inasmuch as the cost would be prohibitive and the profits late in coming. The committee suggested the possibility of a subsidy from the federal government.[69] The day Seward wrote to Sullivan communicating this information, he

[68] March 2, 1868, NA M77, R45.
[69] Cornelius K. Garrison to Seward, Feb. 27, 1868, NA M179, R273. See also Seward to Abram Wakeman, Feb. 13, 1868, Seward Papers.

replied to the committee that he had received their report and would be "pleased to confer" on the matter, proposing New York as a suitable meeting place.[70]

A few days after the tenth of March, the meeting, arranged by Seward's friend, Richard Schell, was held at Thurlow Weed's home in New York City.[71] There is no record of what took place at this meeting, but evidently Seward pleaded persuasively with the committee to continue its efforts to raise the needed capital. In any event, the work went ahead and the Isthmus Canal Company was incorporated under the laws of the State of New York on September 24, 1868. The charter was sent to Seward and he, in turn, forwarded it to the corporation.[72]

According to the charter, the members of the corporation included the following: Peter Cooper, Abram Hewitt, Frederick M. Kelley, William M. Evarts, William T. Coleman, Cornelius K. Garrison, William H. Vanderbilt, Robert H. Pruyn, Marshall O. Roberts, William H. Seward, Jr., Richard Schell, Frederick A. Conkling, William C. Fargo, William H. Appleton, William E. Dodge, and Moses Grinnell.[73] All were residents of New York State and several had been among those who had presented Seward with the Leutze portrait in honor of the purchase of Alaska.[74] A brief look at this veritable Who's Who of influential New York financiers, entrepreneurs, merchants, and commercial men, may reveal something of why they were interested in the Panama project.

[70] Seward to Messrs. Garrison, Cooper, and Coleman, March 2, 1868, NA M40, R64.

[71] Seward to Richard Schell, March 10, 1868, Seward Papers.

[72] Robert Pruyn to Seward, May 4, 1868, *ibid*.

[73] Seward to Peter Cooper, Sept. 28, 1868, NA M40, R64.

[74] They were Peter Cooper, Robert Pruyn, Richard Schell, William E. Dodge, William H. Appleton.

Peter Cooper, President of the Isthmus Canal Company, was the owner of large ironworks in New York and Pennsylvania and the founder of Cooper Union. His associate Abram Hewitt was to be mainly responsible for raising European capital, especially in England. Frederick M. Kelley, a "mystical and imaginative New York capitalist," had for a long time advocated an isthmian canal and had already financed at least ten expeditions to the isthmus and government surveys of it, including that of 1866. William M. Evarts was Attorney General of the United States, a well-known corporation lawyer, and a close friend of Seward's.[75]

William T. Coleman was a member of the New York Chamber of Commerce and an advocate of direct-mail steamship service between San Francisco and China. William H. Vanderbilt, the eldest son of the Commodore, who owned the Accessory Transit Company of Panama, was greatly interested in railroads. Robert H. Pruyn was a close friend of Seward's from their days in the New York legislature, a corporation lawyer, and former United States Minister to Japan. He had guided the incorporation papers safely through the legislature and was an important contact for Seward in New York. Marshall O. Roberts was involved in the New York, Newfoundland, and London Telegraph Company along with Peter Cooper. He was the principal stockholder of the Louisiana Tehuantepec Transit Company, which had a grant to

[75] Hewitt to Seward, Oct. 26, 1868; F. W. Seward to Hewitt, Oct. 29, 1868, Seward Papers. Seward's association with Hewitt goes back to his reelection to the Senate in 1855, when Hewitt wrote to him on behalf of the firm of Cooper-Hewitt to offer an "expression of gratification from those who are simply men of business" (Hewitt to Seward, Feb. 8, 1855, Seward Papers). J. Fred Rippy, *The Capitalists and Colombia* (New York, 1931), p. 45. See also the brief sketch in Parks, *Colombia and the United States*, pp. 334–35. Allen Johnson and Dumas Malone, eds., *Dictionary of American Biography* (New York, 1930), VI, 215–18.

build a railroad across Mexico, and he had been in close touch with Seward over litigation with the Tehuantepec Company, which disputed Roberts' claim. He was also an official of the United States Mail Steam Line running between New York, New Orleans, and Cuba.[76]

William Seward, Jr., was, of course, the Secretary's son and a banker in Auburn, New York. Richard Schell was another of Seward's close friends. A Wall Street "insider" whose "wide circle of friends was ever at Seward's service," he mostly handled liaison between the committee and Seward. Cornelius K. Garrison was president of the Brazil Mail Steamship Company, which ran a line of steamers from New York to Rio de Janeiro by way of St. Thomas. He had urged the acquisition of the latter because it was "destined to become the depot and market for exchanging the products and manufactures of the other nations of the Earth." In the 1850's he was the San Francisco agent for Cornelius Vanderbilt's Accessory Transit Company, which ran steamers from New York to San Francisco via Panama. He had also been one of the sponsors of William Walker's filibustering expeditions in Nicaragua.[77]

[76] New York Chamber of Commerce, *Annual Reports and Proceedings*, Oct. 4; Nov. 1, 1860 (New York Public Library). *DAB*, XIX, 175–76. See sketch in Payson J. Treat, *Diplomatic Relations Between the United States and Japan, 1853–1895* (2 vols.; Gloucester, Mass., 1963), I, 128. New York, Newfoundland, and London Telegraph Co. to Seward, Jan. 30, 1868, NA M179, R271; Mack, *The Land Divided*, p. 137; John F. Kemble, "The Panama Route to the Pacific Coast, 1848–1869," *Pacific Historical Review*, VII (March, 1938), 4; *DAB*, XVI, 11–12.

[77] Van Deusen, *Seward*, p. 264. Lawanda and John H. Cox, *Politics, Principles, and Prejudice, 1865–1866* (London, 1963), pp. 13–14. Seward to Schell, March 10, 1868; Seward to Schell, Jan. 31, 1868; Schell to Seward, Aug. 2, 1866; Seward to Schell, Aug. 3, 1866. All in Seward Papers. C. K. Garrison to C. T. Christiansen, Jan. 30, 1869, Seward

Frederick A. Conkling was president of the Etna Insurance Company; William Appleton was a merchant in New York; Moses Grinell, an old friend of Seward's, was president of Sun Mutual Insurance Company, and one of the managers, along with Evarts, of Seward's campaign for the Republican nomination in 1860; William E. Dodge was a merchant, a member of Phelps, Dodge and Company, copper dealers, and a stockholder in such railroads as the Erie, the Lackawanna, and the Jersey Central. William C. Fargo, the Express man, was President of the Lower California Company, and was involved in land speculation in Mexico.[78]

With the backing of these influential men, Seward was hopeful that the long sought after canal would become a reality, bringing with it a swift, sure means of commercial traffic to Asia. For, as he told Anson Burlingame and the Chinese Embassy at Washington, in July, 1868, although there was a railroad across Panama and a line of steamships from San Francisco to China and the imminent completion of the transcontinental railroad, "there will yet remain besides all these, and more important than all of them, the great work of connecting the two oceans by a ship canal to be constructed across the Isthmus of Darien." [79]

The members of the Isthmus Canal Company doubtless worked overtime attracting investors, and Seward continued to work closely with them, even though for a time it seemed Colombia would not be roused from its lethargy.[80] Because

---

Papers; Mack, *The Land Divided,* pp. 147, 191, 197–98, 200–201; *DAB,* V, 667–68.

[78] Van Deusen, *Seward,* pp. 58, 222; DAB VIII, 5–6; V, 352–53; VI, 271–72. List of officers, dated May 10, 1867, in Cushing Papers (Library of Congress).

[79] Seward, *Works,* V, 589.

[80] Detailed accounts of negotiations are in Parks, *Colombia and the*

of this, Seward was obliged to depart from the practice of negotiating treaties "in mutual confidence" and he expressed the desire for further "consultation with some enlightened capitalists." He proposed to bring along General Santos Acosta, the former President of Colombia and now Minister Plenipotentiary to the United States.[81] The meeting was held in New York sometime around October 20, 1868; Welles' diary records that Seward and Evarts were absent from the cabinet meeting that day and had probably "gone to confer with Peter Cooper and others about canal across the Isthmus." [82]

No record of the meeting survives, but the members were able to assure Seward and Acosta that "men of wealth and enterprise were ready to invest millions." Seward wrote Sullivan on October 24, that having met with "capitalists and other intelligent and enterprising persons" in New York he was "pleasantly surprised [to find] that, in the opinion of those persons, the *projet* of the Darien Ship Canal has manifestly gained favor during the present year." He was now convinced that with a favorable treaty the required capital would be readily secured and the work on the canal speedily begun.[83]

Close cooperation with the members of the corporation continued. When they felt the need for information and advice they asked Seward for "such copies of maps, charts, surveys, plans, etc., as can be conveniently had, & such sug-

United States, pp. 338–47; and Whelan, "William H. Seward, Expansionist," pp. 144–62.

[81] Seward to Cooper, Sept. 28, 1868, NA M40, R64.

[82] Cooper to Seward, Oct. 13, 1868, NA M179, R228; Welles, *Diary*, III, 459.

[83] W. T. Coleman to Seward, Oct. 4, 1868, NA M179, R288; Seward to Sullivan, Oct. 24, 1868, NA M77, R45.

gestions from yourself as occur to you, as to our mode of proceeding, etc.," and Seward obligingly forwarded copies of all departmental correspondence on the subject.[84]

Despite the strenuous efforts of Seward and the Isthmus Canal Company, Colombia still showed little disposition to move. Sullivan reported gloomily that the possibility of a treaty seemed remote.[85] With time running out for the Johnson administration and himself, Seward decided to move swiftly. He sent a special agent, Caleb Cushing, to Bogotá to bring home a treaty at any cost. Cushing was given wide discretionary powers to act "according to your best judgment" and to override any objections from Sullivan. In fact, so broad were Cushing's instructions that he appears to have written them himself.[86]

The choice of Cushing is an interesting one. True, Cushing was an experienced and able diplomat who, in 1844, had negotiated the Treaty of Wanghia with China, which gave

[84] Coleman to Seward, Nov. 3, 1868, NA M179, R290; F. A. Conkling to Seward, Nov. 4, 1868, ibid.; Seward to Coleman, Nov. 12, 1868, NA M40, R64; Seward to Conkling, Nov. 12, 1868, ibid.; F. W. Seward to Cooper, Nov. 13, 1868, NA RG59 (Consular Instructions, Bogotá).

[85] Sullivan to Seward, Oct. 10, Nov. 16, 20, 30, 1868, Jan. 2, 1869, NA T33, R24 (Dispatches, Colombia); Parks, Colombia and the United States, p. 345.

[86] In the Cushing Papers at the Library of Congress, there is a document titled "Draft Instructions, Bogotá, 25 November 1868." It is in Cushing's handwriting and contains numerous additions, deletions, and corrections, also in Cushing's handwriting. The final instructions, with the changes, can be found under date of November 25 in NA M40, R45. A scholarly biography of Cushing is badly needed. Carl M. Fuess, The Life of Caleb Cushing (Hamden, Conn., 1965), is a reprint of the 1923 edition. It is a semi-official biography and is dedicated to Cushing's nieces. There is no mention of Cushing's speculative activities.

the United States equal footing for the first time with European nations. But he was also a speculator of considerable scope with more than a passing interest in an isthmian canal. There was, indeed, an interlocking and overlapping series of memberships in various speculative ventures that shows how complex was the relationship between the State Department and the leading capitalists of the day, and how they all somehow came together on the Panama project.

Cushing was one of the principal stockholders in the Lower California Company of New York. Its objective was to purchase some 35.5 million acres of Mexican territory in the provinces of Sonora and Sinaloa along with adjacent islands and ports. The company sought to acquire quasi-governmental powers in the territory at a cost of $100,000 in gold. Part of the scheme involved importing Chinese coolies to work the land.[87] J. Ross Browne, later Seward's Minister to China, offered to survey the territory with a "corps of experts" for $10,000.[88] The man who acted as liaison between Mathias Romero, the Mexican Minister to the United States, and the Lower California Company was Edward Lee Plumb, *chargé d'affaires* at Mexico City and applicant for the post of Minister; a man who, according to George Wilkes, Secretary

[87] George Wilkes, Secretary to Cushing, May 1, 1865, Cushing Papers (Library of Congress). It will be recalled that this was part of the Mexican territory Seward was anxious to buy in 1861. See Chapter I.

[88] Secretary's Report, Nov. 20, 1866; Wilkes to Cushing, Dec. 11, 1866, *ibid*. The scheme for Chinese immigration had Anson Burlingame's approval. See Cushing, Aug. 25, 1868, *ibid*.; *J. Ross Browne, His Letters, Journals and Writings*, ed. with an Introd. by Lina Ferguson Browne (Albuquerque, 1969), p. 327; J. Ross Browne, aided by a corps of assistants, *Resources of the Pacific Slope . . . With a Sketch of the Settlement and Exploration of Lower California* (New York, 1869), pp. 47–48, 78–80.

of the company, would "be of great service to us as a friend of our Company and its grant." [89] Plumb was enthusiastically supported for the post by Caleb Cushing and by the "first commercial circles" in New York City, who thought his appointment would "be felt in connection with the important interests which are represented in the commercial relations of the two countries." [90]

Caleb Cushing was also one of the founders of the Tehuantepec Company, along with Henry R. de la Reintre, a third-class clerk in the State Department. De la Reintre was more than just a clerk, though, and appears to have had an extraordinarily varied career in the Department.[91]

The connections become even more complex with the appointment of J. Ross Browne as Minister to China in 1868. Browne left for his post in June, accompanied by his old friend and traveling companion, Charles D. Poston, whom Browne characterized as "a daring adventurer amid the shoals

[89] Wilkes to Cushing, Jan. 10, 1866, Cushing Papers (Library of Congress).

[90] Plumb to Cushing, July 22, 1867, *ibid.;* Allan McLane, President of Pacific Mail Steamship Company, to Seward, July 20, 1867; David Hoadley, President of Tehuantepec Railroad Company, to Seward, July 3, 1867, NA M650, R39 (Letters of Application and Recommendation). Admittedly a minor figure, Plumb, nonetheless, had some powerful friends, including Congressman Nathaniel Banks and Senator Charles Sumner. A biography of Plumb would throw much light on the economic penetration of Mexico by Americans, especially railroad interests in the 1860's and 1870's. The Plumb Papers at the Library of Congress are a rich source for these activities. For a brief but excellent sketch of Plumb, see David M. Pletcher, *Rails, Mines, and Progress: Seven American Promoters in Mexico, 1867-1911* (Ithaca, 1958), pp. 72-105.

[91] *New York Herald*, Oct. 17, 1866, in Cushing Papers (Library of Congress). For a summary of de la Reintre's career see F. W. Seward to John Bigelow, Aug. 1, 1864, NA RG59 (Consular Instructions, Paris).

and quicksands of Wall Street." [92] Poston secured, or had secured for himself, the post of United States Commissioner in China for the Department of Agriculture. At the same time he agreed to become the agent of the Lower California Company and "to use the whole of the authority of his position to induce Chinese capitalists to establish colonies . . . upon the Coast of Sonora & Lower Cala. & the interior." In this, according to Wilkes, he "will be supported by J. Ross Browne who is persuaded that such Colonies will furnish markets & be otherwise beneficial to the United States." For his troubles Poston was to get one share of the company's stock.[93]

What an isthmian canal might have meant to the Lower California Company and its investors can be seen in its Prospectus, which pointed out that its lands "lie directly in the new high road of commerce," providing "the short cut by which the Southern inter-oceanic railway can reach the Pacific coast, and take up the China and San Francisco trade." [94]

This interweaving of interests serves to illustrate how crucial an isthmian canal could be to those whose vital interests were tied up, as so many of them were, in transportation and communications. As an instance, several members of the Isthmus Canal Company had more than a passing interest in

[92] Browne, *Letters*, p. 338.

[93] Wilkes to Cushing, June 2, 1868 (Confidential), Cushing Papers (Library of Congress). Wilkes assured Cushing that the "whole strength of the Legation as well as all the influence of the Commr. of Agriculture will be devoted to the promotion of the Compy's interests." If all goes well, "there is no end to the money we may make" (*ibid*). See, also, Wilkes to Browne, June 7, 1868; Browne to Wilkes, June 16, 1868; *For. Rel.* (1868), Pt. 1, pp. 528–30; Seward to Browne, Aug. 17, 1868, NA M77, R39.

[94] "Prospectus" Lower California Company, July 20, 1867, Cushing Papers (Library of Congress).

the fortunes of the Lower California Company. William C. Fargo was President of the Lower California Company, Cornelius K. Garrison and Richard Schell, Seward's close friend, were on the Board of Directors.[95] A further connection between Cushing and the canal company was the fact that Marshall O. Roberts was the major stockholder of the Louisiana Tehuantepec Company, a rival of the Tehuantepec Company. Cushing devoted a portion of his time mediating between them with the announced aim "to unite *all* those interests, which have made expenditures or sacrifices in behalf of interoceanic communications by the Isthmus of Tehuantepec." [96] It would not, therefore, be far off the mark to suggest that Cushing had more than his country's interest in mind when he went to Colombia under those exceedingly liberal instructions.[97]

The Cushing negotiations got underway on January 7, 1869, and under forced draft were completed within a week. Cushing rushed back with the treaty, arriving at Washington on February 13.[98] Seward immediately informed the members of the company, and ten days later addressed a jubilant gathering of the stockholders in Washington.[99]

At the meeting maps of the proposed route were displayed

[95] List of officers, May 10, 1867, *ibid.*

[96] E. L. Plumb to Cushing, July 22, 1867; Cushing to J. L. Barlow, Feb. 8, 1867, *ibid.*

[97] Gideon Welles, in his customary sour manner, asserted that Seward was involved in "extensive private speculations" over the canal route (*Diary*, III, 526–27). Whether Welles meant to suggest that Seward personally invested in these schemes is not clear, but no evidence to support such an allegation has been uncovered. That Seward expected "great glorification and perpetual fame from it" is doubtless true, but this can hardly be considered unethical.

[98] Details in Whelan, "William H. Seward, Expansionist," pp. 152–54.

[99] Seward to Cooper (telegram), Feb. 13, 1869, NA M40, R64.

and there was a general expression of confidence in the success of the enterprise. Seward gave his most complete explication of the significance of the canal. The destiny of America, he said, "can only be attained by the execution of the Darien ship canal." The Suez canal, now approaching completion, would be disastrous to American commerce, forcing it eastward across the Atlantic, the Mediterranean and the Red Seas, and thence through the Indian Ocean to China. This would have realized Seward's worst fears that the United States would become tributary "to ancient and effete Egypt." These fears could be averted by bringing the Mediterranean and West European trade through an American canal. There was a railroad across Panama and soon there would be a transcontinental railroad across the United States connecting New York and San Francisco. But these were only "types and shadows of the Darien ship canal." It was an opportunity to "develop the resources of our own continent, and to regulate and restore the Asiatic nations to self-government, prosperity and happiness." He told the assembled gathering that "every opening of any secluded Asiatic State and nation that has occurred, had increased the zeal and the energy of the friends of progress in favor of a canal across the Isthmus of Darien." He was encouraged that the investors were prepared to supply the hundred million dollars to build the canal, thanked them for receiving him into their "enlightened and noble consultations" and said he was proud to have his name associated with theirs.[100]

The press was enthusiastic. The *New York Herald* announced that "the speculators may now set to work and cut through the isthmus after the eminently magnanimous and liberal service this government has done for them through the

[100] Seward, *Works*, V, 589–92.

medium of Secretary Seward and Caleb Cushing." [101] The *Army and Navy Journal* believed that with the canal "America would become a most formidable rival to Europe in the already rapidly increasing East India trade." [102] And, as a fitting climax to the entire affair, Seward was apprised of his "eminent fitness for the position of President of the Darien Canal Company, with a salary of twenty thousand dollars a year." [103]

The treaty failed of approval owing both to Colombia's

[101] Jan. 30, 1869, Cushing Papers (Library of Congress). The *Herald's* comment should be placed next to Seward's disavowal of such intentions in connection with the Panama Railroad Company in 1862: "It is not known, nor does the President stop to inquire what may be the influences of the Panama Rail Road Company. This Government acts independently of all such influences" (Seward to Allan Burton, Oct. 28, 1862, NA M77, R45).

[102] Feb. 20, 1869, pp. 417–18.

[103] Peter J. Sullivan to Seward, Jan. 14, 1869, Seward Papers. The suggestion was not acted upon, but it should be noted that it was made originally by Sullivan, United States Minister to Colombia, to Caleb Cushing. Had Cushing converted Sullivan to the cause during his special mission? Was Sullivan connected with the Isthmus Canal Company? These questions cannot be answered, but they make for interesting speculation. The New York capitalists did, however, honor Seward with a testimonial dinner on March 8, 1870, given by the New York Chamber of Commerce. The speaker, William E. Dodge (a member of the Isthmus Canal Company) praised Seward for his services to the "commercial classes" and said "they felt that they had his sympathies with them in all honest efforts to restore the commerce of the nation" and were reassured that "his influence and presence abroad would but inure to the general advantage of the nation, and to the interests of American commerce in particular" (New York Chamber of Commerce, *Annual Report and Proceedings* [1870]). Seward expressed gratitude for the "kind congratulations" and went on to say "Your records, I think, are not deficient in evidences of the respect and confidence I have long cherished for your enlightened councils" (Seward to New York Chamber of Commerce, March 1870, Seward Papers).

belief that it had made a bad bargain and could hold out for better terms, and the Senate's reluctance to support a dying administration.[104] But by that time Seward had left office and was traveling leisurely in the Northwest. There, still not believing that the "Colombian treaty will be suffered to fail," he told an audience at Sitka, Alaska, that with the purchase of Alaska only two works were left to connect the Pacific with Europe: "the extinguishment of the colonial system in the West Indies and the construction of a ship canal, adequate to modern navigation, across the Isthmus of Panama." [105]

He was not yet ready to concede defeat on the program that he had told Bigelow in 1867 he was determined to see to a successful conclusion. To this end he had labored long and hard, organized publicity campaigns of great ingenuity and scope, and mobilized the considerable weight of powerful men of wealth and enterprise. Despite all of this effort, only the purchase of Alaska was an unqualified success. The other parts of Seward's program would have to await other men and other days.

[104] Details in Whelan, "William H. Seward, Expansionist," pp. 156–62.

[105] Seward to Cushing, April 19, 1869, Cushing Papers (Library of Congress); Seward, *Works*, V, 571.

CHAPTER VI

Toward the Open Door:
China and Formosa

Asia had a leading role in Seward's foreign policy, since it was there he believed that the crucial contest for commercial supremacy would take place. A victory for the United States would be assured if the Western nations established equality of opportunity in the markets of Asia and if the Eastern nations could be prevented from closing those markets and driving the Western nations out. Seward employed two methods to secure these objectives. The first was cooperation with the other Western powers in order to maintain a common front against the Asians and to prevent any of those powers from acquiring a dominant position. The second was the use of force, if necessary, against those Asian nations which might seek to oust the foreign intruders.

In this scheme, force was not the antithesis of cooperation but its adjunct. To a great extent, its use depended on the receptivity of the Asian nations to the ideas, values, and goals of the West. If the reception was docile and the governments showed a disposition to accept the Westerners, cooperation was likely to be peaceful and uneventful, with a minimum of disturbance to the host country. If, on the other hand, the reception was sullen, grudging, or openly antagonistic, Seward would opt for a more bellicose form of cooperation, with threats, both covert and open, and sometimes the use of military power to enforce acceptance of Western objectives.

At no time did Seward contemplate playing a lone hand in the Far East. Domestic upheaval throughout his time in office and the lack of a navy equal to such a policy left him little choice but to follow a cooperative approach. This was not thought to be a handicap, however, since it was confidently assumed that given an equal opportunity to compete with the other Western powers, American enterprise would easily take first place and leave the others far behind. Furthermore, because commerce also had a civilizing mission, this peaceful triumph would enable the United States to lead the benighted people of Asia out of barbarism and ignorance into the luminous splendor of Western civilization, in return for which the Asians would shower gratitude and trade upon their American benefactors.

The "Protective Tutorship"

When Seward became Secretary of State, the American missionary effort in China was gathering momentum, and the image of the Chinese as childlike, eager, and docile protégés of the United States was assuming its grip on the American mind.[1] Seward had long believed that it would be the Americans who would awaken the nations of Asia "from the lethargy of superstition and caste," and having been so

[1] Paul A. Varg, *Missionaries, Chinese, and Diplomats: The American Protestant Missionary Movement in China, 1890–1952* (Princeton, N.J., 1958), p. 13. For a good general discussion of American views of China, see William L. Neumann, "Determinism, Destiny, and Myth in the American Image of China," in George L. Anderson, ed., *Issues and Conflicts: Studies in Twentieth Century American Diplomacy* (New York, 1959), pp. 1–22.

"roused and invigorated . . . would they spare their European oppressors and smite their American benefactors?" [2]

This benefaction was to consist largely of teaching the Chinese the ways of the West so as to prepare them for participation in world affairs. "It is the distinction of the United States," wrote Seward in 1870, "that they have come to the front of the Western States as the tutors of the decaying Asiatic states." And it was the good fortune of the Chinese, and marked them as apt pupils (in contrast to the obstreperous Japanese), to give way "before the ever-increasing importunity and exaction of the Western nations." [3]

Seward's views were shared by S. Wells Williams, *chargé d'affaires* at Peking during the many absences of Anson Burlingame. It was the American task, he believed, to teach the Chinese to appreciate Western methods and "to help them to carry into effect those measures and enterprises which will do them permanent good." He had no illusions about the "toilsome work" that this tutorship entailed, but, in a revealing statement that stands as an early version of the "white man's burden," he told Seward that he believed "this tutelage, with all its responsibilities, is the best way now available to elevate the Chinese to their proper place among the nations of the earth." [4]

The Chinese manifested their receptivity to the West by accepting Christian missionaries at a time when the Japanese were rejecting them. Williams, himself for many years a missionary in China, took a most favorable view of the situation and assured Seward of the "desire on the part of the imperial government to restrain . . . acts of violence against converts"

---

[2] *Works*, IV, 125.   [3] *Travels*, pp. 93, 133.
[4] S. Wells Williams to Seward, Sept. 26, 1868, *For. Rel.* (1868), Pt. 1, p. 597.

and their American converters.[5] Sometimes, it is true, the Chinese faltered and gave vent to animosity against Westerners in general and missionaries in particular, but Williams counseled Seward against any precipitate action. These outbursts, he said, must be regarded as inevitable when treaties have been "extorted at the cannon's mouth," yet these very treaties were "great charters of civilization and Christianity, and we have need to exercise forbearance and patience while educating a pagan and ignorant people up to their requirements." [6]

Anson Burlingame, who opposed "armed propagandism," was convinced that the Chinese government favored toleration, and he assured Seward that it had always given him a "respectful hearing for the cause of Christianity." The missionaries, he said, "have won their way to the hearts of the people, and secured the central government for their cause." [7] The Chinese, by their prudent acceptance of propagators of the faith, were to be spared more forcible methods.

The desire to teach the Chinese the ways of the West was not entirely altruistic, however. The thought that such instruction might lead to increased economic benefits to the United States was never very far from the minds of the tutors. A case in point is the use that was to be made of the money China had paid on the claims of American merchants for depredations committed by the Chinese in the 1850's. The total came close to a quarter of a million dollars, and its disposition posed something of a problem for Seward and his Ministers. In 1862 Williams made a suggestion to Burlingame, who passed it on to Seward, that the money be used to found

[5] Williams to Seward, Nov. 6, 1865, *ibid.* (1866), Pt. 1, p. 485.
[6] Williams to Seward, May 21, 1866, *ibid.,* p. 515.
[7] Burlingame to Seward, May 27, 1867, *ibid.* (1867), Pt. 1, p. 485.

"an institution in China at which the language and literature" of both countries would be taught to American and Chinese students. Burlingame thought the benefit of the school to the Chinese would be greater, because as he said, Americans were "better able to judge their need" than were the Chinese. But if the academic benefits to the United States would apparently be minor, the economic benefits might be substantial. Burlingame believed that since the school would be run by Americans they would come to exert considerable influence, and the Chinese graduates of the college would, in all probability, carry that influence to "the seat of government in support of peace and commerce throughout all the provinces." [8]

The material benefits to be derived from such a school were further elaborated by Burlingame the following year. He told Seward that Britain, the only country whose trade exceeded that of the United States, had interpreters in all fourteen treaty ports, whereas America had them in only three. A school for interpreters in the Chinese language would better prepare the United States to compete with Britain for the dominant place in the Chinese market.[9]

Seward found the idea an attractive one, and in his draft of President Johnson's first annual message he included a proposal to use the funds to build a college for educating Chinese and American citizens. He made clear to Congress what the objective was: "Persons so educated might be expected to possess great advantages for serving this Government and promoting the interests of American trade and com-

[8] Burlingame to Seward, May 19, 1862, *ibid.* (1861), Pt. 1, pp. 483–86.
[9] Burlingame to Seward, Nov. 18, 1863, *ibid.* (1864), Pt. 3, pp. 846–48.

merce with China." [10] For reasons unknown the proposal was removed from the message before it was delivered in December, 1865, and the scheme was never effected. Still, Seward was heartened by the efforts of the Chinese to emulate the West, and when Burlingame informed him that the Chinese were trying to expand scientific education, he enthusiastically wrote back that it was most commendable. It demonstrated, he said, "a strong tendency on the part of the imperial Government towards assimilation to the institutions and customs of the Western nations." He urged Burlingame to "lend your best exertions to favor this tendency." [11]

The Chinese, then, deserved good marks for making halting but apparently sincere efforts to adopt the customs of the West. By practicing patience, exercising close scrutiny, and administering an occasional pat on the back, Seward hoped to achieve improved commercial relations with China that would lead to the emergence of the United States as the chief trading nation in Asia.

But not everyone agreed with either the means or the anticipated results. J. Ross Browne, Minister to China in the closing months of the Johnson administration, had few illusions about the Chinese attitude toward the United States. Shortly after his arrival at Peking, he wrote to Seward that the "impression seems to have obtained in the United States that the government of China is peculiarly friendly to our country, and that great advantages to our commerce are about to accrue. . . . I need scarcely say these anticipations are without foundation." He tried to disabuse Seward of the notion that the policy of sweet forbearance and friendly instruction

[10] Draft of first annual message, 1865, Seward Papers.
[11] Burlingame to Seward, April 10, 1867, *For. Rel.* (1867), Pt. 1, p. 472; Seward to Burlingame, July 6, 1867, NA M77, R38.

had made the Chinese more favorably disposed to the United States than to the other Western powers. The Chinese, Browne argued, "distrust . . . all who have come in to disturb the administration of [their] domestic affairs." It would do no good to argue the case of American exceptionalism, because it had been tarred with the brush of intervention; all shared equally in the benefits extorted by force, all shared equally in the distrust that resulted.[12] What more could be expected from a people who showed such "inertness and prejudice"? Little could be done "to shake the inherent prejudice of the Tartar race against foreign intrusion" by "a course of inaction." The Chinese, Browne cautioned Seward, "would not be moved so long as they saw no force in the background.[13]

George Frederick Seward the Secretary's nephew and Consul-General at Shanghai, promptly countered Browne's advice. Force will not avail, he replied. Even "if we do not consult morality on this point, policy should dictate to us the advantage of declaring that we will not force matters . . . of assuming a virtue if we have it not. Moral pressure only . . . can be of use here." By relying solely on moral pressure the United States will "so conserve our position and the Empire for our benefit in the long run and ultimate intercourse which I hope is in store for America and China."[14]

[12] Nov. 25, 1868, NA M92, R26 (Dispatches, China).

[13] Dec. 5, 1868; Jan. 22, 1869, *ibid.* For a fuller exposition of Browne's views, see Paul H. Clyde, "The China Policy of J. Ross Browne, 1868–69," *Pacific Historical Review*, I (March, 1932), 312–23.

[14] George F. Seward to J. Ross Browne, Jan. 22, 1869, Seward Papers. He was to change his mind, however, and when he was Minister to China in 1876–1880, he advocated the use of force in China. See Paul H. Clyde, *The Far East: A History of the Impact of the West on Eastern Asia* (New York, 1948), pp. 229–30.

The idea (or illusion) that tutorship would ultimately reap rewards was not to be abandoned. Seward indicated as much in China in 1870. He told the Chinese that the future relations between China and the West would be in the form of a "protective tutorship." He anticipated that there would be "mutual sympathy and respect between the protectors and the protected, the instructors and the pupils." [15] This is the background against which Seward's policy in China must be viewed.

Seward Opens the Door:
The Treaty of 1868

Cooperation in Asia was the traditional policy of American diplomacy. According to one view, Seward merely carried cooperation further than any previous Secretary.[16] This view is, of course, basically accurate, but it minimizes Seward's policy to the point where it tends to disappear. Indeed, Tyler Dennett has suggested that Seward himself did little toward implementing this policy and that it was actually Anson Burlingame who conceived the approach and carried it out, with "Seward's part in Chinese policy limited to approval of Burlingame." [17]

Too much, however, can be made of Burlingame's originality, for as Dennett himself points out, "there were between

[15] Seward, *Travels*, p. 261.

[16] Dennett, "Seward's Far Eastern Policy," pp. 45–46.

[17] Tyler Dennett, *Americans in Eastern Asia: A Critical Study of the Policy of the United States with Reference to China, Japan and Korea in the 19th Century* (New York, 1922), p. 410. Burlingame himself took credit for the policy. See Burlingame to Vice Admiral Sir James Hope, June 30, 1862, *For. Rel.* (1861), Pt. 1, p. 849, for his comment that Seward "has instructed me to follow the line of policy hitherto pursued by me."

them no conflicts, nor even differences of opinion." [18] Since
four to six months might elapse between the transmission of
a dispatch and the receipt of the reply, American diplomats in
Asia inevitably had great discretion and latitude of action. In
Burlingame's case it made little difference, since Seward's
views of China differed in no essential from his Minister's,
and he invariably approved Burlingame's actions.[19]

In China, Seward's policy of cooperation was intended to
preserve equality of commercial opportunity among the
Western powers and maintain the territorial integrity of
China. Seward favored cooperation because he believed the
superior moral position of the United States made it "hardly
necessary for the United States ever to go to war." As he told
his son, Frederick William, "the simple statement on their
part, that they feel that they have been wronged or unjustly
dealt with, brings the offending nation to terms, for none can
stand against the public opinion of the world. That opinion
is on the side of the United States, because they are never
knowingly unjust to any nation: and the world feels we are
entitled to justice." [20]

[18] Dennett, *Americans in Eastern Asia*, p. 410.

[19] Burlingame to Seward, April 10, 1867, *For Rel.* (1867), Pt. 1, p.
472. Dennett is, of course entirely correct in saying that "the customary long letter of instructions usually given to a new minister was
omitted" (*Americans in Eastern Asia*, p. 410). However, what
amounted to such instructions were given a few months after Burlingame arrived in China: "The interests of this country in China, so far
as I understand them, are identical with those of [Great Britain and
France]. There is no reason to doubt that the British and French
ministers are acting in such a manner as will best promote the interests of all the Western nations. You are therefore instructed to consult and co-operate with them, unless, in special cases, there shall be
very satisfactory reasons for separating from them" (Seward to Burlingame, March 6, 1862, NA M77, R38).

[20] Seward, *Memoirs*, III, 474.

With this limitless confidence in the righteousness of the American position, Seward had reason to be pleased that his policy of cooperation met with the approval of the representatives of Great Britain, Russia and France, and he expressed the hope that they would continue to regard cooperation as a "cardinal fact in the policy of all the maritime powers." [21]

The policy of cooperation proceeded smoothly and uneventfully in China, since the Western powers experienced few problems there. The Taiping Rebellion did occasion momentary trouble, chiefly the fear that it might damage the export trade in Shanghai, a trade some believed to be nearly as great as the exports of the entire Russian empire.[22] During this difficult time, Burlingame was prepared to cooperate with the other Western powers for mutual defense should it become necessary, but the threat passed without any need to resort to military measures.[23]

The most significant development in Seward's policy of

[21] Seward to Burlingame, Sept. 9, 1863, NA M77, R38. Seward was less eager for cooperation in the western hemisphere. When the United States Consul at Caracas, Venezuela, sought to join Britain, Italy, and Spain in a request to France to provide a naval vessel for the protection of foreigners during a domestic disturbance, Seward disapproved: "As a general rule representatives of the United States are expected to refrain from formal consultation or conferences with representatives of other foreign countries" (Seward to Erastus C. Pruyn, Aug. 22, 1868, NA M77, R172 [Instructions, Venezuela]).

[22] Burlingame to Seward, Jan. 23, 1862, *For. Rel.* (1861), Pt. 1, p. 833. The Taiping Rebellion was a religious-political movement headed by a Chinese mystic, Hung Siu-tshuen, whose objective was to expel the Manchus from power. It began in the 1840's and gained considerable strength until it obtained control of the entire valley of the Yangtse. It was not suppressed until 1863 (see Dennett, *Americans in Eastern Asia*, pp. 207–10, 396–71).

[23] Burlingame to Seward, Dec. 24, 1861, *For. Rel.* (1861), Pt. 2, pp. 825–26.

cooperation in the interests of commercial opportunity came with the signing of the so-called Burlingame Treaty in 1868. On November 21, 1867, Burlingame resigned as United States Minister to China and, to the surprise of the world, accepted the position of "envoy to the treaty powers." [24] Together with two Chinese diplomats, he left for the United States in February, 1868, on the first leg of a journey that was intended to take him to all the Western nations which had interests in China. The procession of the mission from San Francisco to Washington was little short of triumphant, arriving in Washington the first week of June.[25]

President Johnson received the Burlingame mission on June 6, and made a brief address of welcome which gives every indication of having been written by Seward. He dwelt chiefly on the commercial successes and prospects of the United States, spoke of the impending completion of the transcontinental railroad and construction of an isthmian canal, and urged the Chinese to "take an active part in the general progress of civilization." [26]

After an exchange of greetings, the delegates from China sat down with Seward to draw up a series of articles designed to supplement the Treaty of Tientsin, signed in 1858.[27] The

[24] Burlingame to Seward, Dec. 14, 1867, *For. Rel.* (1867), Pt. 1, p. 494; Williams to Seward, Nov. 28, Dec. 23, 1867, *ibid.* (1868), Pt. 1, pp. 493, 495–97. The genesis of the mission is fully discussed in Frederick Wells Williams, *Anson Burlingame and the First Chinese Mission to Foreign Powers* (New York, 1912), pp. 73–112.

[25] Williams, *Anson Burlingame*, pp. 119–27.

[26] Seward, *Works*, V, 587–89. The speech is misdated July, 1868.

[27] The treaty is in William M. Malloy, comp., *Treaties, Conventions, International Acts, Protocols and Agreements between the United States of America and Other Powers, 1776–1902* (2 vols.; Washington, D.C., 1910), I, 234–36. There is some question about who actually initiated the idea of revising the Treaty of 1858 and to whom

new treaty consisted of eight articles, which may be sum-marized as follows: *Article I* recognized China's "right of eminent domain or dominion" over its "land, and water," except insofar as they had been conceded by treaty. *Article II* recognized China's control over trade and commerce "within the Chinese dominions" except those "stipulated for by treaty." *Article III* recognized the right of China to appoint consuls in American ports. *Article IV* guaranteed freedom of religion to Westerners residing in China. *Article V* permitted "free migration and immigration" of the citizens of the United States and China between the two countries, and out-lawed the coolie trade. *Article VI* guaranteed reciprocal "priv-ileges, immunities and exemptions" to the residents of each nation in the other, but forbade the naturalization of either. *Article VII* permitted each nation to "freely establish and maintain schools in the domain of the other." *Article VIII* recognized the right of China to construct "railroads, tele-graphs or other material internal improvements" without "dictation or intervention" by any outside power.

The significance of the treaty does not lie in the mutual concessions that were made by the two countries. The Chi-nese had shown no disposition to send diplomats to the West on a permanent basis, nor to build schools in America, nor to

---

should go the credit for the "Burlingame Treaty." Dennett is of two minds. On the one hand, he says that it was "written by the Secretary of State with the Envoy of China, as it were, standing at his elbow, telling him what to write." But later he writes that the treaty "might more properly be called the Seward Treaty . . . for Seward . . . ap-pears to have especially desired it and Seward wrote it" (Dennett, *Americans in Eastern Asia*, pp. 380–410). Williams says that the treaty was "drafted by Mr. Seward in accordance with his own ideas of what was right and proper under the circumstances" (*Anson Burlin-game*, p. 144). Regardless of who wrote it, the treaty was a perfect expression of Seward's attitude toward China.

naturalize American citizens. Americans had certainly shown an interest in building schools in China, but none in naturalizing Chinese in the United States. The Burlingame Treaty included no additional privileges not granted in the Treaty of 1858. Americans had been granted the same rights as the most favored nation; the Treaty of 1868 did no more and no less. The only part of the treaty of possible advantage to the United States was the article on immigration, a policy Seward as an advocate of cheap labor favored, but this article would do little to help the United States commercially.[28]

The great importance of the treaty lies in its statement of American attitudes and expectations about China and its relations with the West. Seward's mature thinking on the future prospects of China is reflected in *Articles I, II,* and *VIII.*[29] In them, Seward's position on the territorial integrity of China finds its fullest expression. They embody an unequivocal commitment to respect China's "dominion" over its territory, trade, and "domestic administration" and, in this way, formalize Seward's peaceful approach to China. By so doing, the treaty committed the other Western powers to the principle of equal commercial opportunity since it would prevent any one power from achieving a preponderant position in trade

[28] See Dennett, *Americans in Eastern Asia,* pp. 539–41.

[29] One of the difficulties in dealing with the treaty is the complete absence of documentary evidence. Like the Alaska treaty, the negotiations were conducted without the formal exchange of notes. The reason for this, according to Assistant Secretary F. W. Seward, was "the intense political excitement and bitterness that prevailed in Washington in 1867 and 1868. It seemed as if Congress and the nation had gone daft over the question of impeaching President Johnson. Every other subject was subordinated and misconstrued by some supposed connection therewith. . . . Even our private correspondence had to be jealously guarded" (quoted in Williams, *Anson Burlingame,* p. 145).

with China. Thus, equal opportunity and the territorial integrity of China were erected as the twin poles of Seward's China policy. As Seward was to say later: "The rivalry of the Western nations, with the fluctuations of the balance of their powers, render it dangerous for any foreign state to assume a protectorate" over China.[30]

The door was now slightly ajar. There is evidence, indirect but suggestive, that Seward wished to prop it open permanently. The silence of the official records makes generalizations hazardous, but it does appear that Seward sought formal recognition of the territorial integrity of China from the other treaty powers. In 1871, while in China on his world tour, he remarked to Wan-Siang, the Chinese Minister for Foreign Affairs, that "before the treaty was signed at Washington, its provisions were confidentially submitted to the European courts. They gave us assurances that they would accept them." [31]

The claim is an interesting one. No such assurances can be found in the public archives. Were they given verbally? By whom to whom? Were they given at all? Why would Seward make such a claim if it were not true? Burlingame had gone to Europe with that object in mind, among others, but except for a vague promise from England to refrain from using force in China, he had indifferent success. He died early in 1869, before he could complete his mission.[32] Despite the unimpres-

---

[30] Seward, *Travels*, p. 260.   [31] *Ibid.*, p. 169.

[32] Williams, *Anson Burlingame*, pp. 161–250; Dennett, *Americans in Eastern Asia*, pp. 386–89. There is some question whether Burlingame had not exceeded his instructions in negotiating the treaty for China. The issue is discussed by Knight Biggerstaff, "The Official Chinese Attitude Toward the Burlingame Mission," *American Historical Review*, XLI (July, 1936), 682–701. Biggerstaff does not believe Burlingame was specifically empowered to negotiate the treaty, but that it was acceptable to the Chinese government, which ratified it in 1869.

sive official reception of the mission in Europe, Seward was to claim that he had spoken with several of those who made the trip with Burlingame, and they told him that "the treaty had been virtually accepted by the European states." [33]

What do Seward's comments, made almost three years after the signing of the treaty mean? If Seward's understanding of Europe's view is correct, why is there no record of that fact? Was it wishful thinking? Was he merely trying to make Burlingame's mission sound more successful than it had in fact been, as a tribute to his colleague? Perhaps this is as close to the truth as it is possible to come at present. But the tantalizing thought occurs that, had Seward had the confidence, or perhaps the temerity, of John Hay, he might simply have announced the acceptance of the Burlingame Treaty and thus have promulgated the Open Door a full generation before its actual enunciation. All this is, of course, speculative, but there is no doubt that Seward was moving toward the Open Door, and had indeed prised it open, even if unofficially.

The Rewards of Virtue

The Seward-Burlingame treaty of 1868 was negotiated in an atmosphere of great anticipation of commercial benefits to come. This is apparent in the speech Burlingame gave at the banquet in New York City on June 22, 1868, in honor of the Chinese mission. He used the opportunity to give full

[33] Seward, *Travels*, p. 169. Samuel Flagg Bemis says that William Seward is sometimes thought of as having "set the policy to which the United States came back in the time of the Boxer Rebellion, in 1900: cooperation with the European powers for the guaranty of the structure of treaty rights in Asia." But, he adds, "We cannot say this so securely" (*Short History of American Foreign Policy*, pp. 191–92). Where Bemis minimizes Seward's contribution, others ignore it altogether. Robert H. Ferrell (*American Diplomacy: A History* [rev. and expanded ed., New York, 1969]) makes no mention at all of Seward's Far Eastern policy.

play to the prevailing notions of China as pupil, friend, and market. "Let her alone," he pleaded, ". . . and she will initiate a movement which will be felt in every workshop of the civilized world." China was an inexhaustible market for "your wheat, your lumber, your coal, your silver, your goods from everywhere." China was eager "to trade with you, to buy from you, to sell to you, to help you strike off the shackles from trade. She invites your merchants, she invites your missionaries." [34] Burlingame painted a dazzling picture of the commercial prospects for American merchants in China, and perhaps this accounts in some measure for the enthusiastic reception he received in the United States.

It is tempting to dismiss Burlingame's speech, as Samuel B. Ruggles' speech on the benefits of coinage unification has been dismissed, as so much bombast and empty "eloquence." [35] In truth, the portrait he painted did not comport with the actual attitudes of the Chinese toward the West and the Americans. It was equally wide of the mark in its depiction of the commercial prospects. Nonetheless, it was be-

[34] Quoted in Williams, *Anson Burlingame*, pp. 138–39. An interested participant at the banquet was Samuel B. Ruggles. He used the occasion "to celebrate, by anticipation, the coming interfusion of the commerce, the industry, the law, and last, not least, the money of the two hemispheres of our globe." He heard "with the highest satisfaction and instruction . . . the glowing and noble words of the Chief of the Embassy now before us" and suggested that "our Government at Washington" might "now well ask the Government at Pekin, to receive the metallic money of the United States . . . and to coin for us, in return, the money of the Empire having its peculiar emblems but of equal weight and value." Burlingame apparently assented and, given the identity of Ruggles' views with those of Seward, it is more than likely that the latter had given his consent to this invitation to China to join in the unification of the world's coinage (Ruggles, remarks at dinner for Chinese Embassy, June 22, 1868, NA M37, T22).

[35] Dennett, *Americans in Eastern Asia*, pp. 384–85.

lieved and accepted as a faithful account of the real world. So much is clear from the comments of *Hunt's Merchant's Magazine*, a journal not generally given to printing fiction. In a piece on the "China Trade," written on the occasion of Burlingame's trip, *Hunt's* said: "Lucrative as this commerce has been to the individuals concerned in it, and important so far as regards the wealth and power of Europe, and now America as well, it has only touched the shell of China. In all this, there is room for progress, and promise of it." [36] The pursuit of the *ignis fatuus* of the China trade was not going to be deterred by anything as trivial as reality.

The treaty fired the imagination of Joseph S. Wilson, Commissioner of the General Land Office in the Department of the Interior. He wrote Seward a twenty-five page letter on the "noble mission" of "opening a new era in civilization, bringing four hundred millions of Chinese into social, industrial, and commercial relations with America and Europe" and "inviting maritime enterprise upon a scale hitherto unknown in history . . . enabling us to absorb the enormous productions, and to minister to her home demands." In addition, it would enable the United States to reconstruct Asiatic society "through a normal and harmonious commercial development, without violence to any vested interest." The China trade, he continued, "need only be thoroughly developed and directed in the proper channels to make it a most powerful aid in our movement for controlling the world's commerce." He asked Seward to provide him with data on the nature and resources

[36] LVIII (June, 1868), 458–59. For his part, Seward had firmly fixed his attention on Asia; witness his comment to E. Joy Morris, United States Minister to Turkey, that the United States was not deeply interested in the Eastern Mediterranean "engaged as they are . . . extending their influence upon the Eastern instead of the Western shores of Asia" (Seward to Morris, Aug. 19, 1868, Seward Papers).

of China so that he might more fully develop his ideas.[37] Seward replied favorably and forwarded Wilson's letter to J. Ross Browne with the comment that the "President approves the enlightened and patriotic objects of the Commissioner," and instructed Browne to inquire of the Chinese if they would furnish the information. Nevertheless, Seward played the game of cooperation strictly according to the rules. He told Wilson that he would have to make explanations to the "other Western Powers, who like ourselves are in treaty with China, and with whom it is the habit of this Department to confer frankly upon questions affecting the Empire." He also told Browne to inform the other Ministers in Peking of what he was doing, and he himself spoke to their Ministers in Washington.[38]

Thus, Seward's policy toward China consisted of full cooperation with the other Western nations, the territorial sovereignty of China, equality of commercial opportunity, and the Open Door for all. As his handling of Commissioner Wilson's request shows, Seward scrupulously observed the niceties of cooperation. He wanted no more than "a fair field and no favor" in China, for he believed along with J. Ross Browne that "the citizens of the United States in China, I am happy to say, are not afraid to enter into any fair arrangements where there is an equality of chances." [39] American ingenuity, drive, and moral superiority would permit them to triumph in any fair and equal contest.

As for China, Seward saw little opportunity for change in its status. He told the Chinese that they were not yet ready

[37] July 15, 1868, NA M179, R282.
[38] Seward to Wilson, July 20, 1868, NA M40, R64; Seward to Browne, Aug. 21, 1868, NA M77, R39.
[39] Browne to Seward, Nov. 25, 1868, NA M92, R26.

for "popular revolution" and thus not ready for self-determination. Competition among the Western powers for China's trade was inadvisable since it might result in the preponderance of one of them over the others. The only alternative he could envisage was "the exercise of sovereignty in China by a national dynasty under the surveillance and protection of the maritime powers." He did not think that the role of the Western powers would always "retain its present obnoxious and oppressive character" but was hopeful that "the habit of intervention, and the habit of acquiescence once fixed, surveillance will assume the forms of protective tutorship," with "mutual sympathy and respect" among all.[40] What the Chinese thought of all this is not recorded.

Formosa: The Iron Hand in the Velvet Glove

The most difficult problem in Sino-American relations during the Seward era was that of the depredations by the natives of Formosa upon American shipping. The problem involved China only tangentially, and the way it was handled represented a departure from Seward's peaceful policy toward the Chinese. A discussion of it may help clarify both Seward's policy toward China and his attitude toward non-Chinese peoples in Asia.

Nominally, the Chinese government had jurisdiction over Formosa, but in practice it was either unable or unwilling to maintain control over the island or its native population. As a result, there were frequent attacks on Western ships using the seas around Formosa; seamen unfortunate enough to be shipwrecked on its beaches were maltreated or killed. The situation reached acute proportions in 1866, and Seward in-

[40] Seward, *Travels*, 260–61.

structed S. Wells Williams, *chargé d'affaires* at Peking, to "cooperate with the other powers to suppress piracy in the China seas." [41] The opportunity came when Sir Frederick Bruce, Britain's Minister to China, proposed joint Anglo-American naval operations in the area, and Seward agreed. Secretary of the Navy Gideon Welles, at Seward's request, instructed Rear Admiral Henry H. Bell, Commander of the East India Squadron, "to act in concert with other Powers to the end proposed in consulting with our minister to China and the Commander of Her Brittanic Majesty's forces in Chinese waters." [42]

Effective measures against the Formosan pirates were handicapped, however, by a lack of American naval power in the Far East. Only three steam warships were on station in the area, and Welles could spare only one additional ship for duty there. He told Seward that the squadron "was about as large as can conveniently be assigned to that station in view of the demands for vessels of war in other quarters." Seward relayed the unwelcome news to his Minister in China. [43]

Meanwhile, as matters continued to deteriorate in Formosan waters, Seward asked Williams to call the attention of the Chinese government to the problem "by proper demonstrations" and try to enlist their help. [44] The situation came to a head in April, 1867, when the American barque *Rover* was shipwrecked off the coast of Formosa and thirteen of its crew of fourteen were killed by the natives. The British

[41] Feb. 21, 1866, NA M77, R38.

[42] Welles to Seward, March 3, 1866, NA M179, R234; Welles to Seward, March 5, 1866, NA M472, R11 (Letters sent by Secretary of Navy to the President and Executive Agencies).

[43] Welles to Seward, April 4, 1866, NA M179, R236; Seward to Burlingame, April 9, 1866, NA M77, R38.

[44] Aug. 15, 1866, *For. Rel.* (1866), Pt. 1, pp. 554-55.

promptly sent a vessel to investigate, but it was driven off by the Formosans.[45]

The effort to get the Chinese to remonstrate with Formosa and investigate the *Rover* incident was taken over by the American Consul at Amoy, Charles W. LeGendre. It proved a thankless task. The Chinese temporized and pleaded lack of jurisdiction. LeGendre wrote Seward that little could be expected from the Chinese and that forceful methods might have to be employed. But Seward refused to take any overt action at this time. He remained optimistic that the Chinese would carry out their obligations.[46]

The seeming indifference of the Chinese finally goaded LeGendre into making the threats Seward had preferred to avoid. He wrote a long, intemperate letter to the Chinese governor of Formosa which contained a mixture of threats and advice. The United States, he said, "were a great commercial nation and they are this above all. They desire the extension of trade all over the world, and would certainly not sacrifice their interests to blind friendship for China or any other nations." Should the Chinese persist in their refusal to act, the United States would not object "if any foreign power" took control of southern Formosa "to clear it from the hordes that have interfered with our trade for years past," although he did not think the United States itself would "retain any portion of the territory acquired." Using an analogy that seemed to be standard for Americans in Asia, LeGendre offered the Chinese a bit of advice out of the

[45] Charles W. LeGendre to Seward, April 1, 1867, NA M100, R3 (Dispatches, Amoy); LeGendre to Seward, May 11, 1867, *ibid.*

[46] LeGendre to Seward, May [?], 1967; June 5, 1867, *ibid.* A penciled note in Seward's handwriting in the margin of the dispatch reads: "I hope to hear some satisfactory account of action by Chinese government from Mr. Burlingame."

American frontier experience. "The Formosan savages," he explained, "stand on the same footing with the Indians that yet inhabit a great portion of the United States. What can with truth be said of one under the laws of nations, can equally be said of the other. For the sake of our own interests, the United States have insisted with foreign powers that our Indians should hold their existence as tribes at our exclusive will." If the Chinese wished to avoid any trouble with the foreign powers, it would do well to "imitate us in that respect." [47]

Seward, however, would not be persuaded to sanction force against the Chinese. Instead, he instructed Burlingame to ask them whether they had control of the region, and if so, to urge them again to investigate and punish the perpetrators. If, on the other hand, the Chinese disclaimed jurisdiction, Burlingame was to determine on his own "what form of proceedings should be adopted." Seward stated firmly, though, that "in no case do the United States desire to seize and hold possession of Formosa or any part of said island." [48]

Meanwhile, the United States had taken direct action against Formosa. On June 13, Admiral Bell arrived with two warships, and after a brief encounter retired with the loss of one

[47] LeGendre to General and Taotai of Formosa, June 22, 1867, in LeGendre to Seward, June 30, 1867, *ibid.* Seward's note reads: "We shall await with the solution for the views of Mr. Burlingame." For detailed accounts of LeGendre's activities in Formosa, see Leonard Gordon, "Early American Relations with Formosa, 1849–1870," *Historian*, XIX (May, 1959), 281–87; Sandra Caruthers Thomson, "Filibustering to Formosa: General Charles LeGendre and the Japanese," *Pacific Historical Review*, XL (Nov., 1971), 442–56.

[48] June 20, 1867, NA M77, R38. Similar instructions were sent on July 15, *ibid.*

man.[49] This foray had occurred without Seward's knowledge or approval, but his patience with the Formosans was wearing thin. In August, he wrote to Burlingame of Admiral Bell's report to Secretary Welles, quoting him as saying that the "barbarities of these savages cannot be permanently stopped" until the Western powers persuade the Chinese to seize all the villages and ports on the Southern and Eastern coasts of Formosa and "drive the aboriginals back into the interior." Seward again urged Burlingame to join with the other powers in an attempt to persuade the Chinese to follow Bell's advice.[50] But Burlingame resigned his post as Minister to China before anything was done to implement Seward's instructions. LeGendre, however, still intent on reaching a definitive settlement of the issue, traveled on his own to Formosa and after a meeting with the local chieftains, obtained an agreement from them that in the future, shipwrecked seamen would not be molested.[51]

Throughout the *Rover* affair, Seward had avoided being stampeded into violent action by his impetuous Consul at Amoy. He clung firmly to his announced policy of patience and forbearance toward the Chinese, and aside from diplomatic pressure would use no force against them. Toward the Formosans, however, he felt no such tolerance. They lay

[49] LeGendre to Bell, July 5, 30, 1867; LeGendre to Seward, July 30, 1867, NA M100, R3. LeGendre supported the action, which he thought would "greatly add to the prestige of our flag in the East."

[50] Aug. 23, 1867, NA M77, R38.

[51] A lengthy account of the expedition can be found in LeGendre to Burlingame, Nov. 8, 1867, *For. Rel.* (1868), Pt. 1, pp. 503–10. A short summary of the *Rover* incident "of interest to merchants doing business in the China Seas" may be found in W. Hunter, Acting Secretary to Editor, *Hunt's Merchant's Magazine*, June 20, 1868, NA RG59 (Consular Instructions, Shanghai).

outside the pale, and other measures would be needed to deal with them.

Among the Seward Papers at the University of Rochester, there is part of Seward's draft of President Johnson's third annual message to Congress, delivered on December 3, 1867. In a discussion of the attacks that had taken place on American shipping, there is the following: "A due protection of our increasing commerce on the Pacific Ocean seems to require that the Executive should be empowered, by some general law, to make reprisals; and, if found necessary, to acquire and hold some strong naval port in the region where these outrages so habitually occur." [52]

This item is interesting for several reasons. First, it seems clearly aimed at the Formosa situation (and perhaps also Korea, as will be discussed later), for it falls exactly in the time period when that issue was most acute. Second, it seems to adopt the views of Admiral Bell regarding the proper approach to the problem of protecting American commerce in the Formosa area. Third, it is a complete reversal of Seward's assurance to Burlingame that the United States would seek no territory in the region. And finally, it illustrates Seward's policy toward those peoples of Asia who defied the needs and wishes of the Western powers. It is a complete reversal of his policy toward the accommodating Chinese against whom Seward consistently abjured the use of force.[53]

The proposal was excised from the message which Johnson delivered to Congress. Why it was removed is problematical.

[52] Seward Papers.

[53] Some may find irony in the thought that almost one hundred years before the second President Johnson's Tonkin Gulf Resolution, the first President Johnson came close to submitting a proposal that not only bore some resemblance to it, but dealt with the same general area of the world.

Most likely the news from LeGendre that he had reached an agreement with the Formosans was the decisive reason. Perhaps either Johnson or Seward thought better of it. Whatever the reason, it is a revealing picture of the double aspect of Seward's Far Eastern Policy: the sword and the olive branch.

CHAPTER VII

Gentle Coercion:
Japan and Korea

The Chinese, in their inscrutable way, appeared docile, cooperative, and eager to learn the ways of the West, though in reality, as J. Ross Browne pointed out, they may have harbored feelings of hostility toward America and Europe. But there was nothing inscrutable about the attitude of the Japanese. They were openly resentful and sought, in ways both overt and devious, to resist the incursion of an alien civilization.

Seward firmly believed that the United States had a great civilizing mission in Asia. That mission was to be achieved through the instrumentality of commerce, "which, surviving dynasties and empires . . . continues, as in former ages, to be a chief fertilizer" of both Europe and Asia.[1] Unfortunately, the Japanese did not wish to use Seward's methods of cultivating their soil and they made their resistance unmistakable. The Chinese, with whatever sincerity, showed themselves properly appreciative of his efforts; with them Seward could be generous and patient. The Japanese had the audacity to resist; only a stern visage and a harsh voice would serve.

[1] Seward to Burlingame, May 29, 1862, NA M77, R38.

The Wild East

From the beginning, the Japanese had to be dragged into the family of nations. The United States had been among the chief participants in this tug of war, and Seward was fully aware of it. He used a revealing phrase in his instructions to Robert H. Pruyn, the new Minister to Japan, in 1861, when he spoke of how Matthew C. Perry had "gently coerced Japan into friendship with us." He went on to inform Pruyn that "it is notorious that the people of Japan, especially its ruling classes, have not yet reconciled themselves to the sudden and complete revolution of national habits," but he still believed that the Japanese "have been kinder in their sentiments towards us than towards the other Western powers." [2] Because the Japanese harbored ill-concealed hostility and continued to resist the encroachment of the foreigners, Seward told Pruyn that he must "make the simple people of Japan respect not only the institutions of [the United States], but the institutions of Christianity and Western civilization." [3]

What Seward found most galling was Japan's open opposition to the preaching and practice of the Christian religion. Whereas China accepted the missionaries, albeit not giving them an outright welcome, the Japanese remained adamant in their rejection. Attacks on Christians, native and foreign, the proscription of missionary activities, and the prohibition of Christianity outraged him. When the Japanese government

[2] Nov. 15, 1861, NA M77, R104. Seward held views like this very early. In 1844 he observed, "Japan and China are exclusive states. Great Britain and the United States are social nations. So inconsistent is exclusiveness with progress, that sooner or later, Providence wills the subjugation of unsocial states, thus securing the advancement of civilization" (quoted in Baker, *Life*, p. 230) .

[3] Seward to Pruyn, Nov. 15, 1861, NA M77, R104.

passed an ordinance forbidding the practice of Christianity, he instructed Robert V. Van Valkenburgh, who had replaced Pruyn in 1866, to join the other Treaty powers in an appeal to the Japanese to repeal the law.[4] The United States, he said, could not agree to such restrictions and he advised his Minister to "proceed in the matter with firmness and without practicing any injurious hesitation or accepting any abasing compromise." [5] He did not trouble to disguise the consequences should the Japanese persist in their opposition. "When one foreign Christian shall have suffered martyrdom in Japan," he warned, the Christian world would be rocked to its foundations, and then it "may demand that the policy of forbearance and encouragement which the treaty powers have hitherto practiced in Japan may be reversed." Indeed, Seward held before the Japanese the threat of a holy war. If remedial action were not taken, he told Van Valkenburgh, it "will only prepare the way for fearful and bloody political convulsions, which will not cease until Christianity shall have established its claim to be recognized and maintained by the Government, and shall be universally accepted and adopted throughout the Empire. Humanity indeed demands and expects a continually extending sway for the Christian religion." [6] Thus, "Christian imperialism" took its place alongside commercial supremacy as a worthwhile goal for the United States.

Seward insisted that Japan open itself to Western commerce and influence even if it meant social upheaval and radical institutional change. It was simply part of the price that had to be paid for progress. Recent events were "rapidly

[4] Seward to Van Valkenburgh, Oct. 7, 1867, *ibid.*

[5] Van Valkenburgh to Seward, May 30, 1868, *For. Rel.* (1868), Pt. 1, p. 749; Seward to Van Valkenburgh, July 14, 1868, NA M77, R104.

[6] Seward to Van Valkenburgh, Oct. 5, 1868, NA M77, R104; Sept. 5, 1868, *ibid.*

raising the curtain which has hitherto secured the political machinery of the Empire against the intrusive curiosity of the Western Powers," and he was fully aware of the impact this "curiosity" would have on Japanese society, culture, and political institutions. But he bore the prospects with equanimity. The Japanese, he said, "have a task sufficiently arduous and perilous in the efforts they are wisely making to accommodate their political and civil institutions and customs to the commercial movements of the age and to the principles and policies established by the law of nations." He regretted the dislocation, but conceded that "one can hardly expect anything less than serious political changes as a consequence of the sudden entrance by Japan into relations with the other nations." [7]

Not surprisingly, Seward's views were shared by his Minister to Japan. Pruyn, who was a personal friend of Seward's, was as one with him in his conviction that only force would bring the Japanese to their senses and persuade them to accept the inevitable gracefully. "No conviction of public good," he wrote Seward, "nor respect for other nations, opened this country to residence and commerce. The silent but no less potent utterances of bayonet and wide-mouthed cannon burst away the barriers of isolation, and our foothold here can be maintained only by a firm attitude and with the hand on the sword." [8] Pruyn had no illusions about the cost to the Japanese of forcible change, or the reasons for their desperate resistance. The Japanese, he told Sir Rutherford Alcock, the British Minister to Japan, "must be sensible of the danger to which the institutions of the country are exposed by the continuance of foreign trade and intercourse, and it can

[7] Seward to Pruyn, Dec. 17, 1863, Sept. 5, 1868, Jan. 27, 1868, *ibid.*
[8] July 24, 1863, *For. Rel.* (1863), Pt. 2, p. 1046.

scarcely be expected to welcome cheerfully the presence of silent yet powerful forces, which must eventually endanger its own existance." The choice for Japan was a cruel one: "There can be no doubt that the entire framework of society and government must be remodelled . . . or it will crumble and disappear." But the task of nation-building did not dismay Pruyn; it was merely the unfolding of historical necessity. The current social, economic, and political systems of Japan would have to go the way of feudalism in Europe "in the presence of the representatives of constitutional government, of a wider commerce, and a purer Christianity." [9]

Pruyn and other American diplomats in Asia saw themselves as engaged in a lonely and hazardous enterprise. For them the Western frontier had become the Eastern frontier. The analogy is unmistakable in his comment to Seward that "all the officers of the Western powers in Japan are sentinels in the outposts of civilization. It is here as with our Indian tribes. The first notice of the attack is written in the blood which it causes to flow. The bolt comes out of an unclouded sky." [10] The Wild West had been transformed into the Wild East, where treacherous natives skulked beyond the light of the campfire waiting to pounce on the advance guard of civilization. Under such conditions the only solution that would serve was the one that had been applied to the American Indians—force.[11]

[9] Pruyn to Sir Rutherford Alcock, May 13, 1864, *For. Rel.* (1863), Pt. 3, p. 510.

[10] Pruyn to Seward, June 30, 1862, *ibid.* (1863), Pt. 1, p. 955.

[11] On this point, see Walter LaFeber, *The New Empire*, p. 5. For an interesting and stimulating analysis of the significance of the frontier in American diplomacy, see William Appleman Williams, "The Frontier Thesis and American Foreign Policy," *Pacific Historical Review*, XXIV (Nov., 1955), 379-95.

Conditions within the United States provided Seward with another reason for feeling that he had to deal forcefully with the Japanese. Seward's instructions to Pruyn reminded him that the time "for our trials had come. The nation was divided by Civil War." Seward was worried about the impact of this internal conflict abroad, especially among those peoples newly admitted to civilized society. He dreaded the "influence of the news of our divisions among the semi-barbarians of Japan." Would the Japanese "retain the fear which, perhaps, was the best guaranty of its goodwill towards us?" The Chinese, he said, had heard of our troubles and "have come to underrate our power and to disregard our rights. Is this evil to be experienced in Japan?" Stand firm, he advised Pruyn, and exhibit no uncertainty for the future, else "your distrust will be discovered by the ill-informed and feeble-minded community around you." Should he be able to maintain face with the Japanese, then "their friendly relations towards us may be retained until our domestic differences being ended, we are able once more to demonstrate our power in the East and establish our commerce there on secure foundations." How Seward really felt about the Japanese may be seen in a comment made to Pruyn in 1863 in the midst of a yet undecided Civil War, strained relations with Great Britain, and French machinations in Mexico. "You will be gratified to learn," he said, "that it is only in Japan that we are apprehending collision with a foreign enemy." [12]

Thus to Seward Japan was a stubborn, implacable foe of all that the West represented, and a barrier to commercial expansion in the Far East. Only force would serve to remove that barrier. The point is worth remembering, for, when Seward joined the other Western powers in combined mili-

[12] Nov. 15, 1861, NA M77, R104; Dec. 17, 1863, *ibid.*

tary operations against Japan, some historians would claim that he had been tricked into them by wily British diplomats. The fact is that he recognized the need for force and was prepared to use it whenever he thought it would serve the best interests of the United States.[13]

The Glove Removed

In Japan, Seward followed the same policy of cooperation with the other Western powers that served him so well in China, but because of his more negative attitude toward the Japanese, events there were more dramatic and more militant than they had been in China. No sooner had he taken his place at the Secretary's desk than he began demonstrating his devotion to the use of both cooperation and force in Japan.[14]

The occasion was the murder of C. J. Heusken, an American interpreter at the Legation in Yedo. Although the crime had been committed in the late days of the Buchanan administration, no satisfaction had yet been received from the Japanese. The United States Minister to Japan at the time was Townsend Harris. He was firmly opposed to any forceful retaliation for the murder since, in his view, Heusken had been guilty of contributory negligence by not taking the

[13] See Dennett, "Seward's Far Eastern Policy," p. 48; Van Deusen, *Seward*, p. 521.

[14] The standard history of Japanese-American relations in this period is the two-volume work by Payson J. Treat, *Diplomatic Relations Between the United States and Japan, 1853–1895*, cited in Chapter V. The relevant material is in Vol. I, pp. 105–352. Treat's work, while massively detailed, is disappointing in synthesis and analysis. A good general survey with many pertinent insights is William L. Neumann, *America Encounters Japan, from Perry to MacArthur* (New York, 1965), pp. 51–71, 71–78. Tyler Dennett (*Americans in Eastern Asia*, pp. 391–406) covers the major developments admirably.

proper precautions to guard himself against such an attack.[15] Seward soon made clear what his view was. On his own initiative, he proposed to the other Western powers in Japan— France, Great Britain, Prussia, and Russia—that a joint naval demonstration be made against the Japanese. The objective was to impress upon them the need to "strictly and literally comply with their obligations." Seward proposed that each nation supply "a vessel or vessels of war in the bay of Yedo," and if the Japanese reaction proved unsatisfactory, the powers were to undertake "such hostilities recommended and prosecuted as the naval commanders may deem most likely to bring the Japanese to a sense of their obligations." [16]

But it was not only the murder of Heusken that impelled Seward to urge armed attack on Japan. He was also disturbed by the failure of the Japanese to open the port of Yedo for trading purposes as they were obliged to do under the Treaty of 1858. Failure to compel them to open the port would cause the Japanese to "infer that we are unwilling or unable to vindicate our rights." He insisted that the Japanese not be granted any delay in opening Yedo and instructed Harris that "the other powers consulted would probably be induced

15 For details and Harris' views, see Dennett, *Americans in Eastern Asia*, pp. 396–97; or, more extensively, Treat, *United States and Japan*, I, 106–10.

16 Seward to Baron Edouard de Stoeckl, May 20, 1861, NA M99, R82 (Notes to Russian Legation). Seward made it clear, however, "that as the Constitution of the United States requires the sanction of Congress to the commencement of hostilities against a foreign Power, this convention is not to be considered as obligatory on that Government until that sanction has been obtained." One is curious to know if Seward really thought he could get that sanction in the early days of the Civil War, or if he was merely leaving himself a way out. See also Seward to Harris, May 16, 1861, NA M77, R104.

to cooperate." [17] Harris, however, pleaded for time and the authority to deal with the problem in his own way. He was convinced that the Japanese were doing their utmost to apprehend the killers of Heusken and that serious internal problems as a consequence of foreign trade were partly responsible for Japanese intransigence.[18] Seward, observing that Harris' proposed course of action was "different from what has been contemplated by the President," yet holding Harris' "ability and discretion in high consideration," conceded that "it might be hazardous to every interest already secured to substitute a policy of our own, adopted at this distance, for one which you find necessary on the spot." After due consultation with the other powers, Seward informed Harris that it was agreed he should act on his own discretion.[19]

The Heusken affair was amicably settled by Harris, the Japanese agreeing to pay the late interpreter's widowed mother an indemnity of $10,000.[20] The incident, while a minor one, illustrates Seward's eagerness to engage in a display of power when he thought it would bring results. It also shows that, in Japan, Seward was willing to take the policy of cooperation to its ultimate limits. He told Harris that he had "lost no time" assuring the British Government of the desire of the United States to cooperate with it "in any judicious measures it may suggest" to protect the interests and representatives of the Western powers in Japan.[21] That willingness did not preclude military measures.

American representatives in Japan were enjoined as assid-

[17] Aug. 1, 1861, NA M77, R104.
[18] June 7, July 12, 1861, *For. Rel.* (1861), Pt. 1, pp. 797, 799–800.
[19] July 23, Aug. 1, 1861, NA M77, R104.
[20] Harris to Seward, Nov. 23, Nov. 27, 1861, *For. Rel.* (1862), Pt. 1, pp. 804–806.
[21] Oct. 21, 1861, NA M77, R104.

uously as their counterparts in China to follow a policy of cooperation and equality of commercial opportunity. When Harris, pleading age and infirmity, submitted his resignation in July, 1861, he was replaced by Seward's old friend and associate, Robert H. Pruyn.[22] In his instructions, Seward impressed upon the new Minister the importance of maintaining "friendly and intimate relations" with the representatives of the other Western powers in Japan. "You will seek no exclusive advantages and will consult freely with them upon all subjects," he told Pruyn, so that the "prestige of Western civilization could be preserved." The following month, Seward again reminded Pruyn that he could not "too earnestly enjoin upon you the duty of cultivating the best possible understanding with those representatives and of doing all in your power to maintain harmony of views and policy between them and yourself." Nothing less than the interests of the "civilized world" were at stake in "retaining the foothold of foreign nations already acquired in the Empire of Japan."[23]

Tyler Dennett has remarked that Seward "was willing to pay the price of co-operation," and because of this became an unwitting tool of British diplomats in Japan, thereby departing radically from traditional diplomacy in Asia. To support this view, Dennett cites Seward's note to Pruyn that "some of the agents of some others of the treaty powers pursue, in their intercourse with the Japanese, a course more energetic, if not more vigorous, than that which you have followed under the instructions of this Department."[24]

[22] Harris to Seward, July 10, 1861, *For. Rel.* (1861), Pt. 1, p. 799.
[23] Nov. 15, 1861, NA M77, R104; Dec. 19, 1861, *ibid.*
[24] Dennett, "Seward's Far Eastern Policy," p. 48; Seward to Pruyn, Jan. 31, 1863, NA M77, R104.

If Seward did indeed permit himself to be used to advance the interests of other powers in Japan, it was with his eyes wide open. After all, he had told Pruyn that the United States would cooperate with them "in *all necessary* efforts and by the use of *all necessary* means to maintain and secure the fulfillment of the treaties on the part of the Japanese Government." Pruyn was to "leave no room for the supposition that this Government can separate itself *in any way* from the interests of the other Treaty powers." [25] This view is reinforced by Seward's instruction to A. L. C. Portman, *chargé d'affaires*, that he should cooperate with the other powers, because "concurrence in their action is doubtless more important than even correctness of the decision which may be adopted." [26]

Thus, Seward was not only willing to pay the price of cooperation, he was ready and eager. As the Heusken incident demonstrated, he would not shrink from the use of force, if need be. And under the doctrine of equality of opportunity, whatever one power achieved, by whatever means, would ultimately redound to the advantage of the United States as well.

In 1863 and 1864 the internal situation in Japan began to worsen. The conflict between the government and the antiforeign elements grew sharper, and there was fear in the West that the Tycoon, who had shown himself pliable, might be toppled and the Westerners driven from Japan. Under pressure from the dissidents, he had issued exclusionary decrees, and the treaties with the Western powers were in jeopardy.[27] Seward was perturbed by these developments and

[25] June 6, 1863, NA M77, R104. Emphasis added.
[26] July 7, 1866, Seward Papers.
[27] For details, see Treat, *United States and Japan,* I, 172–76, 193–95.

urged Pruyn "to give every encouragement and support to such of the Tycoon's ministers and to such of the Daimos [*sic*] as are favorable to foreign trade, and thus to lead to the ultimate revoking of the feudal system and the exclusion theory in Japan." [28] Pruyn had come to this view somewhat earlier and had advocated stationing an American fleet permanently in Japanese waters. "It must be obvious to the President," he wrote Seward, "that the presence of Commodore Perry's powerful fleet first opened Japan, and it is both natural and undeniable that the same means must be relied on, for some time at least, to preserve to the world what was thus acquired." [29]

What use Pruyn might have made of such a fleet can be seen in a proposal he made to Seward in 1863 regarding the domestic situation in Japan. The prospect that the antiforeign elements might rise to power in Japan persuaded the representatives of Great Britain and France to offer the services of their naval units to the Tycoon so that he might defeat his opponents. The Tycoon was reluctant to accept aid from foreign governments in his battle against domestic enemies for fear it might compromise his position, but Britain and France were determined to thrust help upon him even if they had "to resort to measures of coercion." Pruyn was of the opinion that the offer of assistance would not be accepted and that "coercive measures" would follow. He knew that if needed, the USS *Wyoming* was in conveniently nearby

[28] Aug. 20, 1864, NA M77, R104. Note also the comment of the Assistant Secretary expressing the hope that "the dangers of civil and foreign war, which threatened to interrupt the commercial intercourse of Japan with foreign nations may have been removed" (F. W. Seward to George S. Fisher, July 13, 1863, NA RG59 [Consular Instructions, Kanagawa]).

[29] June 16, 1863, *For. Rel.* (1863), Pt. 2, p. 1018.

waters. Seward told Pruyn to cooperate with the other treaty powers in whatever problems might arise and assured him that the *Wyoming* would follow his orders.[30]

At the same time the Western powers were trying to force the Tycoon to accept their aid, the British were also trying to collect an indemnity from the Japanese for the murders of several of their subjects. Seward regretted that the indemnity had to be imposed "under coercion," but he told Pruyn that it was his duty to "lend [the Western powers] all the moral support" in his power. The American naval forces "will take care not to hinder, oppose, or embarrass the British authorities in the prosecution of those objects." He doubted the British sought "any conquest or exclusive privilege" and, in any event, whatever one nation achieved would result in "greater security for all." [31]

While these events were taking place, the American legation at Yedo was destroyed by fire on May 24, 1863, and several people were injured. Although the cause of the blaze was never determined, Pruyn could not repress the suspicion that it was deliberately set as part of the campaign to drive out the

[30] Pruyn to Seward, May 8, May 12, 1863, *For. Rel.* (1863), Pt. 2, pp. 1003, 1010; Seward to Pruyn, June 28, 1863, NA M77, R104.

[31] Seward to Pruyn, June 29, 1863, NA M77, R104. Because the incident also involved a purely British grievance, Seward wanted to keep American involvement to a minimum. He informed Pruyn that "the *Wyoming* will not commit any hostile act against the Japanese Government or people except in defense of the Legation or American residents." Pruyn was enjoined to "endeavor to cultivate friendly sentiments on the part of the Japanese Government" (Seward to Pruyn, July 7, 1863, *ibid.*). Evidently Seward hoped in this manner both to display his adherence to the principle of cooperation and at the same time impress upon the Japanese that it was Britain and not the United States which was acting in a hostile fashion.

foreigners.[32] He had lost all patience with the Japanese, and he expressed the hope to Seward that "the situation of affairs at home may soon be so improved as to admit of your proposal of 1861 being carried into effect." This, of course, was Seward's desire to shift American power to Asia at the close of the Civil War. Pruyn went further, however. He wanted "a demonstration at Osacca" by United States naval forces, and if this did not prove immediately successful in bringing the Japanese to heel, it was to be followed by "a land force to move on to Kioto." [33] Thus, a policy of force if followed to its logical conclusion would lead to an armed invasion of Japan. Whatever merit Pruyn's suggestion had, there was little possibility of its being put into effect. Where were those naval vessels, to say nothing of the land forces, to come from while civil war raged at home?

The destruction of the legation at Yedo was followed by a demand for an indemnity to compensate the United States for the loss of property and injury to its citizens. The Japanese at first refused, then temporized, and finally insisted that the negotiations be transferred to Washington. Fretting at the delay, Pruyn lamented the absence of military power because, in his opinion, "nothing has been accomplished here as yet by any nation in the absence of force, or the prospect of its immediate presence." [34] Seward was of like mind, and he urged upon the Secretary of the Navy the necessity for speed in

[32] Pruyn to Seward, May 26, 1863, *For. Rel.* (1863), Pt. 2, pp. 1011–12.

[33] Pruyn to Seward, June 27, 1863, *ibid.*, p. 1036. Pruyn wrote this dispatch four days before the Battle of Gettysburg.

[34] Seward to Pruyn, Sept. 1, 1863, NA M77, R104; Pruyn to Seward, Jan. 5, Jan. 22, 1864, *For. Rel.* (1864), Pt. 3, pp. 466–72, 475–76; Seward to Pruyn, March 18, 1864, NA M77, R104.

giving such orders to United States warships in Asiatic waters "as will enable Mr. Pruyn to enforce the demands which he has been instructed to make." Welles issued the necessary orders to Captain Cicero Price, Commander of the USS *Jamestown,* and Seward was able to inform his Minister that care had been taken to see that he was "not left unnecessarily without adequate force" to achieve his demands.[35] The indemnity was negotiated without need for further pressure from the United States.[36]

The bombardment of Shimonoseki in August, 1864, was both the logical culmination of Seward's penchant for force in Japan and an illustration of how inadequate were the military means to carry out a policy of coercion. The incident was precipitated by an attack on the *Pembroke,* an American merchant vessel, near the Straits of Shimonoseki on June 25, 1863.[37] Although the work of dissident elements in Japan, this direct assault on the presence of the Western powers in Japan could not be permitted to go unanswered. As Pruyn told Seward, "failure to act with energy would be attributed to our inability to act at all . . . and would cause loss of respect."[38] The USS *Wyoming* was dispatched to the Straits

[35] Seward to Welles, March 23, 1864, NA M40, R56; Seward to Pruyn, March 23, 1864, NA M77, R104; Welles to Price, March 30, 1864, Welles Papers (Library of Congress). The weakness of the Navy in the Far East is shown by the fact that the only vessel available was sail-equipped. The *Wyoming,* a steamship, was tracking the Confederate raider *Alabama.*

[36] Oct. 15, 1864, *For. Rel.* (1864), Pt. 3, p. 543.

[37] For details, see Treat, *United States and Japan,* pp. 184–85; Dennett, *Americans in Eastern Asia,* pp. 398–99.

[38] July 24, 1863, *For. Rel.* (1863), Pt. 2, p. 1040. For a full account of the *Pembroke* incident, see George F. Seward to William Seward, July 3, 1863, NA M112, R6.

to investigate, and while sailing through them was fired upon by shore batteries. In the brief engagement that followed, the *Wyoming* destroyed the gun positions, but suffered several men killed and wounded.[39] In reporting the incident, the *Army and Navy Journal* asserted that "the gloved hand is not going to serve with the Japanese," and that "it is probable that nothing but an extensive drubbing will keep the diversified Daimio-oligarch government of Japan in decent good faith. We ought to have more ships there." [40] Seward agreed, and told Pruyn that in a matter of "common defense, or to save a common right, or secure a common object, just and lawful in itself, the naval force of the United States will be expected to cooperate with the other Western powers." [41]

With this instruction in mind, Pruyn agreed to a plan proposed by the British to force the Japanese to open their ports and relent in their opposition to the Western powers. The project was the bombing of the Straits of Shimonoseki by the combined fleets of those powers. Pruyn informed Seward, who was surprised by the news but was not disposed to "disturb the concert of action between the Treaty powers." [42] The combined fleet of seventeen ships sailed for Shimonoseki on August 28 and 29. The bombardment began on September

---

[39] Pruyn to Seward, July 24, 1863, *For. Rel.* (1863), Pt. 2, pp. 1040–47; Treat, *United States and Japan*, I, 231–38; Dennett, *Americans in Eastern Asia*, pp. 400–401. A complicating factor was that the Mikado was emerging as the most powerful political figure in Japan, but he had not ratified the treaties of 1858. The Western powers were trying to get this commitment from him.

[40] Sept. 12, 1863, p. 41.

[41] Oct. 3, 1863, NA M77, R104.

[42] (Telegram), Aug. 26, Sept. 3, Oct. 12, 1864, *For. Rel.* (1864), Pt. 3, pp. 544–45, 553–58; Seward to Pruyn, Aug. 29, 1864, NA M77, R104.

5; it lasted for four days, and, according to Burlingame, was a complete success.[43]

The expedition was well received by the American commercial community. The *New York Journal of Commerce* applauded the "successful attack," but nonetheless was doubtful that the "difficulties attending commercial and social intercourse with Japan" had ended. It advocated keeping within reach a "considerable portion of the naval force which has been used with such beneficial results" and expressed the hope that the Japanese would "submit to the laws of progress and abandon efforts at seclusion." [44]

Out of the bombing of Shimonoseki came the Shimonoseki Indemnity Treaty and the Convention of 1866. The indemnity, agreed upon in October, 1864, was a payment by the Japanese government of three million dollars payable in quarterly installments, to be shared equally by Great Britain, France, the United States, and the Netherlands.[45]

The Convention of 1866, signed on June 25, dealt with tariff duties among the Western powers and Japan. As the

[43] Treat, *United States and Japan*, I, 233–35. The engagement was not without its comic aspects. The *Wyoming* was unavailable and the *Jamestown*, a sailing vessel, could not keep up with the others, which were steamships. The United States was obliged to charter a private vessel and arm her with guns off the *Jamestown* (see Treat, *United States and Japan*, I, 236; and Dennett, *Americans in Eastern Asia*, p. 400). Relevant documents on the Shimonoseki expedition can be found in Senate Misc. Doc. No. 52; House Exec. Docs. Nos. 93 and 219, 40th Cong., 2d sess. (1868).

[44] Dec. 20, 1864. Obviously, the *Journal* was not aware of the nature of the "naval force" that had taken part in the operation. The paper also expressed continued alarm over the impact of the internal conflict in Japan on commerce (see edition of Dec. 11, 1866).

[45] The indemnity treaty can be found in Malloy, *Treaties and Conventions*, I, 1011–12.

treaty delicately put it, the Japanese government was "desirous of affording a fresh proof of their wish to promote trade and to cement the friendly relations which exist between their government and foreign nations." A specified *ad valorem* tariff of 5 percent that was imposed in effect lowered the duties. But the basic importance of the treaty was that it was made for an indefinite period of time, "subject to revision" in 1872 at the pleasure of the treaty powers. In fact, the Convention of 1866 made the Japanese the economic wards of the West. For this reason Dennett calls it "one of the most thoroughly un-American treaties ever ratified by the American government." [46]

By this time, the policy of cooperation in Japan had been extended far beyond anything that had been done in China. Not only had American policy been meshed into the policies of the other powers, but Americans had also participated in joint military operations. Further, the United States had entered into treaty arrangements in concert with European powers. Short of a formal alliance, a more extensive commitment could hardly be envisaged. The true state of affairs was described by A. L. C. Portman in October, 1865, when he informed Seward that "the entente cordiale among the Legations is as satisfactory as can be desired." [47] Doubtless, a certain amount of pride in accomplishment was justified.

Pressures Short of Force

Not every attempt to persuade the Japanese to follow a course of action more acceptable to the United States involved the direct use or even the threat of force. The indirect means used generally took the form of withholding delivery

[46] *Ibid.*, pp. 1012–21; Dennett, *Americans in Eastern Asia*, p. 404.
[47] Feb. 14, 1866, NA M133, R7 (Dispatches, Japan).

of military equipment purchased by the Japanese in the United States.

The first such instance occurred when, in 1863, the Shogunate inquired of Pruyn if the United States would build them three steam vessels to offset those which were being supplied the daimios by Holland and England. Pruyn passed the request on to Seward.[48] Seward in turn was pleased by "this evidence of the high estimation in which the skill of our mechanics is held by the Japanese government" and agreed to provide the vessels. "It is constantly the policy of the government to encourage the resort of foreigners to our manufacturers and markets for all lawful merchandise," Seward told Pruyn.[49]

The exigencies of war, however, delayed the building of the vessels. By the time the first one had been completed, the Shimonoseki incident had occurred. The departure of the ship, the *Fusiyama*, was delayed by President Lincoln because of the "unsettled conditions of the relations of the United States with that Empire." [50] There is a little doubt the delay was intended to apply additional pressure on the Japanese to settle their differences with the Western powers.

Pruyn was disturbed. Although he found the actions of the Japanese most objectionable and urged punitive measures against them, he realized the importance of the Japanese market. He wrote to Thurlow Weed of Lincoln's refusal to allow the *Fusiyama* to sail pending "the amicable settlement of all differences with the Treaty powers." He warned Weed that the Danes, Dutch, Swiss, and French were building ships,

[48] Pruyn to Seward, Oct. 21, 1862, Senate Exec. Doc. No. 33, 37th Cong., 2d sess.

[49] Seward to Pruyn, Jan. 29, Feb. 9, 1863, NA M77, R104.

[50] Executive Order, Dec. 3, 1864, NA M163, R1.

manning machinery and vessels, and selling guns to the Japanese. He feared that a "large market for our merchandise will be closed in this country when our war closes by reason of the foothold others are now gaining. I am sure a large preference will be given our country if we are allowed to compete." He urged the prompt delivery of the *Fusiyama* to Japan.[51]

With the successful expedition to Shimonoseki, and the signing of the indemnity agreement, the reasons for the delay were eliminated. On February 5, 1865, the *Fusiyama* was turned over to Japan. It was the only one of the three vessels ordered that was actually built.[52]

The Japanese government was still in need of naval vessels, however, and in 1867, it dispatched two commissioners to the United States to learn firsthand of modern naval methods and to acquire another warship. Robert B. Van Valkenburgh, who had replaced Pruyn in 1866, cautioned the Assistant Secretary not to let the commissioners "fall into the hands of any sharpers," because their impressions of the United States "will go far to make or mar our immediate and future commercial relations with them." He repeated Pruyn's warning that European countries were "making inroads in Japan and have acquired a great deal of power." However, he praised the Japanese as a "kind, affectionate people who naturally 'take' to Americans." There was, in his view, "no reason why we may not be upon the best terms, and in a great measure control their commerce."[53]

President Johnson received the commissioners on May 3,

[51] March 15, 1865, NA M163, R1.

[52] Executive Order, June 6, 1865, NA M163, R1; *For. Rel.* (1866), Pt. 2, pp. 678–79.

[53] Van Valkenburgh to F. W. Seward (Private), Feb. 20, 1867, NA M163, R1.

1867. He expressed the view that the United States and Japan should be friends because they were so distant from each other that "neither has any reason to covet what the other possesses," and that "neither can find cause to do the other an injury." Having stressed the remoteness of the two powers, Johnson then reminded the Japanese of the purchase of Alaska and pointed out that the Americans were "advancing our frontiers near to Japan, while we are at the same time connecting our ports with hers by a new regular and frequent steamship line. It shall not be my fault," said the President, "if the two countries do not come to esteem each other the more by reason of greater commercial and social intimacy." [54]

The commissioners wished to make it known that they held similar fraternal feelings toward the United States, but pointed out that Japan was "full of rebels" who did not share these feelings and were opposed to improved relations with Western powers. Seward assured them that it was "our principle" that every government "in doing its duty ought to be sustained in its supremacy over its own people, by the good offices and friendship of nations with which it is at peace and with which it has treaties. We do not believe in rebellion at home, and we do not encourage rebellion in friendly states." [55] It was, then, with the idea of strengthening the position of those in Japan who asserted their desire to continue and enlarge their commercial and other relations with the United

[54] Message of Welcome, May 3, 1867, *ibid.* It seems clear that these sentiments were written by Seward. They precisely reflect his thinking and are similar to the comments he had made to the commissioners two days earlier at the State Department.

[55] Interview at State Department, May 6, 1867, NA M163, R1. The Civil War had wrought a great change in Seward's thinking about revolution. Compare these remarks with his speeches on Louis Kossuth (Seward, *Works,* I, 172–85).

States that Seward was amenable to the sale of military vessels to Japan.

The Japanese were given a tour of the naval facilities, paid a visit to Annapolis, were introduced to Admiral David Porter, and finally purchased a former Confederate iron-clad, the *Stonewall*, for $500,000. It was to be taken to Japan under the command of Captain George Brown of the United States Navy, after the Japanese confessed they would be unable to manage a voyage of that length themselves.[56]

Meanwhile, open warfare had broken out in Japan between the antiforeign forces and those who followed a more pacific attitude toward the West. After consultation, the Ministers of the Western powers agreed on a position of neutrality in the conflict. Van Valkenburgh informed Seward of the decision and announced that in keeping with it, he would act to detain the *Stonewall* when it arrived in Japan.[57]

The reason behind this clearly unneutral act was the increasing perturbation of some Americans in Japan. They had begun to reassess the Japanese and what might be in store for the West should they be armed with modern weapons. One of those most disturbed was A. L. C. Portman, *chargé d'affaires* at Yedo. He had followed Van Valkenburgh's instructions to detain the *Stonewall* when it arrived. Now he began to believe it should not be delivered at all. He warned Seward of the "utter unreliability" of the ruling classes of Japan. Supporting them in the hope of commercial rewards could prove a two-edged sword. He pleaded with Seward that "such terrible engines for mischief should never be permitted to get into their possession." No effort should be spared to prevent the delivery of the *Stonewall*. "It is worthy of consideration,"

[56] Seward to Van Valkenburgh, July 6, 1867, NA M77, R104.
[57] Feb. 24, 1868, *For. Rel.* (1868), Pt. 1, pp. 671–72.

he said, "what the effect may be not only on our relations with this country, but perhaps also with China at a future day, if this nation became fully armed." [58] This gloomy view of a militant Japan was shared by Captain Daniel Ammen, on duty with the Far East squadron. He wrote the Assistant Secretary of the Navy that "the moral force of vessels being built, armed and manned there is not to be overlooked in considering the Asiatic who is advancing wonderfully in the modern arts and will far sooner than is generally supposed be formidable." [59]

Seward at first disagreed with Van Valkenburgh and Portman. He informed his Minister that he had no authority in law to hold up the delivery of the vessel. The *Stonewall* had been bought and paid for; it was now the property of Japan and the United States had no jurisdiction over it. But then, having conceded the legal right of the Japanese to the ship, Seward proceeded to take it back in the interests of cooperation with the other treaty powers. Despite the unlawful character of the *Stonewall*'s detention, as long as Van Valkenburgh cooperated "in prudent measures with the representatives of the treaty powers in Japan," he could expect his government's approval since there was a "manifest necessity" to save "lives and property of the citizens of the United States." [60] After admitting that retaining the *Stonewall* was

[58] March 2, 1868, *ibid.*, pp. 681–84. Less than thirty years later, in the Sino-Japanese War, the prophecy would be fulfilled. William Neumann also records the fears of Sir Rutherford Alcock, the British Minister to Japan, that "Japan's aspiration for naval power boded ill for the West" (*America Encounters Japan*, p. 73). But he is inaccurate in saying that "Alcock's was a unique warning voice."

[59] D. Ammen to Edgar Welles, July 22, 1868, Welles Papers (Library of Congress).

[60] Seward to Van Valkenburgh, April 30, May 20, 1868, *For. Rel.* (1868), Pt. 1, pp. 733–35.

illegal, Seward made the remarkable observation that Van Valkenburgh was "understood to have done so with the informal consent and approval of both of the belligerents in Japan and with the view of facilitating the restoration of peace, law and order throughout the empire." That being so, the United States would "expect a full reimbursement" of the expense of maintaining the ship, when it was finally turned over to the Japanese government.[61] Thus, the Japanese, who admittedly had every legal right to the ship, not only were to be refused delivery of it, but, inasmuch as its retention was actually in the best interests of the Japanese, they would have to defray the cost of that retention. With the triumph of the Mikado and the return of peace within Japan, the *Stonewall* was finally released to the Japanese early in March, 1869.[62]

The use of indirect pressure, combined with the more obvious use of power, was intended to persuade the Japanese to accommodate themselves more fully to the needs of the Western powers. Even if those pressures were not productive of any immediate gains, they nonetheless contributed to the success of the United States in maintaining a common front with the other treaty nations and in preserving equality of commercial opportunity in Japan. Seward's penchant for using force in Japan stands in marked contrast with his policy toward China. That he did not employ force more frequently and with more telling effect was probably owing not to any disinclination to use it, but rather to insufficient means for applying it.

After Seward had left office, his views of Japan moderated somewhat. Passing through Japan in 1870 on his world trip,

[61] Van Valkenburgh to Seward, March 8, 1869, NA M133, R11.
[62] See Treat, *United States and Japan*, p. 322; Van Valkenburgh to Seward, March 8, 1869, NA M133, R11.

he observed that the "great problem now is, whether the European civilization can be extended over Japan, without the destruction, not merely of the political institutions of the country, but of the Japanese nation itself." There were but two ways to bring Japan "completely into the society" of the West: "the application of force, or . . . persuasion and encouragement." The answer should not be force, he said, because Japan was "practically defenseless against the Western states." Instead, he went on to say, "commerce has largely taken the place of war, and it is now universally felt that interest and humanity go hand in hand." Fortunately for Japan, the United States had "come to the front of the Western states as tutors of the decaying Asiatic states." [63] Thus, through trade and tutelage Japan might, like China, come to accept peacefully Western civilization and its values. Force had been tried and found wanting. Perhaps the Chinese solution might work in Japan after all.[64]

Korea: Bearding the Hermit

In the eyes of the West, Korea occupied approximately the same position as Formosa. Isolated, wild, hostile, the Hermit Kingdom was *terra incognita*. The Koreans rarely

[63] Seward, *Travels*, p. 93.

[64] The *Army and Navy Journal*, however, continued to lament the weakness of the American Navy in the Pacific. It pointed out that Britain had "three cruising vessels on squadron to our one." According to the *Journal*, the British had 35 ships and 243 guns compared to 14 ships and 137 guns for the Americans. Lecturing the government, it charged that "they cannot understand that a police of the sea—which is what the Navy is—is just as essential as a police of the land; that our commerce—if we are to have any, and if we are going to increase in wealth and importance, commerce we must have—necessitates a Navy somewhat proportioned to its size and extent" (Jan. 2, 1869, p. 305).

emerged from their isolation except to attack the luckless crews of ships wrecked on their inhospitable shores. Nevertheless, French missionaries came into this forbidding land to carry the gospel to unwilling natives. Not unexpectedly, their reception was sometimes less than enthusiastic. In March, 1866, nine French Catholic priests were murdered by the Koreans. In reporting the incident, S. Wells Williams informed Seward that the French were dispatching a naval force to Korea to avenge the massacre. If successful, he said, it would "probably result in opening the last country in the world which still forbids Europeans to travel or settle in it and establishing the dominant influence of Christian nations throughout the entire globe, if nothing worse to the independence of the Corean peninsula." [65]

Williams may have been pleased to see the French in Korea, but not everyone was. The *New York Journal of Commerce* warned that France, if it seized Korea and established a naval depot there, would be in a position to prevent the expansion of Russia southward. This possibility was disturbing to the *Journal*, which held the idea that "the Pacific ought to be controlled by America and Russia." [66]

Seward gave no hint that the French move toward Korea unduly disturbed him. He merely informed Williams that the "proceedings of the French Admiral . . . will be regarded with great interest throughout Christendom." [67] In early November, a French force of several hundred men attacked the Koreans in the vicinity of Seoul. After a brief skirmish they withdrew, apparently without having achieved any substantial success. George F. Seward, Consul-General at Shanghai, expressed the commonly held opinion that the expedition

[65] Aug. 8, 1866, *For. Rel.* (1866), Pt, 1, pp. 536–37.
[66] Nov. 8, 1866.   [67] Nov. 16, 1866, NA M77, R38.

had been a failure and that the French would soon propose a joint expedition to Korea by themselves, Great Britain, and the United States. He did not see "any immediate advantage to trade from opening Corea, but doubtless considerable traffic would grow up in the course of a few years." Meanwhile, protection ought to be given to sailors shipwrecked off the coast of Korea.[68]

The return of the French expedition brought more disquieting news to Seward. An American merchant ship, the *General Sherman*, had put in near Seoul in August, 1866, for water and supplies when, according to Burlingame, it had been treacherously attacked by the natives, who destroyed the ship and killed the entire crew.[69] The news had also been reported to Secretary of the Navy Gideon Welles by Rear Admiral Henry H. Bell, Commander of the Asiatic Squadron. Bell advocated that "prompt punishment be inflicted on the savage King and his willing subjects." He told Welles that "a blow so struck, promptly and efficiently . . . would awe not only Japan and the Court of Peking into profound respect for American views and interests, but would disclose to the world who are the masters of the Pacific." [70]

Anson Burlingame informed Seward that France was preparing another demonstration against Korea with a view toward getting a treaty and opening up commercial relations.

[68] G. F. Seward to W. Seward, Nov. 27, 1866, NA M112, R8.

[69] Burlingame to Seward, Dec. 15, 1866, *For. Rel.* (1867), Pt. 1, p. 426.

[70] Nov. 30, 1867, and Dec. 14, 1867 (Confidential), NA M89, R251 (Squadron Letters). Bell had advocated the seizure of the "Port Hamilton (Nam-Hoo) Islands" south of Korea, for a naval base. He told Welles, "The possession of so small a place does not indicate the least ambition for territorial aggrandizement" (Bell to Welles, Feb. 11, 1867, *ibid.*, R252).

He believed that Great Britain and Russia would join France, and asked Seward for permission to be present, together with Admiral Bell, saying that "our presence there should rather restrain than promote aggression." [71] Burlingame seems to have been unaware of Bell's view of the matter. He was certainly unaware of what Seward was thinking.

On March 3, 1867, though not yet informed of the proposed joint demonstration against Korea, Seward approached the French Minister in the United States, Jules Berthemy, and made a proposal of his own. He invited France to join the United States in a naval attack on Korea in order to avenge the destruction of the *General Sherman* and the murder of the missionaries. The British, however, were not invited. He told Berthemy that he had conceived the idea "in order to affirm publicly the good harmony that existed between the United States and France." Berthemy, in passing this news on to his government, said that since his instructions were to "seize every opportunity which offered itself to establish an understanding with the United States" he felt compelled to submit the proposal to his government. He thought it an excellent

[71] Burlingame to Seward (private letter), Jan. 31, 1867, Burlingame Papers (Library of Congress). The expedition was being fitted out on the assumption that the French attack in October had been a failure. According to Bell, some "retribution" was needed for the West to save face. "If the retirement of the French is not speedily followed by a signal demonstration it will be whispered among the Mandarins and Yaconins that the strength of the foreigner had departed; and in China and Japan the long hoped for moment to expel the foreigner will be fondly imagined to have at last arrived" (Bell to Welles [Confidential], Dec. 27, 1866, NA M89, R251). Actually, the expedition, which was originally thought to have been a failure, had been successful, and the officer who had commanded it was promoted by the French Government. See Dennett, "Seward's Far Eastern Policy," p. 54.

opportunity to improve American public opinion toward France, recoup the losses resulting from the apparent French failure in Korea, and open that country to commerce and prevent its absorption by Russia.[72]

The French declined the invitation. There was no longer any need for punitive action against Korea as far as they were concerned because additional information proved their first attack to have been successful. The only possible reason left for joint action would be to affirm "the mutual and constant sympathy that draws towards each other the French and American people." But this was not a sufficient reason to join in activities "whose distant object and undetermined character could not allow us to specify from the beginning their extent and duration." The "kind intention that has inspired

[72] Berthemy's dispatch to his government is printed in full in French in Dennett, "Seward's Far Eastern Policy," pp. 54–56. The translation is mine. Seward's proposal was undoubtedly made orally since no record of it can be found in the archives. Dennett says it was unknown to anyone alse in the American government until a copy of the reply to Berthemy was shown to the United States Minister to China, Frederick M. Low, in 1873, by the French Minister there. Low passed it on to then Secretary of State Hamilton Fish. It can be found in Low to Fish, Feb. 1, 1873, NA M92, R34 (Confidential).

However, there was another copy extant when Seward was still in office. It can be found in the Seward Papers at the University of Rochester. It is an English translation of the instructions to Berthemy, dated Paris, March 29, 1867, and signed "Moustier," the name of the Minister for Foreign Affairs for France. The reason for its long disappearance from the archives may be found in a penciled note in Seward's handwriting in the margin: "Not to be filed but goes with my private papers." Apparently, Seward had no desire to make public during his lifetime his plan for a Franco-American attack on Korea. Berthemy's instructions are printed in French in Dennett, "Seward's Far Eastern Policy," pp. 57–58. I have used the copy in the Seward Papers.

Mr. Seward's proposal" was appreciated, but politely declined.[73]

The episode is a most interesting and curious one on several counts. First, it provides a revealing glimpse into Seward's methods in Asia. This was the second proposal that Seward had originated for joint military operations with European nations against an Asian country. Neither was merely a lapse, nor can either be charged to the machinations of wily European diplomats. There can be little doubt that Seward believed force an acceptable means of overcoming those who defied the ambitions of the West. In China, none was needed; in Japan, Formosa, and Korea, nothing else would serve.

Second, no one at that time was more dedicated than Seward to cooperation in Asia among the Western powers. What, then, did he mean to accomplish by excluding England from the proposed expedition? There is no satisfactory answer to this question, but one possibility suggests itself. In his proposal, Seward spoke of his desire to "affirm publicly" the harmonious relations that existed between the United States and France. It should be recalled that the last of the French troops left Mexico in the Spring of 1867. The Mexican affair had been a clear-cut diplomatic victory for the United States and just as clear-cut a defeat for France. It is entirely possible that Seward was attempting to achieve two things by his extraordinary proposition: to repair the strained relations between France and the United States, and to get the naval power he lacked to deal with the Koreans.

Finally, Tyler Dennett has raised another significant question which cannot be satisfactorily answered, but which bears

[73] Baron de Moustier to Berthemy, March 29, 1867, Seward Papers.

on an earlier point. Dennett wonders if Seward had meant to
ignore the Congressional prerogative of declaring war and
then present the treaty with Korea as a *fait accompli*.[74] It
will be recalled that the problem with the Formosan pirates
had become acute in late 1866 and that the attack on the
Rover took place one month after Seward's proposal to the
French. The request to Congress for a resolution empowering
the President to act on his own discretion in dealing with
attacks on American shipping in the Far East was intended
to be included in the annual message to be delivered in December, 1867. But when did Seward get the original idea?
Could he have had it in mind as early as March, 1867, and
when the French declined his invitation, saved it for later
that year? It seems unlikely that he would have further
exacerbated an already rebellious Congress by overstepping
its prerogative to declare war.[75] The answer to this puzzling
question will probably never be known, but the possibilities
are intriguing.

With the French rejection of the punitive expedition to
Korea, Seward reversed his field. He wrote to Burlingame in
May that France would probably not send a naval force
against Korea because the earlier attack had been more successful than previously believed. Furthermore, he was "satis-
fied" that France, together with the other powers, "would
cordially agree with the United States in desiring that the
Corean peninsula shall be opened to social and commercial

[74] Dennett, "Seward's Far Eastern Policy," p. 56. Dennett also tries
to tie the Korean expedition to the purchase of Alaska, but there is no
real evidence to suggest this connection (*ibid.*, pp. 59–61).

[75] The Tenure of Office and Reconstruction bills were passed over
Johnson's vetoes on March 2, 1867, bringing the constitutional crisis to
a critical point.

intercourse with all nations." There was, then, no need to join in any contemplated military venture.[76]

This, too, was the view of the Consul-General at Shanghai. He reported to the Secretary the arrival there of a Korean mission to inquire about the wisdom of sending an emissary to the West to offer explanations and to enter into treaties of amity and commerce. The *Sherman* incident could be satisfactorily accounted for, and the need for hostile action avoided. With the Koreans suitably penitent, it would not be necessary "to use force or even the show of force" to negotiate a commercial treaty with the Koreans. He was eager to go to Korea to negotiate it and asked Seward for the authority to do so because "this opportunity is not one that should be lost." He had no doubt that he would succeed.[77]

This was welcome news indeed to Seward. The prospect of a peaceful settlement of the *Sherman* affair was opportune, as he well knew, because he doubted that the other powers would cooperate in a military expedition to Korea. The President was "highly gratified" by the Korean embassy and hoped to see it in America. If, for some reason, the Koreans decided not to make the trip, the Consul-General was authorized to go to Korea and negotiate a treaty opening Korea to American and European commerce. It is significant that the treaty, if obtained, was to be "as nearly similar in its provisions to those now existing between the United States and Japan, as may be found practicable and expedient." This was a reference to the Convention of 1866, which put Japan in economic thralldom to the West. Showing his more pacific

[76] May 6, 1867, NA M77, R38.
[77] G. F. Seward to W. Seward, April 24, 1868, Nos. 281, 282 (Confidential), NA M112, R9.

attitude toward Korea, Seward instructed his nephew to make the visit "a generous and friendly one, reserving the question of force, if found necessary, for the ultimate consideration." He was not to intimidate the Koreans even by a display of force but to "practice discretion, prudence and patience." [78]

Seward's avuncular mood was not to last, however. Efforts by the USS *Shenandoah* to learn the fate of the *Sherman*'s crew were frustrated by the Koreans. The Korean "embassy" proved a hoax. Bitterly, George F. Seward wrote his uncle that he was "now led to believe that no negotiations not supported by a considerable show of force would be likely to be successful." [79] Seward agreed and withdrew his instructions of June 27.[80]

The Consul-General in Shanghai and the United States Ministers to Japan and China held a conference in 1868 on the future course of relations with Korea. They were agreed that conditions were not such as would "render it possible to attain success without the exercise of force." They also agreed that the desirability of a commercial treaty was unquestioned because from it would follow such an increase in trade as would "surprise the most sanguine." The United States was the most logical choice for the project: "France has been unfortunate in Corea. Great Britain had hardly a greater interest at stake than we, and no grievance to redress, Northern Germany . . . has yet no determined policy in the East. We are favorably known and all the circumstances indicate that an attempt to open the country may first be made by us."

[78] Seward to G. F. Seward, June 27, 1868, NA RG59 (Consular Instructions, Shanghai).

[79] G. F. Seward to W. Seward, May 25, 1868, NA M112, R9.

[80] Seward to G. F. Seward, July 22, 1868, NA RG59 (Consular Instructions, Shanghai).

All that was needed was an increase in the naval forces since the one presently in the area was not sufficient.[81]

But before any action could be taken, time ran out on the Johnson administration and on Seward as well. The Korean situation had come full cycle and ended with the *Sherman* incident still unsettled and the use of force still under consideration.

[81] G. F. Seward to W. Seward, Oct. 4, 1868, NA M112, R9. Seward's note on the dispatch reads: "Submit to Sec. Navy for his views upon subject and cooperation."

CHAPTER VIII

Seward's Foreign Policy:
The Great Culmination

On March 3, 1869, a new administration took office in Washington, and a new Secretary took over William Seward's desk at the State Department. Seward returned to his home in Auburn, New York, to begin a brief but active retirement from public life. He spent the few years remaining to him mostly in traveling—a short trip to Mexico, the Northwest, and Alaska in 1869; a lengthy one around the world in 1870–1871. He died on October 10, 1872.

If Seward had any final thoughts on his work as Secretary of State, they have not come down to us. Almost certainly he would have reflected on those years, on the triumphs and the achievements. And there was much that must have given him satisfaction. His piloting of the Union through the tricky shoals of Civil War diplomacy had been competent, if not at all times brilliant. He had seen the French peacefully out of Mexico, turning back the most serious challenge to the Monroe Doctrine until then. He had purchased Alaska, the first noncontiguous addition to the United States, and the largest accession since the Louisiana Purchase. He had maintained and strengthened America's position in Asia, and had kept the door open to commercial opportunity there. All of these were achievements of the first rank; any one of them would have assured him a prominent place in the history of American diplomacy.

Being the sort of man he was, he must occasionally have reflected upon his failures as well. He had tried to acquire commercial depots in the Caribbean, but his plans for St. Thomas and Santo Domingo did not succeed. His project for an isthmian canal across Panama did not come to fruition. The intercontinental telegraph and the unification of the world's coinage were both aborted. They had been among his most cherished objectives; the fact that he never saw them realized must surely have tempered whatever sense of achievement he may have felt.

Seward's inability to complete his program cannot be assigned exclusively to his personal failures either of planning or of execution. It resulted in large part from conditions wholly beyond even his own considerable political skills to overcome. To begin with, Seward's entire approach to foreign policy was predicated on unity and tranquility at home. It was unfortunate for him and his ambitions that he would never know a day when either prevailed, from the moment he took office until he retired. His first term as Secretary occurred during civil war, when the preservation of the Union took precedence over all else. For Seward, the war must have been a vexing obstacle to his primary concern— foreign affairs. Indeed, he made one last desperate effort to return the nation's attention to that interest in his now famous "Thoughts for the President's Consideration," on April 1, 1861, in which he urged President Lincoln to offer challenges to Spain, Russia, Great Britain, and France. This memo is sometimes considered an aberration, but it is perfectly logical in the context of Seward's total program. The effort having failed, Seward devoted as much time and energy to foreign affairs as he could spare (and as has been shown, these were not inconsiderable) and waited impatiently for peace so that he might at last take up his true interests.

He was confident that he would have little difficulty in doing so. On November 11, 1864, he predicted that the postwar period would be "an era of peace and harmony," and that the United States would resume its "proud career among the nations . . . advancing the interests of our country, of freedom, of self-fulfillment, and humanity." [1]

But he was wrong. Seward's second term proved hardly more tranquil than his first. The era of reconstruction was full of divisiveness and contention that distracted Congress and the American people from the urgent tasks abroad to which Seward hoped to devote both himself and the country. It was at least partially for this reason that he advocated and supported a conciliatory attitude toward the South and urged a quick end to Reconstruction, even at the cost of abandoning the freed black men. He wanted to welcome the errant South back into the arms of the country, much as a prodigal son might be welcomed home after a brief but misguided escapade.[2] Why else would he, as early as 1862, favor the quick return of secessionist congressmen to their former positions? [3]

Shortly after the close of the war, Seward wrote to John Bigelow that the "intense popular interest" in the Civil War had "tended in some degree to moderate the solicitude which the situation in foreign affairs was calculated to create," but

[1] Seward, *Works*, V, 513–14.

[2] Van Deusen, *Seward*, pp. 425–27.

[3] On this, see Lawanda and John Cox, *Politics, Principles and Prejudice*, pp. 30, 37–40, 220–23.

that now this interest was "rapidly subsiding." He was hopeful that the "Congress of the United States and the people
in their primary assemblies will give a very large share of attention to questions of an extraneous character." [4] In a way
Seward surely did not intend, the people did indeed find
foreign affairs "extraneous," and he was soon writing to his
Minister in Turkey that "the political councils of this Government in foreign affairs" were controlled "by a sense of
restraint which results from popular anxiety concerning our
domestic reconstruction." To John Bigelow he wrote in a
vein that contrasts markedly with his sanguine mood in 1865:
"How sadly domestic disturbances of ours demoralize the
National ambition." [5] He now warned against any optimism
regarding the future because "public attention sensibly continues to be fastened upon the domestic questions which have
grown out of the late civil war." [6]

Seward's desperation led him to support Andrew Johnson's
lenient policies toward the South, and by so doing he became
identified with the President on fiercely contested domestic
issues. Consequently, his foreign projects came under close
and often hostile scrutiny by a Congress already suspicious of
the Executive branch. Whatever merit his proposals may have
had was frequently lost in the aura of suspicion and mistrust
that permeated the relationship of these two branches of
government. The dilemma was a cruel one for Seward, for
without supporting the President he could not remain in
office, but in giving that support he alienated an equally im-

[4] Seward to Bigelow, Sept. 6, 1865, *For. Rel.* (1865), Pt. 1, p. 413.
[5] Seward to E. Joy Morris, Jan. 2, 1868, Seward Papers; Oct. 8,
1868, *ibid.*
[6] Seward to Z. Spalding, July 5, 1868 (Confidential), NA M77, R99
(Instructions, Hawaii).

portant source of support for himself. Despite this, Seward maneuvered with skill, and the wonder is not that he accomplished so little, but that he was able to get anything at all done.

It was inevitable that the climate of contention and suspicion at the seat of government should spill over into the general public. Seward's program called for broad vision and daring action, but the nation had had a surfeit of adventure. The people longed for a return to quiet times and the ordinary business of life; they paid little heed to the call for national greatness and international competition, however peaceful. Try as he might, Seward could not shake them from this mood.

Continued domestic strife was equally unappealing. Reconstruction came to an end in 1877. But it is significant that the actual unification of the nation was not signaled until the Blue and the Gray fought side by side in the Spanish-American War,[7] the war that presumably resulted in what Samuel Flagg Bemis has called The Great Aberration—America's acquisition of a colonial empire.

Another reason for Seward's failure to implement his entire program is simply that the economic basis for his foreign policy had not yet been fully developed in the United States. If the "take-off" stage was indeed the period between 1843 and 1857, then the economy of the 1860's had not got far enough off the ground to sustain Seward's flight into commercial imperialism.[8] The great age of railroad building, the phenomenal growth of industry and finance capital, the enormous productivity that filled the warehouses, did not occur

[7] On this point see Paul H. Buck, *The Road to Reunion, 1865–1900* (New York, 1959), pp. 318–19.

[8] See Walt W. Rostow, *The Stages of Economic Growth, A Non-Communist Manifesto* (London, 1960), p. 38.

until the seventies, eighties, and nineties. The Seward era was not an "age of excess," with its ever-increasing pressures to seek markets for the endless flow of goods made possible by the full flowering of America's industrial economy.[9]

Of course, even in Seward's era there were voices calling for commercial expansion and new markets for American goods, Seward's among them. But the voices were not as numerous as they would one day be, nor was their influence anything like what it would be in the age of the great industrialists and financiers. Commercial men, railroad and canal entrepreneurs, and bankers gave Seward important, indeed, crucial support. Seward mobilized that support as brilliantly and effectively as any Secretary ever has, but even they could not prevail over the spirit of contention and disillusion that characterized the Seward era.

Furthermore, the frontier was diminishing but not yet gone, as it would be in the nineties. No Frederick Jackson Turner was on hand to warn policy makers of the doom that impended when the frontier was irrevocably closed. It was still possible to believe that the answer to America's problems lay within the continental limits of the nation. A generation later this confidence would be undermined, and America's frontier would be thrust beyond the western shore and across the Pacific.[10]

Finally, the naval power so essential to Seward's designs was never at his disposal. The need to blockade Southern ports and to hunt Confederate raiders on the high seas took

[9] Ray Ginger, The Age of Excess, the United States from 1877 to 1914 (New York, 1965), especially pp. 35–52.

[10] Frederick Jackson Turner, "The Significance of the Frontier in American History," originally delivered at the Chicago Exposition, 1893, most conveniently found in Ray Allen Billington, ed., Frontier and Section, Selected Essays of Frederick Jackson Turner (Englewood, N.J., 1961), 37–62.

all the resources of the navy during the Civil War. After the war, the navy was practically dismantled. What remained was obsolete and insufficient for Seward's purposes. The modern American navy did not get its start until the 1880's, and not until the 1890's was it a first-rate fleet. Others would find uses for it, but like much else, it would come too late to do Seward any good.

But a simple balance sheet of credits and debits does not do full justice to Seward's significance. To appreciate this, it is necessary to look a generation beyond him. For Seward had conceived an idea of empire as serviceable in another day as it had been in his. The idea was simply that the United States should possess the commercial hegemony of the world. By virtue of its superior political, moral, and commercial institutions, Seward believed America was destined to dominate the trade routes and markets of the globe, and especially of Asia. But mere increase in wealth was not the only goal for Seward. In actuality, the commercial empire was the means to other ends, for through commercial domination political and cultural changes could be introduced, American ideals and values transmitted, and the Christian religion spread over the globe. It was, in many ways, a remarkable formulation; so remarkable, in fact, that a full generation would be needed before there would be any chance for its realization.

In the 1890's, with many of the domestic problems that had blocked expansion solved, and with others, equally burdensome but more conducive to expansion, a united nation embarked on imperial ventures. Few thought to look back to Seward; had they done so they would have found some familiar ideas. One historian has described the "large policy" of 1898 as follows: [11]

[11] Julius W. Pratt, "The 'Large Policy' of 1898," *Mississippi Valley Historical Review*, XIX (Sept., 1932), 223. Seward's relevance was

The "large policy" of the leading representatives of this new spirit, Roosevelt and Lodge, aimed at no less than making the United States the indisputable dominant power in the western hemisphere, possessed of a great navy, owning and controlling an Isthmian canal, holding naval bases in the Caribbean and the Pacific, and contesting, on at least even terms with the greatest powers, the naval and commercial supremacy of the Pacific Ocean and the Far East.[12]

What is this if not Seward's commercial empire with all its appurtenances and almost in his very words? The imperialists of 1898 were unconscious Sewardites, their theories ideological glosses on his text.

It has been suggested that Seward, despite his views, was only an expansionist of the old Manifest Destiny school rather than an imperialist, because "even the most grandiose of expansionists hesitated to project their views beyond the bounds of the western hemisphere." But if the argument thus far advanced has any merit at all this view is not tenable. Seward was nothing if not global in his thinking. Indeed, he fully anticipated what one historian has called the two "heritages" of the 1890's: the "establishment of a power commitment that lay outside the North American orbit," and the idea that

---

much in evidence in an article which appeared at the height of the Spanish-American War in which Seward's opinions on expansion were termed "so prophetic as to be almost startling," and that "nearly all his thoughts on the subject have a peculiar interest to us now." Frederick Bancroft, "Seward's Ideas of Territorial Expansion," *North American Review*, CLXVII (July, 1898), 80.

[12] Despite the similarities of approach, there are undoubtedly aspects of the imperialism of the nineties Seward would have found most uncomfortable, notably its militarism and its racism, and he certainly would have looked with some unease upon the Spanish-American War. In addition, Seward's advocacy of the unification of the world's coinage and the intercontinental telegraph reflect a more sophisticated approach than some of the crudities of the 1890's.

the "national mission must be fulfilled, not only by example, but by actual tutelage, not merely at home, but abroad as well."[13] Efforts to distinguish between expansionism as Seward is thought to have practiced it and the imperialism of the 1890's only serve to obscure rather than to illuminate the continuity of foreign policy from the 1860's to the 1890's. This continuity can be seen most clearly in the Open Door Notes of 1899 and 1900. If John Hay had been looking for a base upon which to place his approach to the Far East, he could have rested it quite comfortably on Seward's policy toward China.[14]

The true significance of William H. Seward, the most outstanding Secretary of State after John Quincy Adams, lies not so much in his specific achievements, brilliant as they undoubtedly were, as in the fact that he anticipated the direction of American foreign policy for the next generation and beyond, and with the limited materials and opportunities at his disposal, prepared the way. From this vantage point, The Great Aberration looks more and more like The Great Culmination.

[13] See David Healy, *US Expansionism, the Imperialist Urge in the 1890's* (Madison, Wis., 1970), p. 52; also pp. 36, 49, 254. The very title of Healy's book indicates some confusion of terminology.

[14] Tyler Dennett has claimed that "John Hay found his model, not in Seward's policy in Japan or his policy of 1867 as to Korea, but in Burlingame's frank, kindly, and irenic policy in China" (Dennett, "Seward's Far Eastern Policy," p. 62). This position can be maintained only by assuming there was a distinction between Burlingame's approach to China and Seward's. There was none. The real distinction is between Seward's policy toward Japan and his policy toward China.

Bibliography

NOTE ON SOURCES

The bibliography lists all the materials consulted in the preparation of this book. Some indication of the nature and extent of the unpublished sources may be useful to those who wish to pursue their own studies of foreign policy in the Seward era.

The indispensable source is the William Henry Seward Papers at the University of Rochester, Rochester, New York. No true understanding of Seward or his ideas is possible without a thorough knowledge of this magnificent collection housed in the Rush Rhees Memorial Library and superbly tended by the staff of the Special Collections Division. The Seward manuscripts include not only the preliminary drafts of his speeches and state papers, but also many letters from numerous governmental and private persons, many of whom were instrumental in helping shape Seward's ideas and policies. Among these, the most important for this study were the letters of Admiral David Dixon Porter, Samuel Bulkley Ruggles, and the officials of the Isthmus Canal Company. Sometimes the drafts of Seward's public utterances differ materially from the published versions, permitting a glimpse of his thinking before his editorial pencil struck out some of the more revealing passages.

Other, smaller collections of Seward's correspondence were consulted but, with one exception, proved of little value for this book. Those at the Chicago Historical Society, Yale University, and the Clements Library (all on microfilm at the University of Rochester), and the New-York Historical Society were disappointing, although undoubtedly useful for a study of Seward's domestic activities. However, the collection of Seward correspondence at the Library of Congress proved valuable far beyond its modest size. It is from this collection that S. B. Ruggles' influence on Seward emerges most clearly.

The papers of a number of men who in one way or another were involved with Seward were mined. Those that give especially important insights into Seward's approach to foreign affairs and also into the views and roles of his friends and associates are the papers of Admiral David Dixon Porter, Caleb Cushing, and Edward Lee Plumb, all in the Library of Congress, and the papers of Samuel Bulkley Ruggles, in the New York Public Library. Admiral Porter was Commandant of the United States Naval Academy, a close friend of Seward's, and an unabashed advocate of commercial expansion supported by a strong navy. His papers are an excellent index to the thinking of American naval officers in the Seward era. The Cushing Papers are most important for an understanding of Seward's effort to acquire the Isthmus of Panama, and for revealing the interaction and influence of various promoters, speculators, and commercial men on American foreign policy in the post-Civil War period. The Plumb Papers make clear the machinations of a minor diplomat and his efforts to persuade members of Congress and capitalists to undertake speculative enterprises in Mexico. All of these men deserve modern biographies that would give us a fuller comprehension of the influences that went into the making of foreign policy in the Lincoln and Johnson administrations. Ruggles is a key figure, and he has been well served by D. G. Brinton Thompson, *Ruggles of New York: A Life of Samuel B. Ruggles* (New York, 1946).

A considerable number of State Department records and other government documents were consulted. Much of the diplomatic correspondence, but by no means all, has been published in *Papers Relating to the Foreign Relations of the United States, 1861–1872* (Washington, D.C., 1966). Much that was useful, however, remains unpublished, especially the instructions and dispatches to and from consular and other minor diplomatic posts. These show the thinking and attitudes of lesser figures in the diplomatic service, some of whom, for example, Perry McDonough Collins, were extremely influential. An intensive investigation into these records (admittedly a laborious and tedious undertaking), would tell us a great deal about the methods and objectives of American diplomacy in this period.

Two interesting collections of State Department records which have little to do with the actual conduct of diplomacy are the Domestic Letters, letters from the State Department to other than diplomatic personnel, and the Miscellaneous Letters, letters to the State Department from other than diplomatic personnel. These voluminous collections cover a wide variety of subjects and reveal Seward's views on sundry matters which he often could not express in his formal correspondence. In addition, many of the letters are to and from men close to Seward who sought in one way or another to influence his policies. Another source of great interest, little used by students of American foreign policy, are the Letters of Appointment and Recommendation. These letters from men seeking employment in the State Department and their supporters often reveal the interests of the business and commercial community far better than any other source. All the sources mentioned in this paragraph merit more intensive study by historians than they have hitherto received because they frequently tell us much more of the real basis of American foreign policy than the more formal records that have generally formed the core of foreign policy studies.

UNPUBLISHED SOURCES

Manuscripts, by Repository

Library of Congress

Charles Francis Adams Papers, Nathaniel Banks Papers, Burlingame Family Papers, William Conant Church Papers, Caleb Cushing Papers, James R. Doolittle Papers, William M. Evarts Papers, Andrew Johnson Papers, Reverdy Johnson Papers, Robert Todd Lincoln Papers, Samuel F. B. Morse Papers, Edward Lee Plumb Papers, David Dixon Porter Papers, Porter Family Papers, William Seward Papers, Thurlow Weed Papers, Gideon Welles Papers.

New-York Historical Society

Gustavus V. Fox Papers, William Seward Letters.

New York Public Library

John Bigelow Papers, William Conant Church Papers, Samuel S.

Cox Papers, Henry J. Raymond Papers, Samuel B. Ruggles Papers, George Templeton Strong Diary (Microfilm).
University of Rochester
William H. Seward Papers, Thurlow Weed Papers.
The following collections were consulted on microfilm at the University of Rochester: William H. Seward Correspondence, Chicago Historical Society; William H. Seward Correspondence, Clements Library, University of Michigan; William H. Seward Correspondence, Yale University Library.

National Archives

U.S. Department of the Navy. Letters Sent by the Secretary of the Navy to the President and Executive Agencies, 1861–1869, NA M-472.
——. Letters Received by the Secretary of the Navy from Commanding Officers of Squadrons ("Squadron Letters"), 1861–1869, NA M-89.
U.S. Department of State. Consular Dispatches, 1861–1869, from following posts, with National Archives Microcopy numbers: Amoor River (T-111), Amoy (M-100), Bangkok (T-134), Buenos Aires (M 70), Canton (M 101), Cap Haitien (M-9), Chefoo (M-102), Chinkiang (M-103), Dublin (T-199), Hangkow (M-107), Hong Kong (M-108), Honolulu (M-144), Kanagawa (M-135), Lahaina (T-101), Mexico City (M-296), Nagasaki (M-131), Ningpo (M-111), Panama (M-139), Paris (T-1), Port-au-Prince (T-346), Puerto Rico (M-76), St. Croix (T-233), St. Thomas (T-350), Santo Domingo (T-56), Shanghai (M-112), Swatow (M-113).
——. Consular Instructions, 1861–1869 (National Archives Record Group 59, volumes 28–53) to the following posts: Amoor River, Amoy, Bangkok, Buenos Aires, Canton, Cap Haitien, Chefoo, Chinkiang, Dublin, Hangkow, Hong Kong, Honolulu, Kanagawa, Lahaina, Mexico City, Nagasaki, Ningpo, Panama, Paris, Port-au-Prince, Puerto Rico, St. Croix, St. Thomas, Santo Domingo, Shanghai, Swatow.
——. Diplomatic Dispatches, 1861–1869, from the following posts, with the National Archives Microcopy numbers: Argentina (M-69), Brazil (M-121), Central America (M-219), China (M-92), Denmark (M-41), France (M-34), Great Britain (M-30), Haiti (M-82),

Hawaii (T-30), Japan (M-133), Mexico (M-97), Russia (M-35), Spain (M-31), Venezuela (M-79).

——. Diplomatic Instructions, 1861–1869 (Microcopy Number 77), to the following posts: Argentina, Brazil, Central American States, China, Colombia, Denmark, France, Great Britain, Haiti, Hawaii, Japan, Mexico, Russia, Santo Domingo, Spain, Venezuela.

——. Notes from Foreign Legations, 1861–1869, with National Archives Microcopy numbers: Central America (T-34), China (M-98), Colombia (M-51), Great Britain (M-50), France (M-53), Haiti (T-803), Hawaii (T-160), Japan (M-163), Mexico (M-54), Russia (M-39), Spain (M-59).

——. Notes to Foreign Legations, 1861–1869 (National Archives Microcopy Number 99): Central America, China, Colombia, Great Britain, France, Haiti, Hawaii, Japan, Mexico, Russia, Spain.

——. Domestic Letters of Department of State, 1861–1869, NA M-40.

——. Letters of Application and Recommendation, 1861–1869, NA M-650.

——. Miscellaneous Letters of Department of State, 1861–1869, NA M-179.

——. Reports of the Secretary of State to the President and Congress (State Department Report Books), 1861–1869, Volumes VIII–IX.

——. Special Agents, 1861–1869, NA M-37.

——. Special Missions, 1861–1869, NA M-77.

Dissertations

Sharrow, Walter G. "William H. Seward, a Study in the 19th Century Politics and Nationalism." Ph.D. dissertation, University of Rochester, 1965.

Stutz, Frederick H. "William Henry Seward, Expansionist." Master's thesis, Cornell University, 1937.

Whelan, Joseph G. "William Henry Seward, Expansionist." Ph.D. dissertation, University of Rochester, 1959.

GOVERNMENT DOCUMENTS AND PUBLICATIONS

U.S. Congress. *Congressional Globe*, 1850–1869.

U.S. House of Representatives. Committee Report No. 62 (*Coins, Weights and Measures*). 39th Cong., 1st sess.

——. Executive Document No. 93 (*Shimonoseki Indemnity*). 40th Cong., 2d sess.

——. Executive Document No. 177 (*Alaska Purchase*). 40th Cong., 2d sess.

——. Executive Document No. 219 (*Shimonoseki Indemnity*). 40th Cong., 2d sess.

——. Committee Report No. 35 (*Payment for Alaska*). 40th Cong., 3d sess.

——. Executive Document No. 266 (*Supplemental Report, International Monetary Conference, 1867*). 41st Cong., 2d sess.

U.S. Senate. Executive Document No. 33 (*Construction of Warships for Japanese Government*). 37th Cong., 2d sess.

——. Executive Document No. 62 (*Proposed Routes for Interoceanic Canals and Railroads*). 39th Cong., 1st sess.

——. Executive Document No. 5 (*Paris Universal Exposition*). 39th Cong., 1st and 2d sess.

——. Executive Document No. 14 (*International Monetary Conference*). 40th Cong., 2d sess.

——. Miscellaneous Document No. 52 (*Shimonoseki Indemnity*). 40th Cong., 2d sess.

U.S. Senate. Executive Document No. 79 (*Discovery, Occupation and Character of Midway Island*). 40th Cong., 2d sess.

——. Executive Document No. 52 (*Murder of American Seamen in Formosa*). 40th Cong., 2d sess.

——. Committee Report No. 194 (*Midway Island*). 40th Cong., 3d sess.

Blake, William P., ed. *Reports of the United States Commissioners to the Paris Universal Exposition, 1867*. 6 vols. Washington, D.C.: Government Printing Office, 1870.

Malloy, William M., comp. *Treaties, Conventions, International Acts, Protocols and Agreements Between the United States of America and Other Powers, 1776–1902*. 2 vols. Washington, D.C.: Government Printing Office, 1910.

United States Congress. *Papers Relating to the Foreign Relations of the United States, 1861–1872*. Microfiche ed. Washington, D.C.: Government Printing Office, 1966.

——. *Papers Relating to the Intercontinental Telegraph*. Washington, D.C.: Government Printing Office, 1864.

ARTICLES, MEMOIRS, DIARIES, SPEECHES, LETTERS, PROCEEDINGS, ETC.

Adams, Charles Francis. *An Address on the Life, Character and Services of William Henry Seward.* Albany, N.Y.: Parsons, 1873.

"Alaska, What Is It Worth?" *Lippincott's Magazine,* I (Feb., 1868), 185–91.

Baker, George E., ed. *The Works of William H. Seward.* 4 vols. New York: Redfield, 1853–1861.

——. *The Diplomatic History of the War for the Union, being Volume Five of Seward's Works.* Boston: Houghton, Mifflin, 1884.

Barrows, Isabel C. "Personal Reminiscences of William H. Seward," *Atlantic Monthly,* LXIII (March, 1889), 379–97.

Beale, Howard K., ed. *The Diary of Gideon Welles.* 3 vols. New York: Norton, 1960.

Bigelow, John. *Retrospections of an Active Life.* 5 vols. Garden City, N.Y.: Doubleday, Page, 1913.

Browne, J. Ross, aided by a corps of assistants. *Resources of the Pacific Slope, a Statistical and Descriptive Summary of the Mines and Minerals, Climate, Topography, Agriculture, Commerce, Manufactures, and Miscellaneous Productions, of the States and Territories West of the Rocky Mountains, with a Sketch of the Settlement and Exploration of Lower California.* New York: Appleton, 1869.

Browne, Lina Ferguson, ed. *J. Ross Browne, His Letters, Journals and Writings.* Albuquerque: University of New Mexico Press, 1969.

Clyde, Paul H., ed. *United States Policy Toward China: Diplomatic and Public Documents, 1839–1939.* New York: Russell and Russell, 1964.

Cole, Allan B., ed. *Yankee Surveyors in the Shogun's Seas, Records of the United States Surveying Expedition to the North Pacific Ocean, 1853–1856.* Princeton, N.J.: Princeton University Press, 1947.

National Board of Trade. *Proceedings of the First Annual Meeting, December, 1868.* Boston: Eastburn's Press, 1869.

——. *Proceedings of the Second Annual Meeting, Richmond, Virginia, December, 1869.* Boston: Barker, Cotter, 1870.

New York State Chamber of Commerce. *Annual Reports and Proceedings* (Microfilm).

Porter, David Dixon. "Secret Missions to San Domingo." *North American Review*, CXXVIII (June, 1879), 616–30.

Richardson, James, D. *A Compilation of the Messages and Papers of the Presidents, 1789–1897.* 10 vols. Washington, D.C.: Government Printing Office, 1897.

Ruggles, Samuel B. *American Commerce and American Union.* New York: Appleton, 1856.

——. *Freedom of Ocean Telegraphs.* New York: Bryant, 1866.

——. *Writings and Speeches of Samuel B. Ruggles.* New York: Hall, Clayton, 1860.

"Scientific Expedition to Alaska." *Lippincott's Magazine*, I (Nov., 1868), 467–85.

Seward, Frederick W. *Reminiscences of a War-Time Statesman and Diplomat.* New York: Putnam's Sons, 1916.

——. "Seward's West Indian Cruise." *Godey's Magazine*, CXXVIII–CXXIX (April–Nov., 1894).

——. *William H. Seward: An Autobiography, with a Memoir of His Life, and Selections from His Letters.* 3 vols. New York: Derby and Miller, 1877.

Seward, Olive Risley, ed. *William H. Seward's Travels Around the World.* New York: D. Appleton, 1873.

Seward, William H. *Immigrant White Free Labor, or Imported Black African Slave Labor.* Washington, D.C.: Buell and Blanshard, 1857.

——. *Life and Public Services of John Quincy Adams, Sixth President of the United States, with the Eulogy Delivered Before the Legislature of New York.* Auburn, N.Y.: Derby, Miller, 1849.

Sherman, John. *Recollections of Forty Years in the House, Senate and Cabinet.* 2 vols. Chicago: Werner, 1849.

——. *Selected Speeches and Reports on Finance and Taxation, from 1859 to 1878.* New York: Appleton, 1879.

Tuckerman, Charles K. *Personal Recollections of Notable People at Home and Abroad.* London: Bentley and Son, 1895.

——. "Personal Recollections of William H. Seward." *Magazine of American History*, XIX (June, 1888), 499–503.

Vandersee, Charles. "Henry Adams Behind the Scenes: The Civil War Letters to Frederick W. Seward." *Bulletin of the New York Public Library*, LXXI (April, 1967).

Vevier, Charles, ed. *Siberian Journey, Down the Amur to the Pacific,*

1856–1857. A New Edition of a Voyage Down the Amoor by Perry McDonough Collins. Madison: University of Wisconsin Press, 1962.

Western Union. *Statement of the Origin, Organization and Progress of the Russian-American Telegraph Western Union Extension, Collins Overland Line.* Rochester, N.Y.: Evening Express Book and Job Printing Office, 1866.

NEWSPAPERS AND PERIODICALS

The Commercial and Financial Chronicle (New York)
Hunt's Merchants' Magazine
New York Journal of Commerce
New York Times
The Telegrapher
The United States Army and Navy Journal, and Gazette of the Regular and Volunteer Forces

SECONDARY SOURCES

General Histories, Monographs, and Special Studies

Albion, Robert G. *The Rise of New York Port, 1815–1860.* New York: Scribner's Sons, 1939.

Bailey, Hugh C. *Hinton Rowan Helper, Abolitionist-Racist.* Southern Historical Publications, No. 7. University: University of Alabama Press, 1965.

Bailey, Thomas A. *A Diplomatic History of the American People.* 3rd and 7th eds. New York: Appleton-Century-Crofts, 1946, 1964.

Baker, George E. *The Life of William H. Seward, with Selections from His Works.* New York: Redfield, 1855.

Bancroft, Frederick. *The Life of William H. Seward.* 2 vols. New York: Harper, 1900.

Barrows, Chester L. *William M. Evarts, Lawyer, Diplomat, Statesman.* Chapel Hill: University of North Carolina Press, 1941.

Bemis, Samuel Flagg. *A Short History of American Foreign Policy and Diplomacy.* New York: Holt, Rinehart and Winston, 1959.

——, ed. *The American Secretaries of State and Their Diplomacy.* 10 vols. New York: Knopf, 1928.

Billington, Ray Allen, ed. *Frontier and Section, Selected Essays of Frederick Jackson Turner.* Englewood, N.J.: Prentice-Hall, 1961.

Callahan, James Morton. *American Foreign Policy in Mexican Relations.* New York: Macmillan, 1932.

Cameron, Meribeth E., Thomas H. D. Mahoney, and George E. McReynolds. *China, Japan and the Powers.* New York: Ronald Press, 1952.

Clyde, Paul H. *The Far East: A History of the Impact of the West on Eastern Asia.* New York: Prentice-Hall, 1948.

Cox, Lawanda and John H. *Politics, Principles, and Prejudice, 1865–1866.* London: The Free Press, 1963.

Crouthamel, James L. *James Watson Webb: A Biography.* Middletown, Conn.: Wesleyan University Press, 1969.

De Conde, Alexander. *The American Secretary of State, an Interpretation.* New York: Praeger, 1962.

Dennett, Tyler. *Americans in Eastern Asia: A Critical Study of the Policy of the United States with Reference to China, Japan and Korea in the 19th Century.* New York: Barnes and Noble, 1922.

Dulles, Foster Rhea. *Prelude to World Power, American Diplomatic History, 1860–1890.* New York: Macmillan, 1965.

Ekirch, Arthur A., Jr. *Ideas, Ideals, and American Diplomacy: A History of Their Growth and Interaction.* New York: Appleton-Century-Crofts, 1966.

Farrar, Victor J. *The Annexation of Russian America to the United States.* Washington, D.C.: Roberts, 1937.

Ferrell, Robert H. *American Diplomacy: A History.* Revised and expanded edition. New York: Norton, 1969.

Fuess, Carl M. *The Life of Caleb Cushing.* Hamden, Conn.: Archon Books, 1965.

Graebner, Norman. *Empire on the Pacific: A Study in American Continental Expansion.* New York: Ronald Press, 1955.

Griffin, Eldon. *Clippers and Consuls: American Consular and Commercial Relations with Eastern Asia, 1845–1860.* Ann Arbor, Mich.: Edwards Bros., 1938.

Harlow, Alvin E. *Old Wires and New Waves: The History of the Telegraph, Telephone and Wireless.* New York: Appleton-Century, 1936.

Harrington, Fred Harvey. *Fighting Politician: Major-General N. P. Banks*. Westport, Conn.: Greenwood, Corp., 1970.

Healy, David. *US Expansionism, the Imperialist Urge in the 1890's*. Madison: University of Wisconsin Press, 1970.

Holt, William Stull. *Treaties Defeated by the Senate: A Study of the Struggle between President and Senate over the Conduct of Foreign Relations*. Baltimore: The Johns Hopkins Press, 1933.

Israel, Jerry. *Progressivism and the Open Door, America and China, 1905–1921*. Pittsburgh: University of Pittsburgh Press, 1971.

Jenkins, Brian. *Fenians and Anglo-American Relations during Reconstruction*. Ithaca: Cornell University Press, 1969.

Johnson, Allen and Dumas Malone, eds. *Dictionary of American Biography*. New York: Scribner's Sons, 1930.

LaFeber, Walter. *The New Empire: An Interpretation of American Expansion, 1860–1898*. Ithaca: Cornell University Press, 1967.

Lewis, Paul. *Yankee Admiral: A Biography of David Dixon Porter*. New York: David McKay, 1968.

Logan, Rayford W. *The Diplomatic Relations of the United States with Haiti, 1776–1891*. Chapel Hill: University of North Carolina Press, 1941.

Lothrop, Thornton K. *William Henry Seward*. Boston: Houghton, Mifflin, 1896.

Luthin, Reinhard H. "The Sale of Alaska." *Alaska and Its History*. Ed. Morgan B. Sherwood. Seattle: University of Washington Press, 1967.

Mack, Gerstle. *The Land Divided: A History of the Panama Canal and Other Isthmian Canal Projects*. New York: Knopf, 1944.

McKitrick, Eric L. *Andrew Johnson and Reconstruction*. Chicago: University of Chicago, Phoenix Books, 1964.

Merk, Frederick, with the collaboration of Lois Bannister Merk. *Manifest Destiny and Mission in American History: A Reinterpretation*. New York: Vintage Books, 1963.

Miller, David Hunter. "The Alaska Treaty," Draft Manuscript (Xerox Copy). Seward Papers, Library of the University of Rochester.

Neumann, William L. *America Encounters Japan, from Perry to MacArthur*. New York: Harper Colophon Books, 1965.

——. "Determinism, Destiny, and Myth in the American Image of China." *Issues and Conflicts: Studies in Twentieth Century American Diplomacy*. Ed. George L. Anderson. New York: Greenwood Press, 1959.

Nugent, Walter T. K. *Money and American Society, 1865–1880*. New York: The Free Press, 1968.

Parks, E. Taylor. *Colombia and the United States, 1765–1934*. Durham, N.C.: Duke University Press, 1935.

Parton, James. *The Danish Islands, Are We Honor Bound to Pay for Them?* Boston: Fields, Osgood, 1869.

Paullin, Charles O. *Diplomatic Negotiations of American Naval Officers, 1778–1883*. Baltimore: The Johns Hopkins Press, 1912.

Pierce, Edward L. *A Diplomatic Fiasco, the Rejected Treaty for St. Thomas*. Boston: n. pub., 1889.

Plesur, Milton. *America's Outward Thrust: Approaches to Foreign Affairs, 1865–1890*. De Kalb: Northern Illinois University Press, 1971.

Pletcher, David M. *Rails, Mines, and Progress: Seven American Promoters in Mexico, 1867–1911*. Ithaca: Cornell University Press, 1958.

Pratt, Julius W. *A History of United States Foreign Policy*. New York: Prentice-Hall, 1955.

——. "The Ideology of American Expansion." *Essays in Honor of William A. Dodd*. Ed. Avery Craven. Chicago: University of Chicago Press, 1935.

Rippy, J. Fred. *The Capitalists and Colombia*. New York: The Vanguard Press, 1931.

Rostow, Walt W. *The Stages of Economic Growth, A Non-Communist Manifesto*. London: Cambridge University Press, 1960.

Schonburger, Howard B. *Transportation to the Seaboard, the "Communication Revolution" and American Foreign Policy, 1860–1900*. Westport, Conn.: Greenwood, 1971.

Shippee, Lester B. *Canadian-American Relations, 1849–1874*. New Haven: Yale University Press, 1939.

Smith, Henry Nash. *Virgin Land, the American West as Symbol and Myth*. New York: Vintage Books, 1957.

Smith, Joe Patterson. *Republican Expansionists of the Reconstruction Era*. Chicago: Private ed., distributed by Chicago Libraries, 1933.

Soley, James Russell. *Admiral Porter.* New York: Appleton, 1903.

Sprout, Harold and Margaret. *The Rise of American Naval Power, 1776–1918.* Princeton, N.J.: Princeton University Press, 1944.

Tansill, Charles C. *The Purchase of the Danish West Indies.* Gloucester, Mass.: Peter Smith, 1966.

——. *The United States and Santo Domingo, 1798–1873.* Baltimore: The Johns Hopkins Press, 1938.

Thompson, D. G. Brinton. *Ruggles of New York: A Life of Samuel B. Ruggles.* New York: Columbia University Press, 1946.

Thompson, Robert L. *Wiring a Continent: The History of the Telegraph Industry in the United States, 1832–1866.* Princeton, N.J.: Princeton University Press, 1947.

Treat, Payson J. *Diplomatic Relations Between the United States and Japan, 1853–1895.* 2 vols. Gloucester, Mass.: Peter Smith, 1963.

Van Alstyne, Richard W. *The Rising American Empire.* Chicago: Quadrangle Books, 1965.

Van Deusen, Glyndon. *William H. Seward.* New York: Oxford University Press, 1967.

Varg, Paul A. *Missionaries, Chinese, and Diplomats: The American Protestant Missionary Movement in China, 1890–1952.* Princeton, N.J.: Princeton University Press, 1958.

Warner, Donald F. *The Idea of Continental Union, Agitation for the Annexation of Canada to the United States, 1849–1893.* Lexington: University of Kentucky Press, 1960.

Weinberg, Albert K. *Manifest Destiny: A Study of Nationalist Expansionism in American History.* Chicago: Quadrangle Books, 1963.

Weinstein, Allen. *Prelude to Populism: Origins of the Silver Issue, 1867–1878.* New Haven: Yale University Press, 1970.

Williams, Frederick Wells. *Anson Burlingame and the First Chinese Mission to Foreign Powers.* New York: Scribner's Sons, 1912.

——. *The Life and Letters of Samuel Wells Williams.* New York: Putnam's Sons, 1889.

Williams, William Appleman. *The Contours of American History.* Cleveland and New York: The World Publishing Co., 1961.

——. *The Roots of the Modern American Empire: A Study of the Growth and Shaping of Social Consciousness in a Marketplace Society.* New York: Vintage Books, 1969.

——. *The Tragedy of American Diplomacy*. Rev. and enlarged ed. New York: Dell, 1962.

Wriston, Henry Merritt. *Executive Agents in American Foreign Relations*. Gloucester, Mass.: Peter Smith, 1967.

Younger, Edward. *John A. Kasson, Politics and Diplomacy from Lincoln to McKinley*. Iowa City, Iowa: State Historical Society, 1955.

Articles

Allen, Walter. "William Henry Seward." *Atlantic Monthly*, LXXXVI (Dec., 1900), 849–54.

Bailey, Thomas A. "Why the United States Purchased Alaska." *Pacific Historical Review*, III (March, 1934), 39–49.

Bancroft, Frederick. "Seward's Ideas of Territorial Expansion." *North American Review*, CLXVII (July, 1898), 79–89.

Biggerstaff, Knight. "The Official Chinese Attitude Toward the Burlingame Mission." *American Historical Review*, XLI (July, 1936), 682–701.

Bruce, H. Addington. "The Romance of American Expansion: William Henry Seward and the Alaska Cession." *Outlook*, LXXXIX (July 25, 1908), 687–97.

Carman, Harry J. "William H. Seward in Retrospect." *University of Rochester Library Bulletin*, VIII (Autumn, 1952), 1–8.

Clyde, Paul H. "The China Policy of J. Ross Browne, 1868–1869." *Pacific Historical Review*, I (March, 1932), 312–23.

Dennett, Tyler. "Seward's Far Eastern Policy." *American Historical Review*, XXVIII (Oct., 1922), 45–62.

Dozer, Donald Marquand. "Anti-Expansionism during the Johnson Administration." *Pacific Historical Review*, XII (Sept., 1943), 253–75.

Dunning, William A. "Paying for Alaska." *Political Science Quarterly*, XXVII (Sept., 1912), 385–98.

Dyer, Brainerd. "Robert J. Walker on Acquiring Greenland and Iceland." *Mississippi Historical Review*, XXVII (Sept., 1940), 263–66.

Golder, Frank A. "The Purchase of Alaska." *American Historical Review*, XXV (April, 1920), 411–25.

Gordon, Leonard. "Early American Relations with Formosa, 1849–1870." *Historian*, XIX (May, 1959), 262–89.

Hart, Albert Bushnell. "New Light on Seward." *Political Science Quarterly*, XV (Sept., 1900), 536–46.

Harvey, Charles M. "Seward, Empire-Builder and Seer." *Putnam's Monthly*, II (June, 1907), 267–76.

House, E. H. "The Martyrdom of an Empire." *Atlantic Monthly*, XLVII (May, 1881), 610–23.

——. "The Thraldom of Japan." *Atlantic Monthly*, LX (Dec., 1887), 721–34.

Jones, W. Martin. "Two Great American Treaties: One with Russia—Ratified; One with Denmark—Deferred." *Review of Reviews*, XVII (May, 1898), 549–60.

Kemble, John F. "The Panama Route to the Pacific Coast, 1848–1869." *Pacific Historical Review*, VII (March, 1938), 1–13.

Koht, Halvdan. "The Origins of Seward's Plan to Purchase the Danish West Indies." *American Historical Review*, L (July, 1944), 762–67.

Lamb, Martha J. "A Great Public Career, 1801–1872." *Magazine of American History*, XXV (May, 1891), 349–70.

Lodge, Henry Cabot. "William H. Seward." *Atlantic Monthly*, LIII (May, 1884), 682–700.

Monroe, James. "William H. Seward and the Foreign Affairs of the United States." *Oberlin Review*, XIX (Feb. 23, 1892), 291–99.

Parry, Albert. "Cassius Clay's Glimpse into the Future." *Russian Review*, II (Spring, 1943), 52–67.

Perkins, Dexter. "William Henry Seward." *University of Rochester Library Bulletin*, VII (Autumn, 1951), 1–6.

Persinger, Clark E. "Internationalism in the '60s." *Historical Outlook*, XX (Nov., 1929), 324–26.

Pratt, Julius W. "The 'Large Policy' of 1898." *Mississippi Valley Historical Review*, XIX (Sept., 1932), 219–42.

Seward, Olive Risley. "A Diplomatic Episode," *Scribner's Magazine*, II (Nov., 1887), 585–602.

Sharrow, Walter G. "William H. Seward and the Basis for American Empire, 1850–60." *Pacific Historical Reivew*, XXXVI (Aug., 1967), 325–42.

Supplee, Henry H. "William Henry Seward—A Sketch." *Junior Munsey*, XX (Nov., 1900), 207–19.

Thomson, Sandra Caruthers. "Filibustering to Formosa: General

Charles Le Gendre and the Japanese." *Pacific Historical Review*, XL (Nov., 1971), 442–56.

Vevier, Charles. "American Continentalism: An Idea of Expansion, 1845–1910." *American Historical Review*, LXV (Jan., 1960), 323–35.

———. "The Collins Overland Line and American Continentalism." *Pacific Historical Review*, XXVIII (Aug., 1959), 237–53.

Welch, Richard E., Jr. "American Public Opinion and the Purchase of Russian America." *American Slavic and East European Review*, XVII (Dec., 1958), 481–94.

Williams, William Appleman. "The Frontier Thesis and American Foreign Policy." *Pacific Historical Review*, XXIV (Nov., 1955), 379–95.

Index

The Foundations of
the American Empire

Designed by R. E. Rosenbaum.
Composed by Vail-Ballou Press, Inc.,
in 11 point linotype Janson, 3 points leaded,
with display lines in monotype Janson.
Printed letterpress from type by Vail-Ballou Press
on Warren's 1854 text, 60 pound basis,
with the Cornell University Press watermark.
Bound by Vail-Ballou Press
in Columbia book cloth
and stamped in All Purpose foil.